ALOHA ʻOE
By Queen Liliuokalani

Ha aheao ka ua i na pali
Ke nihi aʻe la i kanahele
E uhai ana paha i ka liko
Pua ahihi lehua a o uka,

Aloha ʻoe, aloha ʻoe
E ke onaona noho i ka lipo
One fond embrace, a hoʻi aʻe au
Until we meet again

Translation:

FAREWELL TO THEE

Proudly the rain on the cliffs
Creeps softly up the forest
Seeking perhaps the bud
Flower ahihi lehua of inland

Farewell to thee, Farewell to thee
Sweet fragrance dwelling
*   in the blue depths*
One fond embrace, before I leave
Until we meet again

Liliuokalani, a prolific composer, wrote *Aloha ʻOe* in 1877, inspired by the parting embrace of two lovers—her sister and an American colonel—on the Nuʻuanu Pali.

She became Hawaiʻi's first woman monarch in 1891 and two years later was Hawaiʻi's last monarch—imprisoned in her own palace after the overthrow of the government. The haunting chorus of *Aloha ʻOe* has become an international farewell song and also, in the islands, a bittersweet tribute to the Kingdom of Hawaii.

OAHU TRAILBLAZER
Where to Hike, Snorkel, Surf
From Waikiki to the North Shore

Second edition
Text by Jerry Sprout
Photographs, design, and production by Janine Sprout

For Kate, Nancy, and Sarah Moser; Annie and Beth Brissenden; Jeremy and Greg Purdy; Norah Harvey and Greg Hanson; Sarah Harvey; Spencer and Blair Hyde; Sam and Julie Scott; Laura Gotz; Nikki Rowley; Trevor and Oscar Hagstrom; Jennifer and Michael Camargo; Rebecca, Carrie, and Jonathan Spring; Ben and Daisy York; Whitney Hartzell; Jess, Jasmine and Autumn Rose Carlisle; Heather and Cameron Barr; Kyle Cohen; Nathan and Josh Gillespie; and Collin, Owen, Holly, Dane, and Katie Rickford.

Special thanks to our Trailblazer ohana: Jimmy Dunn and Paula Pennington; John and Patty Brissenden; John and Suzanne Barr; Gregory Hayes and Joan Wright; Ellen Scott and Joseph Stroud; Richard and Kate Harvey; Marge and Jerry Purdy; Rob Moser; Margaret and Dennis Daniels; Anna and Derek Rickford, Carol Mallory, Jim Rowley, Barbara and Gary Howard, Judy Farnsworth, Virginia York, Mark and Vicki Hyde, John Manzolati, Linda Kearney, Elsa Kendall, Lea Duchein, Vivienne Bekeart, Sandy and Jack Lewin; Cynthia, Michael, Matthew and Amy Sagues, and Edwin O. Hagstrom.

Diamond Valley Company, Publishers
89 Lower Manzanita Drive, Markleeville, CA 96120
P. O. Box 422, Kilauea, HI 96754
www.trailblazertravelbooks.com
trailblazertravelbooks@gmail.com
www.trailbazerhawaii.com

ISBN 10: 0-9786371-2-7
ISBN 13: 978-0-9786371-2-5
Library of Congress Catalog Card Number 2004099013

Printed in Canada
Copyright ©2005, 2007, 2009 by Jerry and Janine Sprout

Proofreader: Greg Hayes
Cover: North Shore

Mahalo Nui!

Haleiwa Jane Duncan and Greg Koop; Barry and Alice Zacherle; John Cruz and Leslie Trugilo; William Kaiheʻekai Maioho at the Royal Mausoleum; Buffalo and the Keaulana family of Makaha; Sandi Yara and Michael Paulin at Aqua; Anne Wharton, Shaun Chillingworth of Bishop Museum; Maria Borgess and Deborah Dunn at Iolani Palace; Charlie Aldinger, Honolulu Academy of Art; Donald and Jean at the Hawaii Maritime Center; B.J. Whitman, Moana Surfrider; Guy at the 'W'; The late Dino Ching at Kuhio Beach Park, Mark Heckman at the Waikiki Aquarium; Ron Kamano, Loke Lani, and Kananiola at Kuhai Halau hula; Maile Drake at the Bishop Museum; John Alford, Bike Hawaii; Martha Yent, Debbie Ward, and Aaron Lowe at the Department of Land and Natural Resources; Kalani at the Hawaii Nature Center; Ray Baker at Lyon Arboretum; Anne at Hanauma Bay; Max and Doug at HURL; Gary Carr at Oceanic Institute; Olive Vanselow, Hoʻomaluhia Botanical Garden; Will Ho, Honolulu Park & Recreation; David Morgan at Kualoa Ranch; Emma at Tropical Farms; Shiela at Kahana Valley; Sister Tan at the Mormon Temple; Scott and Denise from Salem; Charlie Silva at the Turtle Bay Resort; Gary Gill, Kiromi Suenaka, and Aunty Kaula at Waimea Valley; Steven Gould at the North Shore Surf Museum; Floren Elman and Jo Ann Fakler at Hawaii's Plantation Village; Keith Awai and Matthew Tuahivaa the Polynesian Cultural Center; Brian Melzack at Bestsellers; Winnie Singeo at Foster Garden; Brooks Baehr at KGMB; Charles Hinman, Bowfin Submarine Museum; Maile Lowery, Halemanu Plantation; Gloria and Susan, Dole Plantation; Pat Johnson and Ken at Deep Ecology, Chuck Dudley, Camp Timberline; Steve Mayher, Koʻolau Golf Club; Grant Gomes, Town & Country Surf; James Ho, Hawaiian Chinese Museum; Gary Hosaka, Hilton Hawaiian Village; Stephanie Hardy and Ray Baker at Lyon Arboretum; Penny Dumont at Sugar Kane Realty; Caroline Witherspoon, Becker Communications; Maura Jordan, Rebecca Pang, and Jennifer at Oahu Visitors Bureau; Ron Artis; Travis Talemano; Emma at Tropical Farms; Megan at Bookends; Karol and Teresa at Hawaiian Railway Society; Arthur Wong, and Arnold at City and County of Honolulu.

North Shore

*OAHU TRAILBLAZER is dedicated to the beauty of the
land and the sea and to all the people working with aloha
in their hearts toward a vision of a new Hawaii.*

OAHU

Trailblazer

WHERE TO HIKE, SNORKEL, SURF
FROM WAIKIKI TO THE NORTH SHORE

JERRY AND JANINE SPROUT

DIAMOND VALLEY COMPANY

MARKLEEVILLE, CALIFORNIA

PUBLISHERS

TABLE OF CONTENTS

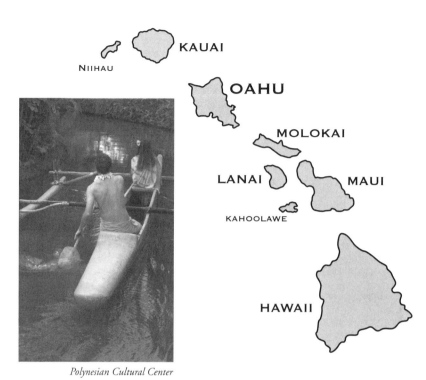

KAUAI

NIIHAU

OAHU

MOLOKAI

LANAI

MAUI

KAHOOLAWE

HAWAII

Polynesian Cultural Center

INTRODUCING OAHU

Most of the five million people who each year jet into Honolulu seek the dream of swaying palms and beachside reverie, of moonlit- and rum-enhanced bliss—one week inside a bubble of pleasure at Waikiki, perhaps taking guided outings to Oahu's headline attractions. For them, Oahu is a fantasy escape, a Las Vegas minus the slots, plus the surf and sand.

A second group of visitors are independent adventurers who want all the attractions, but also want to get outside the bubble and see an Oahu of surprises and intrigue beyond the brochure headlines. Then there's a third group. They are also independent and get outside the tourist bubble, but then it bursts, leaving them lost in traffic, waiting in lines, annoyed, sweaty, hassled, disappointed, and wishing they'd stayed home.

Oahu Trailblazer is for the independent adventurers wanting to graduate to group number two, those who want shed the cowbells to be free of the tourist bubble, but avoid donning the shackles should the bubble burst.

Most of those five million have chosen Oahu, rather than a neighbor island, because it has the cheapest vacation packages and the most available rooms. Some newcomers may not be aware that Hawaii is made up of islands with differing personalities. Only later do these oblivious visitors realize that they've joined a legion of Hawaiian aficionados who have seen all the islands and keep coming back to the 'Gathering Place' for a host of very good reasons.

Many of Oahu's charms are expected. It does have the glimmering entertainment and nightlife, a wealth of restaurants, many of the state's top museums, and one of the world's most dynamic walk-around cities with a bustling Chinatown. Add to that some of Hawaii's top attractions—the USS Arizona Memorial at Pearl Harbor, Waikiki, Polynesian Cultural Center, and Diamond Head among them. At Hanauma Bay, nature has carved a perfect undersea park—the most popular in the world—but snorkelers can also fnd the beach of their dreams at several out-of-the-way spots on the Windward Coast and pocketed into the North Shore.

Oahu's other charms are more surprising. Most of the island's 112-mile coastline is sandy beach, more than any other island, including the Big Island, which is seven times larger in area. Beachcombers can kick off their shoes and go, go, go. And, although surfing originated in Hawaii and it is big on all the islands, Oahu is the wave-riding capitol of the universe. Along that sand-and-coral coastline are more than 150 named wave breaks, from the 50-footers to the little rollers, from Waikiki to the big-time surf on the North Shore at Waimea Bay and the Banzai Pipeline. Beaches like Sandy and Makaha, unknown to most visitors, also attract surfers from all points on the globe.

Kualoa Regional Park

Yokohama Beach

Just as surprising are the opportunities for land-lovers, who can lace up the boots at more designated public trailheads than on any other island. Many of the trails are within the Honolulu metro area, and hikers will not be wanting for rain forests, waterfalls, and ridges with a view. Visitors may be surprised to see the rural life outside of metro Honolulu, where a series of county and state parks present hikers with an array of trails that will turn a day into a get-away adventure.

For nature fans wishing to stroll rather than sweat, Oahu also delivers. The island has five botanical gardens including Foster, which is downtown; huge Ho'omaluhia underneath the towering pali; and Koko Crater, a primordial world unto itself. Throw in spectacular Waimea Valley gardens and resplendent Lyon Arboretum in Manoa Valley, and you've got a lineup that argues for Oahu to be tops in the state.

Oahu also is quite fetching as pure eye-candy, which, again, is surprising for an island that has freeways and high-rises, more than 80 percent of the state's million-plus residents, and gets more tourists than the other islands combined. Only Oahu has glamorous Waikiki and Diamond Head, a skyline as recognizable as New York, Paris, or San Francisco. Oahu has the Windward Coast with the rippling green wall of the Ko'olau Range, through which drivers penetrate on the space-aged H-3 freeway and off which are a string of seabird islands and jagged spur ridges that evoke the romance of the South Seas. In the Valley of the Temples, even agnostics can find religion. And Oahu has a second range, the Waianaes, with mountainous valleys that fall to wild seascapes and long beaches.

So, even visitors who get here by throwing a dart at a map will have made a smart choice. For those already in love with Hawaii, the love will not be complete until they've come to Oahu. Yes, Hawaii stalkers, Oahu will complete you.

Lanikai Beach, Moana Surfrider, Diamond Head and Waikiki

GETTING TO AND AROUND ON OAHU

See *Transportation*, page 240, and *Driving Around*, page 222.

AIRLINES—Most major airlines fly into Honolulu. Shop around for the lowest price, and don't forget to look online. Some airlines have good fares and direct flights from many smaller airports in the West, but be advised you may fly in a smaller jet, not one of the jumbos. Hawaiian Airlines will always be competitive, especially for stays longer than 30 days. Also check with a travel agent or in your Sunday newspaper's travel section for vacation packages.

CAR RENTALS—If you are staying in Waikiki, especially for a week or less, you may not need a rental car. Many attractions are within walking distance of Waikiki. For independent travelers, active visitors staying longer than a week, and those staying outside of Waikiki, a car will be nearly essential. Make sure to ask your hotel about parking availability and cost.

PUBLIC BUS—TheBus, Oahu's public system, is very good and also inexpensive. Coverage is very thorough and the schedules are convenient and easy to understand. You can easily design your own around-the-island "tour" at a fraction of the cost. Almost all buses are equipped to take bicycles. Adventure travelers can take a bus ride, pedal around, and then hop a ride back.

SHUTTLE BUSES—A number of private shuttle buses run from Waikiki to the airport, downtown, and USS Arizona Memorial at Pearl Harbor. Cost is reasonable, around $15 one-way. You'll also find a number of tour buses that have various packages. The Polynesian Cultural Center has buses that pick up at locations around Waikiki.

WAIKIKI TROLLEY—Open-air cars serve greater Waikiki—from as far east as Hanauma Bay to as far west as the Bishop Museum. Cost is cheap ($2 per ride) to get around Waikiki, Ala Moana, and to Aloha Tower downtown. But to get farther away (Diamond Head, Hanauma Bay, Bishop Museum) tickets get pricey—about $25 for a day pass and $45 for a four-day pass. You can get the four-day pass at half-price online (two for one). Public buses will be cheaper, and so will a rental car, for parties of two or more persons. The trolley makes the most sense for getting downtown and around Waikiki. Urban hikers can cover greater Waikiki on foot.

BICYCLES—You can rent a bike in Waikiki and on the North Shore for around ten bucks a day, at a weekly rate (see *Bike Rentals* in *Resource Links*). For trips of a few miles, a bike will be the fastest and cheapest way to get around. Buses have bike racks, so the two modes work well together. Make sure you have a sturdy lock, and ask the rental company about theft insurance. Much, not all, of the North Shore has a bike lane, and the Kamehameha Highway is cyclist-friendly. Around Waikiki and downtown, bikers will have to pay attention to traffic, but there are many places that are far easier to navigate on a bike than in a car.

DRIVING TIMES FROM WAIKIKI TO:

Diamond Head	10 min. (2 mi.)	Wahiawa	38 min. (25 mi.)
Honolulu	15 min. (4 mi.)	Waimanalo	45 min. (21 mi.)
Nu'uanu Pali	20 min. (8 mi.)	Haleiwa	55 min. (34 mi.)
Airport	30 min. (9 mi.)	Sunset Beach	70 min. (44 mi.)
Kailua	25 min. (13 mi.)	Makaha	75 min. (40 mi.)
Hanauma Bay	30 min. (12 mi.)	Laie	80 min. (42 mi.)
Pearl Harbor	35 min. (14 mi.)		

the island of OAHU

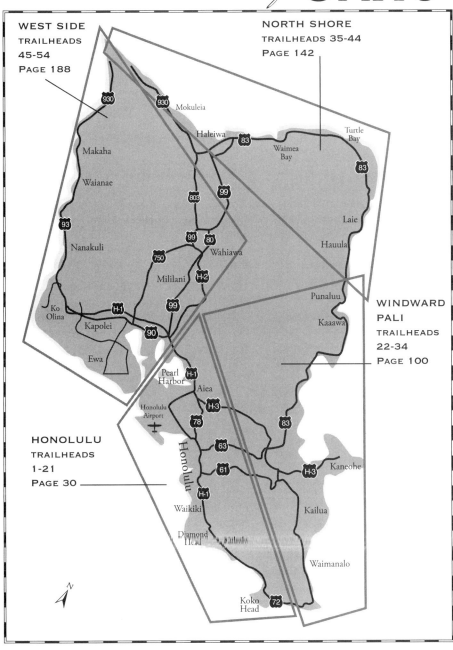

WEST SIDE
TRAILHEADS
45-54
PAGE 188

NORTH SHORE
TRAILHEADS 35-44
PAGE 142

**WINDWARD
PALI**
TRAILHEADS
22-34
PAGE 100

HONOLULU
TRAILHEADS
1-21
PAGE 30

Mokuleia

Haleiwa

Waimea
Bay

Turtle
Bay

Makaha

Waianae

Laie

Nanakuli

Hauula

Wahiawa

Mililani

Punaluu

Ko
Olina

Kaaawa

Kapolei

Ewa

Pearl
Harbor

Aiea

Honolulu
Airport

Honolulu

Kaneohe

Waikiki

Kailua

Diamond
Head

Waimanalo

Koko
Head

930 930 83 83 93 803 99 99 80 750 H-2 99 H-1 90 H-1 H-3 78 63 61 H-1 83 H-3 72

HOW TO USE THIS BOOK

Use the INDEX to locate a trail or place that you've already heard about. Use the TABLE OF CONTENTS and MASTER MAP to focus on a particular region of the island. Then go to the TRAILHEAD MAP for that region to focus further on a particular spot in that region, and read the trailhead descriptions to pick out a hike or other activity that looks appealing.

Use the ACTIVITIES BANNER in the TRAILHEAD DIRECTORY to see which recreational opportunities are available, and where. Or, go to the BEST OF section to find a hike or other activity that suits your interests, mood, and the day—and also is conveniently located.

Use RESOURCE LINKS to find listings and phone numbers for public agencies (including camping and hiking permits), organizations, museums, attractions, tours, outfitters, and visitor information contacts. For overall advice on planning your trip to Oahu, see STRATEGIES FOR VISITING.

KEY TO READING TRAILHEAD DESCRIPTIONS

23. TRAILHEAD NAME   **ACTIVITIES BANNER**
WHAT'S BEST:
PARKING: (SAMPLE)
HIKE: Hike Destination (distance, elevation)   Hike Description
Be Aware: *More Stuff:*
SNORKEL: SURF: Snorkeling and surfing descriptions

"23." Trailhead Number: These correspond to the numbers shown on the four Trailhead Maps. Numbers begin with Map 1, Honolulu, and continue to Map 4, West Side. In most cases, trailhead numbers that are close together numerically will also be close geographically. There are 54 trailheads, listed sequentially.

Trailhead Name: Each trailhead offers one or more of the recreational opportunities—hiking, snorkeling, and surfing. Some trailheads offer one parking spot and a single activity. Other trailheads have two or more parking spots, close together, and several recreational activities.

ACTIVITIES BANNER: This shows recreational activities available at this trailhead.

HIKE: Includes both long and short treks in parks, gardens, forests, beaches, and all other natural settings. Also includes strolls and longer walks at museums, attractions, and in city settings.

SNORKEL: Includes fish-viewing with mask and fins, as well as safe places to get in and take a dip.

SURF: Surfing with long or shortboards, bodyboards, bodies. Also includes windsurfing and kiteboarding locations, along with the best place to be a spectator.

WHAT'S BEST: A thumbnail description of what to expect at this trailhead.

PARKING: Gives directions from the nearest highway or freeway to the parking spot for the trailhead's primary activity. Secondary parking directions are also given for nearby activities.

HIKE: The first paragraph after the Hike: symbol lists each Hike Destination for this trailhead, followed by the (distance, and elevation gain) for each hike in parentheses. Distances are to the nearest .25-mile. Only elevations of 100 feet or more are noted. All hiking distances in parentheses are ROUND TRIP. *Note:* Hikers will average about 2 m.p.h. on strolls and flat hikes. *On ridge hikes with elevation gain*, plan an hour for every mile of trail.

The second and following paragraphs after the Hike: symbol often gives background and history for the trailhead. Then come the hiking directions. The first reference to a **Hike Destination** is boldfaced. Descriptions include junctions with other trails, the type of terrain, as well as landmarks along the way. **Second Destinations** follow in subsequent paragraphs, boldfaced and described in the same order as listed in the first Hike: paragraph.

Be Aware: Notes special precautions and difficulties associated with a hike or other activity. Precautions that apply to all activities—like always following a clearly visible trail and turning back to a known point should you lose the trail—are not mentioned repeatedly. Also see *Free Advice & Opinion* for rules and hazards

More Stuff: Gives other hikes and activities available at this trailhead. Normally these are out-of-the-way spots, sometimes with questionable access, difficult terrain, or requiring a special permit. Fewer visitors will be at these places. These activities will appeal more to Oahu locals and repeat visitors.

Talk Story: Gives historical or other background information. Rooted in the islands' oral traditions, 'talk story' is the term locals use for reminiscing about the old days.

SNORKEL: SURF: Descriptions include where to go for theses water sports, as well as notations for precautions. Parking directions often will have been included in the hike directions. For instance, a beach hike parking may be the same as for snorkeling or surfing. If not, additional parking directions will be included. Several snorkeling or surfing spots may be given for a single trailhead.

Pokai Beach Park

What do you want to do today?
Choose an outing to suit your mood and the day.
ACTIVITIES ARE LISTED ACCORDING TO TRAILHEAD NUMBER.

ATTRACTIONS

WHERE THE KINGDOM OF HAWAII LIVES ON
Iolani Palace, TH1, page 32
Bishop Museum, TH12, page 69
Royal Mausoleum, TH13, page 72
Pu'u O Mahuka Heiau, TH41, page 163
Kukaniloko Birthstones, TH46, page 191
Kaneaki Heiau, TH53, page 205

ALL-STAR RED, WHITE, AND BLUE
Army Museum, TH4, page 45
USS Arizona Memorial-Pearl Harbor, TH8, page 59
Punchbowl-National Memorial Cemetery of the Pacific, TH14, page 77
Tropic Lightning Museum, TH45, page 189

MUSEUMS & CULTURAL ATTRACTIONS
Hawaii Maritime Center, TH1, page 32
Honolulu Academy of Arts, TH1, page 38
Bishop Museum, TH12, page 69
Polynesian Cultural Center, TH36, page 145

NOTABLE FREEBIES
Aloha Stadium Swap Meet, page 234
Aloha Tower, Chinatown, TH1, page 31, 37
Hawaii State Art Museum, TH1, page 34
Ali'iolani Hale, Kawaiahao Church, TH1, page 34
Top of Waikiki, Oceanarium TH4, page 47
Royal Hawaiian, Moana Surfrider, Dukes, TH4, page 46
Kahala Mandarin dolphins TH7, page 57
USS Arizona Memorial, Pearl Harbor, TH8, page 59
Makai Research Pier TH23, page 104
Windward Open Market TH32, page 125
Pacific Skydiving Center TH44, page 179

TROPICAL TREKS

GARDENS

PEOPLE-WATCHING BEACH HIKES

WALK A WILD COAST

WATERFALLS

WALK AROUND TOWN

SNORKELING

BEST ALL AROUND
Sans Souci Beach, Makalei Beach Park, TH5, page 53
Cromwell's Cove, TH6, page 56
Hanauma Bay, TH20, page 89
Makai Research Pier, TH23, page 105
Kailua and Lanikai beaches, TH25, pages 110, 112
Shark's Cove, Three Tables, TH41, page 164

YEAR ROUND SAFE PLACES
Magic Island TH3, page 42
Kahanamoku Beach, Kuhio Beach Park, TH4, page 48
Waialae Beach Park, Mother's Beach, TH7, page 58
Kaiona Beach Park, Pahonu Pond, TH24, page 109
Secret Island TH33, page 130
Kulima Cove, Kaihalulu Keiki Pool, TH38, page 156
Ko Olina Lagoons, Lanikuhonua Cove, TH50, page 199
Pokai Beach Park TH52, page 203
Kaena Keiki Pond TH54, page 213

A SWIMMING DAY AT THE BEACH
Queen's Surf Beach, TH5, page 53
Ka'alawai Beach, TH6, page 56
Laumilo access, Waimanalo, TH24, page 109
Lanikai Beach, TH25, page 112
Kualoa Regional Park, TH33, page 130
Malaekahana-Goat Island, TH37, page 153
Kawela Bay, TH38, page 156
Haleiwa Beach Park, TH43, page 175
Makaleha Beach Park, TH44, page 181

NOT FOR BEGINNERS, BUT NOT HARD
Eternity Beach, TH21, page 93
Punalu'u Beach Park, TH34, page 134
Laniola Beach, TH34, page 150
Mokuauia Beach, Goat Island, TH37, page 153
Alligator Rock, Turtle Beach, TH42, page 169
Pu'uiki Beach, TH43, page 175
Kahe Point-Electric Beach, TH51, page 200

FOR MORE EXPERIENCED
Rainbow Reef, TH3, page 42
Lanai Lookout, TH21, page 92
Chinaman's Hat, TH33, page 130
Wananapaoa Islands, TH42, page 169
Mokuleia Beach Park, TH44, page 181
Kea'au Beach Park, TH53, page 207

SURFING

OAHU'S WORLD RENOWNED FOR KAHUNAS
Sandy Beach, TH21, page 93
Sunset Beach, TH39, page 157
Pipeline, TH40, page 160
Waimea Bay, TH42, page 169
Haleiwa Ali'i, TH43, page 175
Makaha Beach, TH53, page 206

BEST PLACES TO WATCH
Kapahulu Groin (The Wall), TH5, page 53
Koko Kai Beach Park, TH20, page 87
Middles, Makapu'u, TH23, page 105
Pali Kiloia, Pounders Beach, TH36, page 150
Kaunala Bay, TH39, page 160
Pipeline, TH40, page 163
Puaena Point, TH43, page 170
Haleiwa breakwater, TH43, page 176
Waterhouse Estate, Kepuhi Point, TH53, page 209

FOR BEGINNERS
Waikiki Beach Center, TH4, page 49
Waimanalo Recreation Area, TH24, page 109
Pidley's, TH42, page 170
Puaena, Haleiwa, TH43, page 176
White Plains Beach, TH48, page 197

EXPERIENCED, NOT EXPERT
Point Panic, TH3, page 43
Kaisers, Pops, TH4, page 49
Tonggs, TH5, page 54
Cliffs, TH6, page 57
Paiko Drive, TH19, page 87
Rainbows, TH33, page 131
Bongs, TH38, page 157
Velzyland, TH39, page 160
Silva Channel, TH44, page 181
Tracks, TH51, page 201

BOOGIE BOARD AND BODYSURFING
The Wall, TH5, page 54
Sandy Beach, TH21, page 93
Makapu'u Beach Park. TH23, page 105
Bellows Field Beach Park, TH24, page 109
Pounders, TH36, page 150
Kahuku-Malaekahana, Hukilau, TH37, page 154
Papaoneone Beach, TH53, page 206
Yokohama Bay, TH54, page 213

TRAILHEAD DIRECTORY

HIKE: All walking, from short strolls to full-fledged day hikes. Includes both nature walks and man-made attractions.

SNORKEL: Includes fish-viewing with mask and fins, as well as places to swim.

SURF: Board, bodysurf, bodyboard, windsurfing, kiteboarding.

Honolulu

Windward Pali

Honolulu

Waikiki from Diamond Head

While packing for vacation, most people conjure a fantasy of Honolulu—the blue-white heat of Waikiki Beach, the rippling-green profile of Diamond Head crater, the tiki-torched romance of a tropical Pacific seaport—only to arrive and realize almost immediately that, sure enough, the fantasy is true.

No city delivers its postcard image more truly.

Millions of visitors spend a sunburned week by the pool and leave contented. Makes a lot of sense. But others nose around a bit, finding new adventures daily just within the metro Honolulu area, one place leading to another, so that the more they discover the more they have left to uncover, and by the time their jumbo jet bids aloha, they only know that Honolulu is one of the world's dynamic cities, superlative in many ways, which can absorb a lifetime of active vacations.

Before the invasion of Kamehameha the Great in 1795, Honolulu was a village of secondary importance, a rise of land treading above high tides and the floodwaters of the marshlands that were inland. More than 95 percent of Oahu's population lived elsewhere. Today, more than a million Americans call Hawaii home, 90 percent on Oahu, and most of them live in Honolulu. In the 1920s, the Ala Wai Canal was dredged inland from Waikiki, creating a lot of dry beachfront. American servicemen by the thousands fell in love with Hawaii during World War II, and, after statehood in 1959, tourism shot through the roof as the resorts rose toward the clouds.

If staying in Waikiki, watch out. You can easily spend a week hitting the highlights and forget there is another, vastly different Oahu to explore. The biggest draw is to the west of Honolulu at Pearl Harbor, site of the USS Arizona Memorial that is now run by the National Park Service. Despite the crowds, the memorial manages to deliver an unforgettable experience.

Downtown Honolulu—not to be confused with Waikiki—is Oahu's pleasant surprise for urban hikers. This is a big city with a small-town personality. Before homing in on the details, you can get a portrait-quality look from across the harbor at Sand Island Recreation Area. Then put on your walking shoes for a long day or three exploring the vintage buildings, glass towers rising above parks and plazas, and a wealth of museums that are housed in historic sites—the Iolani Palace, Honolulu Academy of Arts, the Hawaii Maritime Museum, and the Royal Mausoleum, to name, as they say, just a few. At Honolulu harbor, Aloha Tower still greets cruise liners, just as in the glory days of Matson's *Lurline*, and just a few blocks away, beyond the eateries and shops of Fort Street Mall, is a thriving Chinatown that is a world apart. Into the mix, add galleries and quirky shops, reflecting Hawaii's blend of cultures, and you've got a world-class, walk-around city.

Aloha Tower, Waikiki

A few blocks to the west of downtown is Bishop Museum, on a campuslike setting of historic and modern buildings. The Bishop holds a phenomenal repository of Hawaiian and South Pacific keepsakes, both ancient and from the more modern epochs that began with the arrival of Captain Cook in the late 1700s. The museum has grown from the personal collection of Princess Bernice Pauahi Bishop, King Kamehameha's great-granddaughter.

Between historic downtown and touristy Waikiki is Ala Moana Beach Park, a sprawling, sunny green space with tree-lined jogging paths, a swimmer's beach, and the snorkeler's pool at Magic Island. Surfboards and sailboats dance along near-shore waters. Across the boulevard is Ala Moana Shopping Center, four-stories of open-air haute couture, an opportunity to complete a surf 'n' shop experience unique to Honolulu. Ala Moana blends with Waikiki, which is actually comprised of five separately named beaches covering a mile or so of oceanfront. Resort towers front the beach and extend inland for about six blocks to the Ala Wai Canal. Two vintage hotels—the Surfrider and the Royal Hawaiian—are reminders of bygone days, as is the memorabilia at Duke's Canoe Club, a bar and restaurant named for Olympian and legendary surfer, Duke Kahanamoku. Waikiki's beaches are all safe for swimming, and tailor-made for beginning surfers. The revolving Top of Waikiki Restaurant serves up a splashy view, while at street level are swank shopping, the International Marketplace, and a blue-glowing aquarium set amid a restaurant. Heads will gimbal on a walk down Kalakaua Avenue, especially on one of the many special event days, such as the Honolulu Festival Grand Parade in March.

Diamond Head, the iconic crater that frames Waikiki, is now a state park. Reachable via a quirky and memorable hike, it looks a lot different from inside, and from on top is a jewel of a view. Between Diamond Head and Waikiki is Kapiolani Park, a bookend to Ala Moana, only this one comes with several attractions like Waikiki Aquarium, the Honolulu Zoo, and the Waikiki Shell, all providing entertainment within walking distance. Visitors looking for a quieter day at the beach need walk no farther than Kapiolani's Sans Souci and Queens— sunning, surfing, and snorkeling.

The biggest surprises for adventure seekers in Honolulu are the metro mauka (mountain) trails, beginning at some 15 different trailheads in the Ko'olau Range that rises to 3,000 feet above Honolulu. Nearby are several

Koko Crater stairs, Waikiki longboards

Ala Moana Beach Park

botanical gardens—Foster and Lyon Arboretum among them—as well as a stroll in Punchbowl, a green crater that holds the National Memorial Cemetery of the Pacific. Other hikes penetrate jungle valleys to waterfalls or up skinny ridgelines to the crest of the range. In minutes, visitors go from the freeway to native forest. The trailheads begin in the west, above Pearl Harbor in the Ewa Forest Reserve, and extend eastward to Koko Head, where the Kuliouou Trail scales the eastern most end of the Koʻolaus.

In between these trailheads is the Moanalua Valley trail along a sylvan stream past seven decrepit bridges of a former estate. Above Waikiki, Tantalus Drive is a 10-mile rain forest loop, a tunnel of greenery that is a gateway to a dozen or more interconnected footpaths. Past the University of Hawaii is a trail through a floral fairyland to Manoa Falls, and on the ridge above is Waʻahila Ridge State Recreation Area, starting point for the island's best view hike to the top of Mount Olympus.

Beaches don't end when you round Diamond Head going east. Kahala is a long run of sand at the doorstep of some ritzy homes, but with plenty of public access. At the Kahala Mandarin Oriental Hotel, visitors can sidle up and do face-time with dolphins, there as part of an educational program. At the far end of Kahala is Koko Head, a pretty sister of Diamond Head, into which nature has carved the most-popular snorkeling venue in the world—Hanauma Bay. Of volcanic origins, the protected bay now shimmers aquamarine, hosting coral and dazzling fish. A companion landform, Koko Crater, rises just inland, where hikers can climb 1,000 steps of an abandoned railway line to the top. Inside and far below is Koko Crater Botanical Gardens, brimming with native palms, weird cacti, and colorful birds.

Around the point from Koko Crater are the whale-watching vistas of the Halona Blowhole. You can see the neighboring islands of Maui, Lanai, and Molokai, on clear days. Sandy Beach is the big draw on this strip of coast, with scorched sand and a shore break that draws some of the world's best bodysurfers.

Sandy Beach, Lyon Arboretum, Cherry Blossom Queen, Honolulu Festival parade

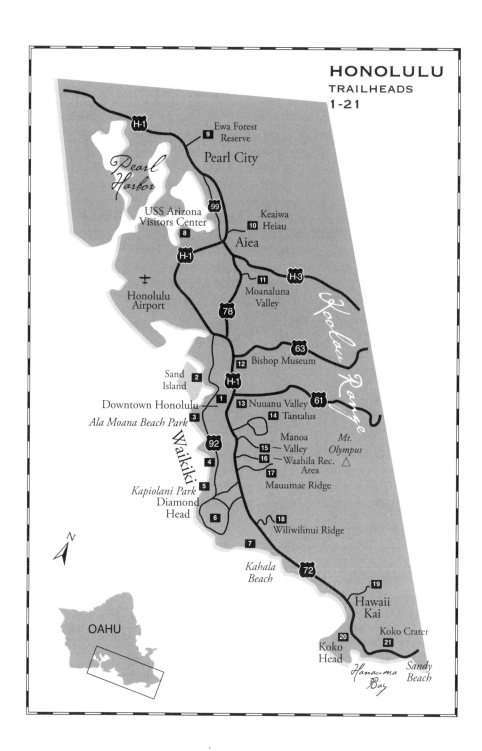

HONOLULU
TRAILHEADS
1-21

Ewa Forest Reserve
9

Pearl City

Pearl Harbor

USS Arizona Visitors Center
8

Keaiwa Heiau
10

Aiea

99

H-1

H-1

H-3

Honolulu Airport

Moanaluna Valley
11

78

63

Bishop Museum
12

Sand Island
2

H-1
1

Downtown Honolulu

Nuuanu Valley
13

61

Ala Moana Beach Park
3

Tantalus
14

92

Manoa Valley
15

Mt. Olympus

Waahila Rec. Area
16

4

Mauumae Ridge
17

Kapiolani Park
5

Diamond Head

6

Wiliwilinui Ridge
18

7

Kahala Beach

72

Hawaii Kai
19

Koko Crater
21

Koko Head
20

Hanauma Bay

Sandy Beach

Koolau Range

Waikiki

N

OAHU

HONOLULU
TRAILHEADS 1-21

TH:	TRAILHEAD
HIKE:	ALL WALKING, FROM SHORT STROLLS TO FULL-FLEDGED DAY HIKES
SNORKEL:	BOTH FISH-VIEWING WITH MASK AND FINS, AND PLACES TO SWIM
SURF:	BOARD, BODYSURF, BODYBOARD, WINDSURFING, KITEBOARDING
MAKAI:	TOWARD THE OCEAN
MAUKA:	INLAND, TOWARD THE MOUNTAINS
MM:	MILE MARKER, CORRESPONDS TO HIGHWAY SIGNS

PLEASE NOTE:
All hiking distances in parentheses are ROUND TRIP. Elevation gains of 100 feet or more are noted. See *Resource Links* page 232 for telephone numbers for all attractions and public agencies. Admission prices listed are for full-price adults. Leave your car free of valuables at every parking spot.

1. HISTORIC HONOLULU   HIKE

WHAT'S BEST: Museums and vintage buildings blend with modern plazas and urban gardens to create one of the world's best walk-around cities. This is a big city with a warm heart. Start at the waterfront and tour either historic museums, or wander through galleries and the old buildings of bustling Chinatown.

PARKING: *From Waikiki*, go west on Ala Moana Blvd. and turn left on Richards toward Aloha Tower, Piers 4-11. Trolley service is available. *From H-1 eastbound*, use Exit 21A, Pali/Bishop. Go right on the Pali Hwy. Then turn right on Vineyard Blvd. and then left on Nuʻuanu. Follow Nuʻuanu all the way to Nimitz-Hwy. 92 and go left. Then turn right toward Aloha Tower. *For both approaches*, use the parking lot in front of Aloha Tower, or the larger lots next to the Maritime Museum at Pier 6. *Notes*: To greatly reduce parking fees, be sure to get your parking stub validated, with minimum purchase, at the Aloha Tower Marketplace or selected museums. You'll wind up paying around $5 for all day.

HIKE: Aloha Tower to: Historic Museums (2 mi.), or Chinatown (1.5 mi.); Honolulu Academy of Arts (.25-mi.) *Notes:* The city hikes can be done in combination. Start with the Historic Museums; directions to Chinatown and the Academy of Arts follow the end of that hike. See map, page 36.

For all hikes, begin with a free elevator ride to the top of **Aloha Tower**, which has clocks on all four sides inscribed with "Aloha," a welcome to cruise ships since 1926. From the 10th floor observation decks, you'll get a literal overview of the urban hikes to follow. Then descend and take a stroll next door through the double-terraced Aloha Tower Marketplace, an open-air assortment of high-end gift shops and restaurants, where at a minimum you'll want to get your parking ticket validated.

Then, for the **historic museums hike**, head to the right as you leave the marketplace. Walking along Honolulu Harbor, you'll come upon the **Hawaii Maritime Center**, formerly King Kalakaua's huge two-level boathouse, with space for large exhibits that come alive with video and audio without being too techy. The islands' entire seaborne past is depicted, from the first Polynesian voyagers right on through to the arrival of Captain Cook in the late 1700s and the onslaught of the sandalwood traders and whalers in the 1800s. Matson's golden age of luxury ships, the 700-passsenger *Lurline* among them, evokes the romance of post-war Waikiki. *Note*: Admission to the nonprofit museum is under $10.

Now get ready to walk six or seven blocks toward **Iolani Palace**. Go left, back toward the Aloha Tower, and hang a right on Bishop Street. Palms sway, as only palms can do, alongside Depression-era buildings, and rising above are the glass towers of white-collar Honolulu. After crossing busy Halekauwila Street, the Dillingham Building is on the right, and the Alexander & Baldwin, is on the left after Queen Street. Very retro. Then veer right on Merchant Street and walk several blocks to wide S. King Street. Across King is the queen of Honolulu's historic buildings, Iolani Palace. *Notes:* You are welcome to stroll the palace's spacious grounds, but the interior is open only to guided tours. At a cost of about $20 per adult, the tours run every 30 minutes from 8:30 to 2, Tuesdays through Saturdays. Call ahead or take your chances as a drop-in. Children under five are not allowed. For less than $10, you can also see the introductory video and visit the Hawaiian crown jewels and artifact galleries in the basement of the palace—but this self-guided option is less satisfying than just taking in the sights on the palace grounds.

Talk Story: For the Kingdom of Hawaii, Iolani Palace represents both great joy and great sadness—and today the tenor there is the bittersweet realm in between. The palace was the residence for the "Merrie Monarch," King David Kalakaua, from 1882 until his death in 1891. Kalakaua was a Renaissance man—composer, author, inventor, and statesman—recognized by leaders around the globe. Iolani Palace, artfully furnished, was also state-of-the-art construction, tricked-out with electricity and telephones a while before the White House. Upon his premature death, Kalakaua's sister, Queen Liliuokalani, acceded to the throne. Her two-year reign ended with the overthrow of the monarchy by mostly American businessmen and politicians—a move questionable on both legal and moral grounds that is debated in the legal system to this today. When royal loyalists continued to protest the overthrow, their queen was imprisoned for eight months in an upstairs bedroom of the palace. The new provisional government, led by American tycoon Sanford Dole and his "Committee of Safety" took over, in spite of a protest by then-President Grover Cleveland. After Cleveland left office in 1898, the U.S. annexed Hawaii, and from then until 1968, the palace was the capitol for the Territory and later for the State of Hawaii. During that period, art and furnishings were sold at public auctions. In 1969, the politicians moved to the nearby Hawaii State Capitol and the palace was returned to the newly formed, nonprofit Friends of Iolani Palace which began tours in 1978.

Iolani Palace, King Kalakua, Coronation Pavilion, Maritime Museum, Royal Hawaiian Band

Near the King Street gate of the palace is the Coronation Pavilion, built for Kalakaua's and Queen Kapiolani's coronation. If you time your visit for a Friday at noon, you'll be treated to a free concert by the Royal Hawaiian Band, which has been together since 1836, founded by King Kamehameha III. To the left of the palace is the Iolani Barracks, the former guardhouse. This is where you buy tour tickets. On the lawn area to the right and in front of the palace is Pohukana, a burial mound holding the sacred remains of ali'i (ancient chiefs), and near that is a rock altar of stones from all the islands that symbolizes one nation among islands. *Be Aware*: The Iolani Palace and its grounds are revered by the Hawaiian people. It's not a tourist attraction per se, so step lightly.

Behind the palace, toward the modern columns of the capitol building, you'll find a statue of beloved Queen Liliuokalani. To the left as you face the front of the palace—at the corner of Richards and S. Hotel streets—is the **Hawaii State Art Museum**, an underrated attraction. A treed courtyard invites you into the old Spanish-Mission style beauty, a former YMCA that was acquired by the state and opened as a museum in 2002. Two galleries await upstairs. In the Ewa Gallery, look for painter Herb Kane's epic *Discovery of Hawaii*, and Madge Tennet's *Two Sisters of Old Hawaii*, powerful in different

Queen Liliiuokalani, Iolani Barracks

ways. *Note:* Admission is free. Hours are 10 to 4, Tuesday through Saturday. Nearby, the YWCA at 1040 Richards may also catch your eye. It was designed in 1927 by Julia Morgan of Hearst Castle fame. Step inside and take a restful break by the indoor pool.

To take in more Hawaiian history through architecture and art, backtrack to the front of the palace and run for your life across King Street. Waiting are the open arms of the life-sized statue of Kamehameha the Great, who became the first ruler of all the islands in 1810. Behind the Great One is the underrated Judiciary History Center, a.k.a. **Ali'iolani Hale**, or Chief unto Heavens. Designed by King Kamehameha V, the building was opened in 1874, the year after his death. It housed the kingdom's legislature and supreme court. Inside today you'll find a gallery explaining how Hawaii's laws have changed with the times. *Note:* Admission is free. It's open Monday through Friday, 9 to 4.

Okay, keep moving. To the left as you face the Judiciary Center is the 1920s-era Territorial Building and then, across Punchbowl Street, is the small stone building and garden that is the King Lunalilo Mausoleum. Ruling for just one year, beginning in 1873 after the death of Kamehameha V, Lunalilo is the only modern monarch not interred at the Royal Mausoleum in Nu'uanu Valley. Rising next to this gravesite is **Kawaiahao Church**. The coral-block beauty was built in 1842, the vision of influential missionary, Hiram Bingham. The truss-beamed interior rises three stories and is ringed by portraits of monarchs, and a who's who of Hawaiian historic figures. This church is quietly one of the most interesting of Hawaii's historical sites.

Across Kawaiahao Street from the cemetery, still heading away from the palace, is **Mission Houses Museum**. Most people have had it with museums at this point, so it doesn't get the play it deserves. The gift shop is first-rate, and you'll find no better depiction of the missionary period in Hawaii. The coral homes have stood here since 1830, among the first permanent structures in Honolulu. Journals and exhibits detail how the missionaries and post-Kamehameha I monarchs shaped an enlightened period in Hawaiian history. The print shop is one of the earliest places to put the Hawaiian language on paper. *Note:* Admission is $10. Tours are offered daily at 11, 1, and 2:45.

Kamehameha statue at Aliiolani Hale

From Mission Houses, backtrack the four or five blocks on Merchant Street to Fort Street, which is one street past Bishop. On the left after crossing Bishop are several period structures; the Stangenwald, Judd, and Star-Bulletin buildings, all built around 1900. At Fort Street, you can go left through Pioneer Plaza back to Aloha Tower, or slide your soles toward Chinatown, as described below.

For the Chinatown hike, put Aloha Tower at your back and cross busy Nimitz Highway to Fort Street. This route description is just a template—virtually every step of the way in old Honolulu presents an opportunity for diversion. You'll pass small Walker Park and come upon the Fort Street Mall. The mall is a six-block, closed-off section of Fort Street, fringed by the city's high-finance towers, as well as some vintage structures. At the lower

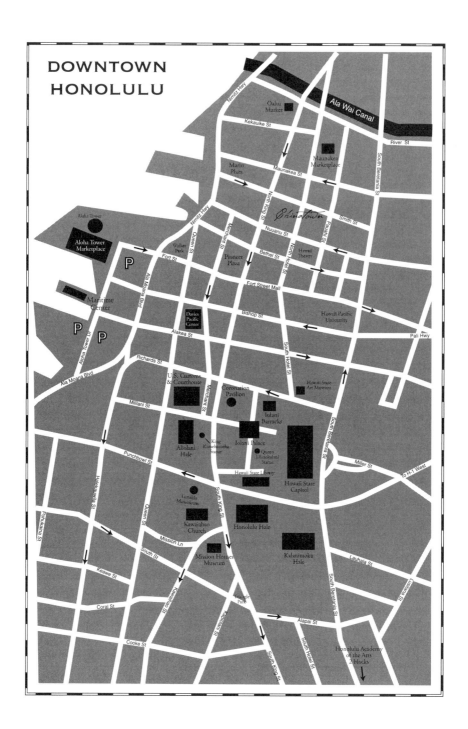

DOWNTOWN HONOLULU

Ala Wai Canal

Nimitz Hwy

Oahu Market

Kekauike St

River St

South Beretania St

Maunakea Marketplace

Marin Plaza

Maunakea St

Aloha Tower

Nimitz Hwy

Smith St

Chinatown

Nuuanu St

North Hotel St

Pauahi St

North King St

Aloha Tower Marketplace

Queen St

Merchant St

Walker Park

Fort St

Pioneer Plaza

Bethel St

Hawaii Theater

Maritime Center

Ala Moana Blvd

Fort Street Mall

Bishop St

Hawaii Pacific University

Davies Pacific Center

Alakea St

South Hotel St

Pali Hwy

Ala Tower Dr

Richards St

Ala Moana Blvd

U.S. Customs & Courthouse

Merchant St

Coronation Pavilion

Hawaii State Art Museum

Mililani St

Iolani Barracks

South Beretania St

Aliiolani Hale

King Kamehameha Statue

Iolani Palace

Queen Liliuokalani Statue

Miller St

To H-1 West

Punchbowl St

Hawaii State Library

Hawaii State Capitol

Haleknuani St

Queen St

Lunalilo Mausoleum

South King St

Pohukaina St

Kawaiahao Church

Mission Ln

Honolulu Hale

Kalanimoku Hale

Laukala St

South Beretania St

US Rampart

South St

Mission Houses Museum

Keawe St

S Ramparts

Triangle Park

Alapai St

Coral St

South King St

South Hotel St

Cooke St

Honolulu Academy of the Arts 2 blocks

end is Pioneer Plaza, welcoming walkers with palms, benches, and outdoor art. The middle of the mall hosts an open-air market Tuesdays, Wednesdays, and Fridays from 8 to midday. You'll also find a strip of cheap ethnic restaurants catering to students and the downtown crowd. At the lower end of the mall, go left on Merchant Street. (If you do the entire mall first, you'll have to double back.)

On the left on Merchant Street you'll see two Bishop Estate buildings that date from the late 1800s. Then you reach Bethel, where all four corners could be part of a film-noir flick. The Kamehameha V Post Office was built in 1870 of iron-reinforced concrete blocks, a modern method that had yet to be utilized in the United States. Notice the cannons used for hitching posts, planted there after being moved from Honolulu Harbor. The post office's corner mates include the 1854 Melchers Building, the Yokohama Bank of 1909, and the former Honolulu Police Station, dating from 1931. From here, turn right on Bethel, go one block to King, turn left. When you reach Nuʻuanu, go right and continue one block to Hotel Street. *More Stuff:* Visitors in search of offbeat galleries can cross Hotel and continue up Nuʻuanu. You'll pass the Hawaii Theater, an old gal dating from 1922, but charming as ever. Near the corner of Nuʻuanu and Pauahi are eight or nine shops and galleries.

From the corner at Nuʻuanu, walk left on Hotel Street and admire cheese-and-sleaze favorites, like the Golden Gate Lounge and Brandy Lee's Black Pearl; this neighborhood can be rough, not fun for the whole family. Continue to Maunakea Street, where to your left you'll see Wo Fat, the funky, photogenic market at the center of things since 1900. Go right on Maunakea, and then look left for the brick façade for **Maunakea Marketplace**, your portal to exotica. Surrounding a two-story interior courtyard are trinket shops, herbalists, Asian restaurants, and a fish-and-vegetable market that is old-world all the way. The Korean Kitchen is plate-lunch city, with long tables and a range of Pacific faire—Vietnamese, Filipino, Korean, Thai. Then, say good-bye and angle left though the marketplace. You'll pop back out on Hotel Street.

Jog right on Hotel and saunter down the pedestrian-only walkway that is Kekaulike Street. Palm trees rise above a concoction of sights, smells, and sounds—sing-song voices, veggies and fruits you won't recognize, chicken feet in jars, live fish in tanks, exhaust fans and tinny music, trays of ornate sweets. Each doorway is a trip. At the end of Kekaulike is **Oahu Market**, which is more of the same, much more of it. The place hums in the early morning and has since 1904. Growers and fishermen stock the indoor array of the island's freshest bounty, an overload of quirky items that will be new to tourist taste buds—pickled, salty, smoked, sweet, spicy, and combinations thereof.

After Oahu Market, it's time to freelance back toward Aloha Tower. You might want to walk King Street and jog right on Smith. You'll see some antique shops in this area. Then cut through Marin Plaza to Merchant Street, which will join up with Fort Street Mall. It's a pleasing return route on Fort Street, past the fountain at old AMFAC gate with Aloha Tower beckoning ahead.

The **Honolulu Academy of Arts** is listed here at the bottom, but it's one of Oahu's top attractions. The American Institute of Architects named its Mediterranean design as Hawaii's best building. Try it on rainy day as showers splatter the tiles in the courtyard gardens. Galleries on two floors hold some 40,000 works of art (someone counts these things) including a credible representation of the best European and American artists, and early Italian classics. The Buddhist, Asian, and Pacific Island art collections are among the most extensive in world. Then you have the only-in-Hawaii offerings, like a three-walled painting *Captain Cook and the Pacific*, Theodore Wores' haunting *The Lei Maker*, Charles Furneaux's illuministic *Old Hawaiian Village*, not to mention volcano paintings that glow in the room. *Note:* Admission is about $7. Wednesdays are free.

A visit to the Honolulu Academy of Arts comes with noteworthy extras: The museum's Academy Shop will have artwork, books, and collectables not found elsewhere. Also within the courtyard is the Doris Duke at the Academy, an art house theater. The Academy Shop is also the place to secure $25 tickets and ride the mini-van to tour Shangri La, heiress Doris Dukes' Islamic-inspired mansion at Black Point. See TH6, Diamond Head, page 56 for more on the dynamic DD. Across the street from the museum is Thomas Square, an acres-large green space to take a break.

Oahu market, Mission House Museum, Wo Fat, Kawaiho Church

Parking for the Academy of Arts: The museum is walking distance, about a half-mile, from Iolani Palace. Walk toward Diamond Head on Beretania. *Driving from Waikiki*, take Ala Moana west to Ward Street and turn right. Continue to King, turn right, and then make your first left on Victoria. *From Eastbound on H-1*, take Exit 22, Kinau Street, continue straight two blocks and turn right on Victoria. *From Victoria*, turn at the T-intersection with Young Street and make a left into the annex parking lot. Parking is free with museum validation.

2. SAND ISLAND STATE PARK   HIKE, SNORKEL, SURF

WHAT'S BEST: Industrial Sand Island won't be featured in travel magazines, but it is *the* place to snap a cover-shot of downtown Honolulu from across the water.

PARKING: *From Waikiki*, take Ala Moana Blvd., which becomes Nimitz Hwy. 92, toward the airport. Before reaching H-1, turn left on Sand Island Access Rd. and follow it 2.5 mi. to the gated park entrance. Park in the lot to the left. *From H-1 Eastbound*, take Exit 18A-Nimitz Highway, and make your first right on Sand Island Access Rd. *Note:* Park hours are from 7 to 6:45 pm.

HIKE: Sand Island loop (1.25 mi.)

You'll have second thoughts, maybe thirds, along the road to **Sand Island**, as you pass warehouses, slag yards, and fuel tanks—but those doubts will be dispelled when you depart the car and jog left to the shoreline path. The view is of downtown Honolulu, its high-rises and Aloha Tower dwarfed by the Ko'olau Mountains. **For the loop**, head to the right along the path, leading along the harbor, where gigantic cruise ships dock below skyscrapers. The 140-acre recreation area sports numerous picnic pavilions spread out under ironwoods, palms, and other beach trees. The path takes you around the point to the wave-washed south shore of the park, where the treeless coast extends about 1.5 miles. Go right where the greenery ends and weave through the picnic areas back to the parking spot. *Talk Story:* Somewhere on those sands, the first blow of the Pearl Harbor attack was struck, ironically by U.S. forces who destroyed a midget Japanese submarine. No one realized the midget was part of a larger attack to come about 90 minutes later. *More Stuff:* On weekdays, stop in a the Universtiy of Hawaii Marine center at 1 Sand Island Access Road to see the *Hokule'a*, the vessel that has been traveling the Pacific, recreating the voyages of ancient Polynesians. Call 842-1100.

SNORKEL: Due to the proximity of industry, **Sand Island** is not known for its swimming. There is, however, a better-than-decent snorkel spot. Go to the mouth of the harbor and to the right you'll see a little beach with **swimming oval**, protected from the open seas by little man-made islands. On the right day, you'll be tempted to take a dip.

SURF: Again, you won't see hoards of board riders, but the reefs off **Sand Island** make for a peaky break, mostly in the summer.

3. ALA MOANA BEACH PARK   HIKE, SNORKEL, SURF

WHAT'S BEST: Come here for Oahu's big-four S's: surf, swim, sand, and shop. On weekends the place is hopping with beachgoers. Midweek and evenings it's perfect for a scenic stroll or jog, or some lap swimming in protected waters.

PARKING: *From Waikiki,* go west on Ala Wai Blvd., take a left on Kapiolani, and veer left immediately on Atkinson. When Atkinson reaches Ala Moana Blvd., go left into the park on Ala Moana Park Dr. A large parking lot will be on your left, or find a spot along the drive. You can also park across the street in the Ala Moana Shopping Center; veer right from Atkinson into the multi-level, free garage. *From H-1 Eastbound,* take Exit 22, Kinau St. and make the first right, on Ward Ave. Follow Ward all the way to Ala Moana and go left. Then turn right on Ala Moana Dr. into the park. Or, to park at the shopping center, continue, turn left on Pikoi, and then right into the garage. *Note:* From Waikiki, the beach park is a .5- to 1-mile walk, depending on where you're staying. You can also ride the Ala Moana pink line trolley, which runs about every 10 minutes at a cost of $2, one way.

Honolulu from Sand Island

HIKE: Ala Moana Beach Park-Ala Moana Shopping Center (up to 3 mi.); Kaka'ako Waterfront Park-Hawaii Children's Discovery Center (.75-mi.)

Located on the west end of Waikiki, across the Ala Wai Canal, **Ala Moana Beach Park** is about a mile of beachfront buffered by a wide, grassy park. Aina Moana Park, better known as Magic Island, is a 30-acre peninsula that juts from the Waikiki side of the park, sprinkled with a dozen picnic areas that host up to 100 persons per site on weekends. Huge, bird-filled banyans, mango trees, and palms are pleasingly spaced. You might start your walk by heading to the tip of Magic Island to behold the Diamond Head as yachts and outrigger canoes glide by into Ala Wai Harbor. Then hug the shore of the peninsula and follow the long stretch of hard packed sand. You'll pass several lifeguard stations and two pavilions—McCoy and Ala Moana—sites for weekend entertainment. At the far end of the beach park is Kewalo Basin, a state park with a promenade and trestled picnic areas. Sunset cruises and fishing charters depart from the basin's harbor. Then double back through the green spaces of Ala Moana. Two ponds on either end of the park are connected by a long canal, with benches and bridges along the way. Most of the locals are here for recreation—softball, tennis, Frisbee, volleyball, and jogging galore.

If you're ready for a plate lunch or perhaps a pair of $200 frayed jeans, bop across the boulevard at the Waikiki end of the beach park. At the **Ala Moana Shopping Center**, escalators and glass elevators interconnect four levels of walkways amid tropical greenery and 250 shops that await your perusal. It's America's largest open-air mall. The shops include the usuals, like The Gap and Nordstrom; but are noteworthy for the heaping helpings of the couture—Chanel, Hermes, Tiffany, Prada, DKNY, and so forth. Mixed in with luxury fashion are shops distinctly Hawaiian. Try The Hawaiian Quilt Collection and Loco Boutique on the fourth level, and Blue Hawaii Surf on the third. The food court is on the ground floor near Macys. Spend hours hanging at this place and you may be jarred by irony when you re-emerge into the tropical air in the middle of the Pacific.

Toward Magic Island at Ala Moana Beach Park

Just west of Ala Moana, **Kaka'ako Waterfront Park** has a wide promenade flanked by vintage light posts and 35 acres of lawn. Go left for a big look toward Diamond Head and Waikiki just across from Kewalo Basin. This spot, called Point Panic, is where local news photographers stand to get scenic shots without fighting the Waikiki traffic. *Directions to Kaka'ako Waterfront Park:* Take Ala Moana Blvd. (Highway 92) west from Ala Moana Park and turn left on Ohe Street. Follow Ohe several blocks to its end.

On the left on Ohe Street, just before the waterfront, is the **Hawaii Children's Discovery Center**. Intended for the whole family, the center uses high-tech and humor to make learning fun. An introductory puppet show will tell you all about it. Local school kids love the place; visiting families are welcome. *Note:* Admission is charged. Tuesday through Friday it opens at 9; on weekends, hours are from 10 to 3.

SNORKEL: Ala Moana Beach Park has some of the best pure swimming in Hawaii, and several decent snorkeling areas. A deep channel just offshore was dredged in the 1920s for boat traffic, and runs for hundreds of yards. It's marked by buoys and protected by a reef farther out, perfect for lap swimmers. Families and dippers like the large man-made swimming oval at the tip of **Magic Island.** Entry is gentle, and the 200-yard long pool is protected by rock islets and a breakwater.

When surf is low, snorkelers can venture out of the protected pool to explore the coral reef. The colorful zone to the right is called **Rainbow Reef**. Snorkeling is also good on the Ala Wai side of Magic Island near a short breakwater, but you need to be mindful of boats. At the other end of Ala Moana, offshore Kewalo Basin, is **Turtle Reef**, where snorkelers may spot large fish along with the hard-shell reptiles. Depths range to 50 feet. *Be Aware:* Don't be shy about asking the lifeguards for tips and precautions about swimming or snorkeling.

SURF: The tip of Magic Island, on the Ala Wai side, is the spot to watch surfers ride a left-break called **Bowls**. On the park side closer in is a 6-foot right break, **Baby Haleiwa**. When the swells get bigger, the break reverses and is called **Big Lefts**. Farther down the beach, offshore the tennis courts, bodyboarders like a long right-break named **Tennis Courts**. (Surfers don't waste valuable wave time thinking up place names.) **Shark's Hole** is inshore to the right of Tennis Courts. Farther offshore is **Concessions** (look for the concession stand), a shortboarder's special. Head to Kaka'ako Waterfront Park for a front row seat of the wave riders at **Point Panic**. Stairs lead down to the water. Some of this zone is limited to bodysurfing.

4. WAIKIKI   HIKE, SNORKEL, SURF

WHAT'S BEST: The name says it all and the place delivers. High-rise resorts, parks, and vintage hotels are packed along a mile-plus of beachfront and backed by luxury shops and restaurants. Iconic Diamond Head frames the scene.

PARKING: For most Oahu visitors, seeing the sights won't involve driving. *From H-1 Eastbound,* Take Exit 22, Kinau St. and make your first right on Ward. Follow Ward all the way to Ala Moana Blvd. and turn left. Continue past Ala Moana Park, cross the canal, and turn right on Hobron. Jog left on Holomoana and turn right into the large, free lots at the harbor. *From H-1 Westbound,* take Exit 25B, Kapiolani, continue on and turn left on Kalakaua Ave. Cross the canal and turn right on Ala Moana. From Ala Moana, turn left on Hobron and continue to the harbor parking lot.

Alternate Waikiki parking: If the harbor lot is full, get back to Ala Moana Blvd. and turn right. Just past the Hilton complex, go right again, on Kalia Rd. You'll find two large lots: one is left on Maluhia Rd. and the second is a little farther on the left, across from the Army Museum. To begin the stroll, angle to the right toward the Hilton's towers. *For Ala Wai Canal from H-1 Eastbound,* take Exit 25A, King St. Continue straight (it becomes Harding for a short distance) and turn right on Kapahulu. Follow Kapahulu past the golf course and turn right on Ala Wai Blvd. Park on Ala Wai or at the library, just before Ala Wai.

Kuhio Beach Park

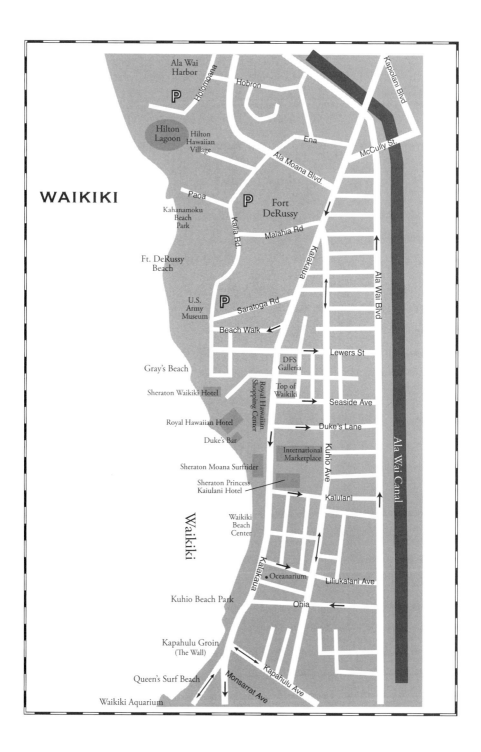

WAIKIKI

Waikiki

Ala Wai Harbor

Holomoana

Hobron

Hilton Lagoon

Hilton Hawaiian Village

Ena

Ala Moana Blvd.

McCully St.

Kapiolani Blvd

Paoa

Kahanamoku Beach Park

Kalia Rd

Fort DeRussy

Malahia Rd

Kalakaua

Ft. DeRussy Beach

Ala Wai Blvd

U.S. Army Museum

Saratoga Rd

Beach Walk

Gray's Beach

DFS Galleria

Lewers St

Sheraton Waikiki Hotel

Royal Hawaiian Shopping Center

Top of Waikiki

Seaside Ave

Royal Hawaiian Hotel

Duke's Lane

Duke's Bar

International Marketplace

Sheraton Moana Surfrider

Kuhio Ave

Sheraton Princess Kaiulani Hotel

Kaiulani

Waikiki Beach Center

Ala Wai Canal

Kalakaua

Oceanarium

Liliukalani Ave

Kuhio Beach Park

Ohia

Kapahulu Groin
(The Wall)

Queen's Surf Beach

Kapahulu Ave

Monsarrat Ave

Waikiki Aquarium

Talk Story: The bald facts are that Waikiki is made up of a half-dozen or so beaches and thousands of hotel rooms extending six blocks inland to the Ala Wai Canal, and bordered on the east by Kapiolani Park and the Diamond Head crater. Although most visitors will sense the romance of Waikiki, few realize the layers of its past now hidden by resorts. But remnants remain. Though hardly a nature stroll, you will follow the Waikiki Historic Trail, so designated by upright surfboard interpretive makers. Only a century ago, Waikiki was a barrier beach, subject to flooding by two streams, an island of sorts, with a vast marsh inland. Around the turn of the century, Hawaiian royalty held residences along the shore's higher ground. In the 1920s, the Ala Wai Canal was dredged, which created dry land ripe for development by ever-expanding tourism. The walk takes you along the beach and loops back on Kalakaua Avenue, the one-way street that fronts Waikiki.

From the harbor parking, begin the **Waikiki stroll** by looping right around the inviting Duke Kahanamoku Lagoon next to the **Hilton Hawaiian Village**, which has the rainbow mosaic on one of the towers. Don't expect to see a Hawaiian village. The Hilton plans a new boardwalk, restaurant, and shops near the lagoon. In front of the Hilton is **Duke Kahanamoku Beach**, named to honor Olympian and all-around superstar Duke Kahanamoku, whose family owned the 20-plus acres on which the resort now stands. You may want to make a loop into the resort, to take a gander at its pink flamingos and black-footed penguins and the shops of Rainbow Bazaar.

From the Hilton, loop out to the beach through a pretty postage-stamp of a park, again named for Duke Kahanamoku. You'll reach **Ft. DeRussy Beach**, a quarter-mile stretch with several acres of lawn and leafy trees that provide breathing room on this end of Waikiki. At the far end of the beach is the **U. S. Army Museum**, housed under a large grassy mound that was formerly a gun emplacement, Battery Randolph, built in 1911. An army museum might be furthest from your thoughts, but this one gets high marks—especially to escape the rain or sun. Its exterior walls are 12 feet thick, from which large guns could fire projectiles the weight of a Volkswagen 14 miles out to sea. All of Pacific warfare, from Kamehameha's invasion in 1795 to Vietnam, is represented as you roam the low lighting of its subterranean hallways, perusing an array of weaponry and battle regalia. If you can't visit, at least walk by the front to see the giant ki'i, statuary carved from ohia trees that are a sacred memorial to Hawaiian warriors called a kukalepa. *Note:* Museum admission is free.

After DeRussy comes the beach-blanketed sands of **Gray's Beach**, virtual acres of pale flesh absorbing Hawaiian sunshine. The name derives from an early-1900s boarding house, though long before that it was called Kawehewehe, place of healing for the ancients. The resorts (including the premier, 500-room Halekulani, founded in 1917) encroach on the sand, and you'll have to step along a railed walkway before coming to the sands of the Sheraton, and then another section of railed walkway. You then reach the beach fronting the venerable **Royal Hawaiian Hotel**. The Pink Lady dates from 1927, originally built by Matson to host cruise ship passengers.

Kalakaua Avenue, Royal Hawaiian Hotel

After the Royal Hawaiian is the Outrigger Waikiki, home to **Duke's Restaurant & Barefoot Bar**. It is dedicated to Duke and his wife, Nadine, and the interior walls are coated with photos of everyone who loved the Duke—Amelia Earhart, Ed Sullivan, Will Rogers, JFK, Duke Wayne, Shirley Temple, you name it. Other black-and-whites of Duke and his more prosaic friends depict without words the meaning of aloha. Next door to the Outrigger is the grand dame of Waikiki, the **Moana Hotel**, now called the Moana Surfrider, A Westin Resort. This hotel was Waikiki's first, built in 1901. Upstairs is a small (free) museum room with a video, and a veranda that overlooks the entrance.

After the Surfrider, the beach opens to Kalakaua Avenue at **Kuhio Beach Park**, the center of things at Waikiki—and not just because it's midway upon the curving shoreline. Here, steps from lapping surf, are the glass towers of a city built exclusively for tourism. Kalakaua Avenue is a stream of luxury boutiques, activity barkers, tiki-torch restaurants, opulent lobbies, street-art vendors—limos and surfmobiles and trolleys cruising by sidewalks full of visitors whose fashion ranges from sunburned bodies in bathing suits to full-blown bridal regalia. Unless you first need a quick draft beer, latte, shrimp tempura or double-fudge cone, take some time to roam around Kuhio Park and watch Waikiki happen. Most evenings at sunset you'll be treated to a free concert.

Kuhio Park is also focal because it's the most obvious place to access the beach for most of the tourists staying at non-beachfront Waikiki. Sitting patiently among the peopled-hubbub is one of Oahu's treasured sites, the Wizard Stones. These are the four, hog-sized rocks chosen by four Tahitian chiefs of the 1500s to represent their mana, or spiritual power. Two statues tell of a more-recent Oahu. One is Duke Paoa Kahanamoku standing before a towering longboard, his arms outstretched toward a Waikiki that was considerably sleepier when the Duke reigned. Down the park is the bronze of the park's namesake, Prince Jonah Kuhio Kalanianaole. Taken in as a son when he was young by his aunt, Queen Kapiolani, and her husband, King David Kalakaua (they were childless), the young prince did jail time, years later, trying to restore the monarchy after the overthrow of Queen Liliuokalani by American businessmen. After his release, Prince Kuhio went on to be a Congressional delegate for the Territory, serving until his death in 1922. Kuhio Park was his home site, which he made public.

At the far end of Kuhio Park, a wide concrete **Kapiolani Groin** (breakwater) protrudes seaward, and you can take a walk out to admire the view from its pavilion. Then, continue your stroll into Kapiolani Beach

Duke Kahanamoku statue

Park—see the next trailhead section—or double back down **Kalakaua Avenue**. The homeward leg is best at dusk or evening. Your first stop should be the Oceanarium, at Pacific Beach Hotel on Liliuokalani Avenue. The 300,000-gallon fish tank is a backdrop for the hotel's diners, but it's okay to go in and gawk—it's three-stories high. Then, back on Kalakaua Avenue, you'll probably want to stop in at the International Marketplace, on the right just past Kaiulani. A massive banyan and waterfall preside over an inner courtyard chockablock with jewelry and art vendors, and a restaurant or three. Then, a block or so farther at Seaside Avenue, is Waikiki Plaza, where you can take an elevator ride to the Top of Waikiki, a revolving restaurant. Dinner is a hot ticket, but they'll let you take a walk around—ride the elevator to the 18th floor and take an escalator up two more floors.

Back on the avenue, across from the Royal Hawaiian, you'll pass the DFS Galleria and can window-shop the fancy stores, like Fendi and Vuitton. At Lewers Street, you'll want to go left, through the latest shopping extravaganza, the double-decked **Waikiki Beach Walk**. Restaurants and high-end shops gleam in the shadow of a Trump Tower. At the far end, is beach access, where you go right to the harbor. (If you parked near Ft. DeRussy, go right on Kalia, before the beach.) *One last tip:* At cocktail time the resorts' beachfront bars are alive with entertainment, and you can compose

Royal Hawaiian Band concert on Kalakaua Avenue

your Waikiki medley by cruising along the beach. One of the best sunset spots, also a favorite for local TV, is the far end of Kahanamoku Beach, at the end of the breakwater adjacent to the harbor parking area. Joggers should enjoy the path along **Ala Wai Canal**. Benches and palms punctuate the way, and outrigger canoeists stroke the waters. You can make the walk a loop by going makai and taking in the tourist commerce along Kuhio Avenue, running parallel, midway between the ocean and the canal.

SNORKEL: Protected by an offshore reef, all the beaches of **Waikik**i are safe for swimming most of the time, although none can brag about snorkeling. The **Duke Kahanamoku Lagoon** is a very inviting swimming spot, mostly off the tourist radar. In front of the Hilton, **Kahanamoku Beach** is a huge calm area, with the best snorkeling offshore to the right nearer the breakwater. To the left of Hilton Pier, you'll find welcoming waters at **Kahanamoku Paoa Beach Park**, and be able to enjoy the green space between swims. The same is true for the long run of sand at **Ft. DeRussy Beach**, although its park is not as intimate. The encroaching hotels at **Gray's Beach**, a.k.a. Halekulani Beach, are a turnoff, but families like the sandy nook between here and the Sheraton. A lone hau tree marks the spot, and, remember, these are the healing waters of ancient times.

Waikiki Center Beach, a.k.a. Moana Beach, running from the Sheraton to the Moana Surfrider, has great sand and swimming waters. The downside is sardinelike sunbathers, and fine sand can mean cloudy waters. The best bet for Waikiki swimming is probably **Kuhio Beach Park**, in spite of its heavy use. Fronting the shore are two large concrete, rectangular pools, the **Kuhio Breakwater**, that provide safe swimming in shallow water. The right side of the breakwater walls have an opening to the sea, where snorkelers might spot a rare fish, lost and frantic. The left-side pool abuts the Kapahulu Groin, "The Wall" built to convey a storm drain and to prevent sand from floating away.

SURF: Waikiki was the home surf for Duke Kahanamoku, the Father of Modern Surfing. Waikiki's breaks are among the best places is Hawaii to learn. The big boys like **Kaisers** in the summer, offshore the breakwater and yacht harbor at Kahanamoku Beach, which is also a good place to watch. A boat channel through the reef creates a right tube. Windsurfers as well as surfers try **Fours,** near the Hilton Pier at Kahanamoku Beach Park. **Threes,** a summer break, is a long paddle out in front of Ft. DeRussy Beach. Off of Gray's Beach is **Populars,** or **Pops,** a well-known fast ride for shortboarders. **Canoes,** in front of the Royal Hawaiian, is the most-consistent break in this zone. It's named for the site's popularity among outrigger surfers—which is a sight to behold. Surfing instruction is available at the **Waikiki Beach Center** at **Kuhio Beach Park.** Just off the sand are racks with hundreds of surfboards, eagerly awaiting their owners. **Queens,** offshore Kuhio, serves up a long right-break for beginning surfers.

5. KAPIOLANI PARK   HIKE, SNORKEL, SURF

WHAT'S BEST: Between the high-rises of Waikiki and the rising-high Diamond Head is a huge green space. Featuring Waikiki Aquarium and the Honolulu Zoo, this is the place for weekend festivities. Kapiolani also has the best snorkeling and hang-around beaches on the Waikiki shoreline.

PARKING: The park is walking distance from Waikiki resorts, beginning on the Diamond Head side at Kapahulu Ave. *To drive from Waikiki* go east on Kalakaua Ave. *From H-1 Eastbound,* take Exit 25A, King St. Continue straight (it becomes Harding for a short distance) and turn right on Kapahulu. Follow Kapahulu all the way to its end at Kalakaua Ave. and turn left. Park on the street. *From H-1 Westbound,* take Exit 26, Waialae and follow all the way past First Ave. and turn left on Kapahulu Ave. Proceed as per directions above.

HIKE: Kapiolani Park stroll (up to 2 mi.)

Headed for Canoes

Talk Story: There are as many routes through Kapiolani Park as there are people and days on the calendar. The nearly 200 acres in the shadow of Diamond Head were given to the public in 1877 by King Kalakaua, in honor of his wife, Queen Kapiolani.

This **Kapiolani Park stroll** begins on the west end, at the corner of Kalakaua and Kapahulu avenues. Start by getting your bearings with a walk out long Kapahulu Groin, a wide concrete wall that gives you a surfer's view of the Waikiki coastline. Then come to shore and get a different perspective. Across the street is **Kahi Halia Aloha**, "Place of Loving Remembrance," which is a burial mound for some of the remains of the native Hawaiians that were dug up during the development of Waikiki. Then begin along the palm-lined beach path. **Queen's Surf Beach** (sometimes just "Queens") is on the Diamond Head side of the groin. It's named for a now-defunct restaurant, which may have been in honor of Kapiolani. The name did not escape the ironic sense of humor of Oahu's gay community, who favor the lawn area of Kapiolani Beach Park on the other side of a breakwater that separates the two shorelines.

At the far end of Kapiolani Park, the beach path passes the outer fences of **Waikiki Aquarium**. Though not large or flashy, the University of Hawaii-operated aquarium has superlative living coral displays (they supply biologists throughout the world). The aquarium is also the only place you can get eye contact with a pair of the endangered Hawaiian Monk Seals, adorable 600-pounders whose ancestors are the only mammals to make to these islands without a boat. Enter the darkness inside and observe the iridescent jellies' tank, the swirling blue waters full of cute sharks and large blunt-nosed Bluefins, and the impossibly complex and colorful displays of coral-reef life. Sit a spell. You won't be wandering by endless tanks filled with this and that, but keen eyes will see 2,500 species of marine life. The Waikiki Aquarium hosts both day and night reef wades, kids' activities, coastal hikes, and other programs; give them a call. *Note:* Admission is about $9. Hours are daily from 9 to 5.

Along the path beyond the aquarium are the art-deco walls of the **War Memorial Natatorium**, which encloses a 100-meter pool that was supposed to be an Olympic site when built in 1927. Though medalists Johnny Weissmuller and the Duke both dipped here, the Oahu Olympics were never realized, and the saltwater pool shut down in 1979. On the other side of the Natatorium is Kaimana Beach, a locals' favorite better known as **Sans Souci Beach**—the name of Frenchman Allen Herbert's 1884 boarding house, meaning "without a care." The beach ends after more than a hundred yards at a reef and some of Oahu's swankiest resorts—The New Otani Kaimana, The W, and Michaels Colony Surf. The blue-blood Outrigger Canoe Club is also in this complex.

Head inland now, crossing the avenue where **Kapiolani Park** comes to a point at circular Louise Dillingham Fountain. Spaced about sprawling green fields are picnic tables under huge banyans and other leafy giants, perfect spots to appreciate a close-up of Diamond Head's famous profile—bring a blanket and book and spend the day. Or, get up and make an aimless walk back through the park. Inland to the right is **Waikiki**

Kapahulu Groin, Queen's Surf Beach, Waikiki Aquarium, Natatorium

Shell, an amphitheater that hosts big-name entertainment, but, alas, the hokey hula shows that were staged nearby for decades came to an end in 1999. Farther down the park is the **Kapiolani Park Bandstand**, an entertainment venue since 2000, built to support the park's various festivals. On the Sundays, the Royal Hawaiian Band will be on hand for a concert. Joggers and soccer teams frolic in the fields, and the serious folks gather yearly for the Honolulu Marathon.

Kapiolani's ongoing events include Sunset at the Beach (that's why the huge screen is set up near Queen's Surf Beach), where locals and tourists gather Saturaday and Sundayto sample an array of plate dinners and watch a free, first-run movie. Another standing favorite, at least among kids, on this end of the park is the **Honolulu Zoo**. The Hawaiian nene lives anxiously next door to the Komodo dragon, flamingos strut, elephants of Africa check out those of Asia, and giraffes ponder the meaning of

Korean dancers at Kapiolani Park Bandstand

it all with the zebras and the rhinoceros. It's all happening. The Honolulu Zoo puts on special talks and walks for kids. It's stroller friendly and has a special playground lawn. *Note:* Admission is $6, less for children and locals. Along Monsarrat Avenue, outside of the zoo, is another ongoing event, the Art Fence, where craftspeople man booths. Now that your Kapiolani stroll is complete, take a break across the way at Lulu's. The second-floor awnings are always open at this beer-and-pupus celebrity hangout.

SNORKEL: Part of the Waikiki Marine Life Conservation District, the waters offshore Kapiolani Park are Waikiki's best for snorkeling. The conservation district begins at the **Kapahulu Groin**, and some fishes live at its tip, but surfing is the main event here. Snorkeling is fair and swimming is good on the left side of the **breakwater** that separates **Queen's Surf Beach** from **Kapiolani Beach Park**. The conditions improve at **Sans Souci Beach**, one of the island's better spots. Walk down to wide sand beach to the right and flipper on out. Coral is close to shore. Under calmer conditions, look for a channel and swim out to your right to explore the reefs in front of the Natatorium and Waikiki Aquarium. You can also explore this zone from the Diamond Head side of **Kapiolani Beach**, but the entry is not as good.

Best for last: Since there's no parking, not many tourists make it to sweet **Makalei Beach Park**. It's on Diamond Head Road, a few blocks from where Kalakaua Avenue ends at the tip of Kapiolani Park. (Park near Poni Moi Road or Coconut Avenue and walk.) To the right of the park's little grass patch is **Kaluahole Beach**, protected by seawalls with near shore coral and a sandy, shaded backshore. Once is not enough for

Kapiolani Beach Park

this beauty. A railed path goes left along a seawall to Leahi Park—a nice stroll past zillion-dollar homes to another neighborhood park with no parking and no beach.

SURF: **The Wall**, a.k.a. Walls, off the tip of Kapahulu Groin is bodyboard central. Walk out to the end and watch these guys peel off waves before doing a header into the concrete. Stand-up boarders try the bigger-wave left break called **Cunha's**, which is pretty much straight out from The Wall. Bodyboarders also drift over to **Publics** (named for the public baths that were near the shore at Kapiolani Park until 1961). From Sans Souci Beach, a channel in the reef leads to **Old Man's**, a longboarders' choice in front of the Outrigger Canoe Club. During the summer, surfers use Makalei Beach Park to access several reefy breaks, including **Ricebowl**, **Tonggs**, and the long paddle out to **Graveyards**.

WHAT'S BEST: Everyone recognizes the 'peak' that is Waikiki's trademarked backdrop, but the up-close view is surprising—and the view from the top is stunning. Afterwards, save some energy to walk a surfers beach along the base of Diamond Head to the shores of Shangri La. An excellent and unusual man-made snorkeling cove awaits.

PARKING: *Diamond Head from Waikiki,* take Kalakaua Ave. past Kapiolani Park. Keep right as it becomes Diamond Head Rd. Circle around past the overlooks and keep left at Kahala Ave. Turn left at signs for Diamond Head State Monument, continue through the tunnel to trail parking. *From H-1 Eastbound,* take Exit 25B, 6th Ave., turn right and continue as 6th becomes Alohea Ave. At Diamond Head Ave. turn left, circle around, and turn right toward Diamond Head. *From H-1 Westbound,* take Exit 27, Kahala and turn left immediately on Kilauea Ave. Follow and then turn left on 18th Ave., which ends at Diamond Head Rd., opposite the road leading to the monument. *Note:* A $5-per-car admission is charged. *Kuilei Cliffs:* From Waikiki, take Diamond Head Road. On an uphill grade, past Beach Road, park where you see a sidewalk and a paved turnout. *For Cromwell's Cove (and direct Ka'alawai Beach):* From Waikiki, follow Diamond Head Road past Kuilei Cliffs and down to where it veers left at tiny Ft. Ruger Park. At this junction, Kahala Avenue continues straight, but you want to veer right on Kulamanu. Park on-street not far after the turn, where Kulamanu Place in on right. Walk down the short road to the bulkhead—Ka'alawai Beach will be to the right, and Cromwell's Cove to the left.

HIKE: Diamond Head summit (1.75 mi., 550 ft.); Kuilei Cliffs to Ka'alawai Beach (1.5 mi., 150 ft.); Cromwell's Cove-Shangri La (.5-mi.)

Talk Story: What appears as a peak from Waikiki is actually the uppermost rim of an oval-shaped crater that is tilted at an angle. You drive through a tunnel to the 350-acre crater floor, which today is arid and covered with dry-land scrub. Diamond Head was formed about 300,000 years ago, several million years after the larger eruptions that formed Oahu, a secondary cone spewing from the southeastern end of the Ko'olau Range. Hawaiians called it Leahi, because it looked like the fin of a yellowfin tuna. British sailors in the early 1800s called it Diamond Head after they mistook for jewels the calcite crystals that sparkled in the sand of its beaches. In the early 1900s, the U.S. military burrowed into Diamond Head, creating a four-level system of gun batteries and observation posts, all of which were outmoded almost before completion. *Be Aware:* Bring water and prepare for sun exposure. Also prepare for crowds. Out-of-shape folks from around the world huff along and there's little passing room. For more solitude, try the early and later hours; the park is open from 6 to 6.

The oddball trail to **Diamond Head summit** starts out innocently enough as a wide paved path that transitions to a switchback trail. Less than halfway to the top is a first lookout, following which is a steep set of stairs leading to a long tunnel, with low lights to aid passage. After the tunnel is a lookout to the left, where winded hikers might pull out before ascending the next long set of stairsteps. At the top of these, you enter a short tunnel that ends at a spiral staircase, leading to a low-ceiling bunker through which everyone squeezes to daylight. From there metal stairs lead to the observation deck at the summit. The view is anything but confining—a toy model of Waikiki is laid out in an expanse of Oahu, from Koko Head to the West Side. To the south across the water, if the day is clear, you'll see Molokai and Lanai, with Maui rising behind them.

To hike from **Kuilei Cliffs to Ka'alawai Beach**, head up from the turnout to a railed path that leads down to the beach. At the first turn of the path is a view of Diamond Head Lighthouse. Down below, Kuilei Cliff Beach Park is a surfers haunt, a grass patch and shower that includes

Diamond Head Trail

11 acres of cliff. Walk left on the narrow strip of sand with cliffs rising inland and Black Point protruding in the distance. After .5-mile along the beach, as the cliffs descend toward sea level, you reach Ka'alawai Beach, a dreamy swath of sand fringed by greenery and curving palms, and by exclusive homes. A reef protects its coral-patched waters. *Be Aware:* Avoid this hike at high tide.

For the short walk to **Cromwell's Cove-Shangri La**, head down Kulamanu Place to the end and go left along a lava-wall path. One crumbly spot midway takes on seawater, but you'll quickly round a point and come upon the man-made cove, which is named for Duke's husband, James. You approach from the closed end of the big lava-rock oval. At the far end, where the Shangri La mansin looms above, is a a 12-foot wide stairway to the water. The pool opens to the sea, protected by a breakwater. *Be Aware:* Watch for breaching waves on the breakwater. *Talk Story:* Formed when an eruption of lava flowed toward the base of Diamond Head, Black Point is the setting of some of Oahu's posh homes. Primary among them is Shangri La, set on a five-acre estate. Cute Doris Duke, a fabulously wealthy tobacco heiress, was only 22 when she set out to build the mansion, which was inspired by her love of Islamic art and culture: Think Paris Hilton meets Citizen Kane. She was a great supporter of the arts on the island until her death in 1993. *Note:* Tours of Shangri La begin at the Honolulu Academy of Arts; see *Resource Links*. *Be Aware:* It's okay to swim the waters along Shangri La, but the grounds are off-limits and only open to tour groups.

Cromwell's Cove

SNORKEL: Ka'alawai Beach is ideal for a day packing the sand, puncuated by dips in clear water. Fish viewing is good. *Be Aware:* When the surf's up, rip currents can be a factor. Local kids like **Cromwell's Cove**, mainly on weekends. Swimming here will be a highlight of a visit to Oahu. Enter on the steps below the estate and swim in toward the protected pool. You will be joined by fish.

SURF: Tour vans pull off at Kuilei Cliffs to watch surfers ride the offshore reef breaks, called **Cliffs**. Surfers heft their boards down the path. Offshore the reef **Ka'alawai Beach**, is a popular big-wave break known as **Browns**. Off Black Point are two other breaks called, yes, **Blacks** and **Kiko'os**. These spots are accessed via a hidden right-of-way that leads to a rocky shore. Follow Kulamanu, go right on Papu Circle, and keep right on Papu Circle Place. You reach a cul-de-sac, now named Kiko'o Place for some reason—just before which is the right-of-way.

Surfers also like the breaks at **Diamond Head Beach Park**, called **Suicides**, **Lighthouse,** and **Diamond Head**. The "park" is off Diamond Head Road, after you pass little Leahi Park heading away from Kapiolani Park. Veer right on Beach Road, a steep one-lane job that ends at a sea-washed shoal with just enough space to turn around. You have to park along the wall on the way down. This is the spot to check out tide pools, but it can be too crowded on good surf days.

7. KAHALA BEACH   HIKE, SNORKEL

WHAT'S BEST: Few tourists see this mile-long beach in the ritzy neighborhood of Kahala. Snorkel with a view of Koko Head, and then get out to sojourn with the dolphins at Kahala Mandarin Oriental.

PARKING: At Waialae Beach Park. *From Waikiki*, take Kalakaua Ave. toward Diamond Head and keep right on Diamond Head Rd., passing the overlooks. Then veer right on Kahala Ave. and continue another 1.25 mi. to the beach park. *From H-1 Eastbound,* take Exit 26B, Kahala. Go straight a short distance, turn right on Hunakai, and follow all the way to Kahala Ave. Turn left to beach park. *From Hawaii Kai*, take Hwy. 72 toward Honolulu and exit at the beginning of H-1, which is Exit 27, Kahala. Go left on Kilauea Ave. and left again, past the elementary school, on Pueo. Take Pueo to Kahala and turn left to the park.

HIKE: Waialae Beach Park to: Kahala Beach hike (up to 1.75 mi.), or Mandarin dolphins (.5-mi.)

The lawn of **Waialae Beach Park** is cleaved by Kapakahi Stream, which is tamed by a canal and footbridge. At the beach, a breakwater shunts the stream offshore, making a pretty cove in front of the park's picnic arbor. Weekends can get active, but Waialae is a weekday special. To walk **Kahala Beach**, take off to the right as you face the water. A nice strip of sand fronts shallow waters—a protective reef is offshore between Diamond Head and Koko Head. High end homes are set back from the sand, and false kamani, palms, and other beach vegetation provide private sunning nooks along the way. *More Stuff:* Kahala Beach may be accessed at several right-of-ways along the avenue coming from Diamond Head: at Kala Place, Hunakai, and two paths near Koloa. Parking is ample and safe.

Koko Head rises before you on the short walk to see the **dolphins** at the **Kahala Mandarin Oriental** hotel. Go left at the park, stepping through coral chunks on the beach past the country club. You'll reach a scenic peninsula with its tiny palm island,

Waialae Beach Park

which frames one end of the resort's man-enhanced beach. Take a walk across the beach to the other little peninsula, where a secluded bench provides an opportunity to sit down and be happy to be in Hawaii. Then wander into the resort. An inner lagoon is surrounded by the Mandarin's two-level rooms and a waterfall. At least a half-dozen of our mammalian friends streak and cavort in its calm waters, occasionally coming up to exhale or for a stare-down with curious humans. To actually get in and meet theses creatures, contact Dolphin Quest on-site, which has programs three times daily for kids and adults. Feeding time is a show itself, often taking place at 11 a.m. Although the architecture is boxy, the Kahala Mandarin Oriental is on the short list among Oahu's premier resorts, with lots of quiet space as well as cultural activities.

SNORKEL: Low tide can be a bummer at **Waialae Beach Park**, but when conditions are right, the snorkeling is better than good. Try to the left of the breakwater in front on the park, or walk left and enter nearer the Mandarin. The **Kahala Mandarin Beach** is a fun swim, but you most likely will see fewer fishes. Go to the peninsula closest to the beach park and swim around the little island, or lap swim the long man-made channel in front of the resort. **Kahala Beach** (see the access points in *More Stuff* above) is an ideal place for staking out a private piece of sand and occasionally taking a dunk to cool off. Since all of the above appeals to moms and toddlers, Kahala is known locally as **Mothers Beach.**

WHAT'S BEST: "Remember Pearl Harbor" was the battle cry that put America into WWII. Today, the USS Arizona Memorial is an unforgettable experience.

PARKING: *From Waikiki*, take H-1 West to Exit 15A, USS Arizona-Stadium (not 15B, Pearl Harbor). Continue straight on Kamehameha Hwy. 99. Continue over bridge past Halawa Dr. and turn left at Kalaloa Dr. Then jog right into a large, free parking lot. *Note*: Public buses #20 and #42 run from Waikiki to the memorial, as do a commercial transportation companies. *From H-1 Eastbound*, take Exit 15, Pearl Harbor-Hickam AFB, and stay right toward Pearl Harbor. Turn right *before* the gate booths and drive through the parking lot—you don't need a day pass. Turn left on the other side of the lot, and then go right at a stop sign on 6ᵗʰ- Center Dr. Take Center to a light at Kamehameha Hwy. 99 and go left. After about a mile, take a left toward the memorial on Kalaloa Dr.

HIKE: USS Arizona Memorial and Bowfin Submarine Park (up to .5-mi.)

Be Aware: People rave about this national park, and it can be a zoo during the summer, spring break, winter holidays, and when the cruise ships are in, which includes most of the time. Call ahead to get a reading from rangers. Hours are from 7:30 to 5, with the last program beginning at 3. During crowded times, arrive early or in the afternoon. You may wait an hour or two to begin your program—but this is good thing. The time is needed to take in the visitors center and grounds before your program. Backpacks, fanny packs, large camera bags, and even diaper bags are not permitted inside. Put them in your trunk (two security guards on bicycles patrol the lot), or use a manned, $2 security locker that is next to the parking lot. Admission to the memorial is free, first-come, first-served.

Talk Story: In 1950, nine years after the "Day of Infamy," a flagpole was erected over the sunken Arizona, thus establishing the memorial. The famous white, broken-backed building that straddles the vessel was approved by President Dwight Eisenhower, and dedicated in 1962. In 1979, the National Park Service took over from the Navy, and, a year later, the visitors center complex was completed.

Upon passing security, you are given a ticket that states your program time for the **USS Arizona Memorial**. At the stated time, line up at the theater to watch a well-made movie that precedes the brief open-boat ride to the memorial building itself— all of which takes about 75 minutes. Buy the $5 audio tour and use the walk time to cruise around the abundance of displays, which include a 50-foot mural of the *USS Arizona*. With a variety of recordings, the audio tour awakens December 7, 1941. A two-acre outside area has shore-side exhibits and a view across the water to Battleship Row, where nine American warships were anchored bow-to-stern.

The memorial's theater is comfortable and the movie is damned moving. Even blasé visitors may have fresh emotions. Navy personnel narrate the short cruise across to the memorial building. A faint trickle of oil still rises from the *Arizona*, which lies just beneath the surface. The memorial building, at a right angle to the ship, has open railings. A room at the far end has a marble wall etched with the names of all those who were trapped below.

Talk Story: No fewer than 60 books have been written about that Sunday morning in Pearl Harbor, covering an attack that lasted about 2 hours. The barest of facts are these: In the 1930s, the United States formally protested Japan's expansion into China and the Pacific, which Japan considered its "Southern Resources Area." Japanese generals determined they needed to cripple the U.S. forces with a quick strike so that the larger country could not interfere with the expansion—they never intended to further the attack on the U.S. Early warnings of the attack were not acted upon: In the fall, the U.S. intercepted communications from Tokyo to the consulate in Honolulu, asking about the position of ships in Pearl Harbor. On the morning of the attack, a Japanese midget sub was destroyed off Pearl Harbor, but no defensive maneuvers were taken in the ensuing 90 minutes before the bombs fell. Later that morning, radar on Oahu's north shore spotted aircraft an hour out, but the invaders were mistakenly thought to be a returning fleet of American B-17s.

Just before 8 a.m., the first wave came. Five minutes later, The *USS Arizona*, a "city at sea," was struck, and only nine minutes later she went down, taking a crew of nearly 1,200 to the bottom. These were to be half the American losses on the day. Some 400 sailors died when the *USS Oklahoma* rolled a few minutes later. The *California* and *West Virginia* sank at their moorings, while the *Nevada* made a run for open sea, but was sunk, blocking the the harbor mouth. Meanwhile Japanese planes assaulted aircraft on the ground at six airfields all over Oahu. There was a lull at about 8:40, while Americans scrambled to respond. About 15 minutes later, a second wave of attackers scuttled these efforts. The skies were quiet again at 10 a.m. In all, 21 vessels were sunk or damaged, the airpower on the island was virtually wiped out, and nearly 2,400 lives were lost. The Japanese lost 29 planes carrying 55 airmen.

The **USS Bowfin Submarine Park & Museum** is steps away, across the parking lot from the USS Arizona Memorial. Look for the upright Navy missiles on display. After the memorial, you'll need a breather before reentry to modern-day Oahu. Outside is a Waterfront Memorial to the 52 subs and 3,500 crewmen that were lost during WWII. Picnic tables and a snack bar will also be welcomed. The *USS Bowfin*, all 300 feet and 2,000 tons of her, is moored in front of the museum. Known as the "Pearl Harbor Avenger," the submarine sank 44 enemy ships during the course of nine patrols. The large museum details not only the Bowfin and the WWII era, but also the history of submarines from the dicey beginnings in 1776 on through to today's nuclear-propelled marvels. Dive suits, control panels, and large model cross-sections all but put you under the water. *Note:* Admission to the sub is $8. The museum charge is $4. All fees go to the nonprofit Pacific Fleet Submarine Memorial Association.

USS Arizona Memorial, USS Bowfin Submarine Park

Moov Staff The *USS Missouri* survived Pearl Harbor and her decks were the later site of the ceremonial surrender by the Japanese to the United States in Tokyo. (In a famous gesture, General Douglas MacArthur responded to the enemy's offer of a handshake with a jerk of his thumb: take a hike.) You can see the *Missouri* from the memorial building, moored at the shore of Ford Island, where only military personnel are allowed. Tours of the *USS Missouri* cost about $16 and last about 2.5 hours. Tickets and shuttle bus service are available at a booth near the Arizona lot and pack-check locker.

WHAT'S BEST: For serious trekkers, the Manana and Waimano trails are an all-day ascent to the Koʻolau Ridge. Or, less-ambitious hikers can choose between a waterfall with dipping pools and a loop through a luscious valley.

PARKING: *From Waikiki*, follow H-1 West past the airport to Exit 10-Pearl City. Continue straight to Moanalua Rd. and turn right where it ends at Waimano Home Rd. *From H-1 Eastbound*, take Exit 10-Pearl City. Just after exiting, go left on Moanalua Rd., and then turn right on Waimano Home Rd. *For the Manana Trail*, continue on Waimano Home Rd. for .6-mi. and turn left at a light on Komo Mai Rd. Continue for 3 mi. through Pacific Palisades to road's end. Park on the street. *For the Waimano Trail*, stay on Waimano Home Rd. for 1.75 mi. until it ends at a security gate. Park in the assigned area.

HIKE: Manana Trail to: Waimano Falls (3.25 mi., 725 ft.), or Koʻolau Ridge (12 mi., 1,750 ft.); Waimano Trail to: Waimano Valley loop (2.25 mi., 325 ft.), or Koʻolau Ridge (14.25 mi., 1,600 ft.)

For both Manana Trail hikes, pass the Na Ala Hele trailhead sign and continue up the inviting road under the shade of large eucalyptus trees and ironwoods, passing a water tank. The road becomes a trail, open and airy. About .5-mile in, keep left at an arrow sign on a rooted mound. The trail drops to the left, and then contours to the right, soon reaching a trail sign with a double set of arrows. For the **Waimano Falls**, go right. You will descend steeply under a leafy canopy and over an eroded, root-snarled surface. The trail then enters an even steeper section, through a thick strawberry guava forest, dappled with leafy ti plants. A rope aids the way down one short rocky section. You contour left for a while, and then drop some more—more than you'll want to. In the rainy season, you will hear the falls before seeing them.

Waimano Falls drops about 40 feet into a rock cavern. The lowest pool is the best for swimming, but you can't see the waterfall due to a bend in the stream. A five-foot cascade, with a rope swing, separates the lower pool from an upper. You can climb around to it, but a pesky eight-foot drop at the end adds difficulty. The prime spot is the top of the falls, reachable via a short hands-on route. At the sunny top, the stream flows over bedrock, a good spot to explore farther upstream. *Be Aware:* This is a long 3 miles, with poor footing and a steep climb back, but it's not dangerous.

To reach **Koʻolau Ridge on the Manana Trail**, keep left at the double arrows, where the falls trail drops to the right. The trail eventually reaches a 2,700-foot ridgetop, visible for much of the route, but the going gets tough not long after the falls trail junction. Leg scratches are likely. Many hikers consider this trail the island's toughest, and that's saying something. The up-and-down ridge leaves the eucalyptus and pine forests and enters native dry-land habitat, a mix of uluhe fern with ohia and koa trees, among others. Two view knobs, spaced apart about halfway up, are worthy destinations for hikers not wanting to go the distance. *Be Aware:* Only hearty hikers traveling in pairs should attempt this hike. Prepare for a full-on trek, and give yourself all day. Avoid this trail on weekends, when hunters may be present.

For aesthetics, the start of Na Ala Hele's **Waimano Trail** couldn't be much worse. **For both hikes**, you begin squeezed between brush and the garbage-strewn Cyclone fence along the grounds of a law-enforcement-training center. Ignore the initial left-forking trail junction (the return route for loop hikers) and continue for about .5-mile along an old irrigation ditch. **For the Waimano Valley loop**, go left at a junction atop an eroded view knob. Descend through eucalyptus, aided by switchbacks that end at a trail junction amid large mango trees. Go left, as the trail descends some more and parallels Waimano Stream. A rock section near the water is a good sit-down spot. Okay, get up. You'll pass a hau thicket, after which begins the gradual climb, a traverse through guava and Christmas berry that ends at the trail junction near the trailhead.

The **Waimano Trail** leads to a 2,200-foot notch in the **Ko'olau Ridge** revealing a big look at the leeward coast from Chinaman's Hat to Kaneohe Bay. It takes at least 6 hours, but the footing is good on this mostly graded route. Keep going past the valley trail junctions. You'll contour above Waimano Valley, roughly following the path of an abandoned irrigation ditch that disappears into tunnels, reaching an intake in the east end of the valley. From there, you climb over a ridge and continue along a stream to a decrepit dam. Native vegetation is a marvel. From the old dam, the trail curves to the right and then does most of its climbing on several switchbacks. The last part is a more gradual ascent to the saddle in the ridge. *Be Aware:* Watch your footing in places, mainly on two

Waimano Falls trail

rooted, rock faces. Trail-reading skills are required, especially at stream crossings. Always double-back to a known point if you lose the trail.

10. KEAIWA HEIAU STATE RECREATION AREA   HIKE

WHAT'S BEST: Take a break at the healing heiau in a well-kept park. Or get the juices flowing on a forested, 5-mile loop hike.

PARKING: *From Waikiki,* follow H-1 West past the airport and then take Exit 13A-78 West-Aiea. Loop around to Hwy. 78 and then keep right on Moanalua Rd. After a short distance, turn right on Aiea Heights Dr. *From H-1 Eastbound,* take Exit 13A-Aiea-Moanalua-H-78. Stay right toward Aiea. Loop around toward Hwy. 99-Stadium and keep straight toward Aiea. You wind up on Moanalua Rd. Then turn right on Aiea Heights Dr. *Follow Aiea Heights Dr.* for 2.5 miles up to the state recreation area. *For the heiau stroll,* park immediately after entering the park. *For the loop trail,* keep right on the park road and continue for .6-mile to the trailhead and the upper end of the road—which makes a 1-mile loop.

HIKE: Keaiwa Heiau stroll (up to .25-mi); Aiea Loop Trail (4.75 mi., 850 ft.)

The remains of **Keaiwa Heiau,** which was the health clinic of its day in the 1500s, are to the left after you pass the sign for the recreation area. Here, the kahuna, or doctor-priest, would use herbs from the surrounding gardens and forest to treat what ailed the local people. The 1,600-square-foot enclosure, now just low walls, used to contain a large thatched structure. Today's heiau was partially restored in 1951, after soldiers had removed stones for roadwork during the war. The Keaiwa Heiau State Recreation Area, some 385 acres, is beautifully forested with Norfolk and Cook pines, as well as other non-natives. The picnic pavilions near the heiau are a pleasant stroll. The mile-long loop road around the park is a good choice for joggers and strollers.

Beginning at the upper trailhead, the **Aiea Loop Trail** is a locals' favorite, and includes options to both lengthen and shorten the hike. You start out amid bird chirps in a eucalyptus forest and reach a first view of Honolulu just minutes from the car. About .5-mile into the walk, after crossing under power lines, you'll get a look at the Koʻolau Range ahead. *More Stuff:* About a half-hour into the walk, in a sparsely treed open section, is an unsigned junction for the Bisectional Trail, which cuts the longer loop in half. To use this trail, drop down on a traverse back toward the trailhead and cross the stream (if it's running) and push through some denser foliage. You reach an obvious junction with the loop trail; go right back to the trailhead.

Staying on the main trail after the Bisectional Trail junction, you'll pass through bamboo and ferns, and the trail narrows in spots as you continue toward the head of the valley. You have to scramble under a tree that spans the trail, not long after which is a junction with the Aiea Ridge Trail. *More Stuff:* The Aiea Ridge Trail, a difficult slog in places, snakes up another 1,000 feet to the Koʻolau Ridge. Noise from the H-3 detracts from the wilderness experience, but the views are A-plus. From the parking lot, the Aiea Ridge Trail is a little over 10 miles, round-trip.

The loop trail's highpoint, Puʻu Uau, is a little more than 2 miles from the trailhead, at about 1,600 feet. Here, amid native ohia and koa trees, the route hooks right around the top of the valley. On the homeward leg, you'll look over the next ridge into the Halawa Valley and the remarkable H-3 freeway. You then descend through mangos and eucalyptus, some of which give off a lemony aroma. If you see the wing section of a B-24 aircraft in a gully, don't report it. The crash took place in 1944. Cook and Norfolk pines, kukui trees, and some snarled ginger grow along the ephemeral streambed below, which you cross. Ahead, to the right, are the several switchbacks over tree roots that climb to the park's loop road. You come out at the lower trailhead and need to walk right for about .5-mile to complete the loop.

Aiea Loop Trail

11. MOANALUA VALLEY   HIKE

WHAT'S BEST: Once the grand entranceway to an estate, the Moanalua Valley hike takes you over old stone bridges beside a forest of exotic plants gone wild —and a petroglyph rock that make these ruins seem new. You won't find many tourists at this beauty.

PARKING: *From Waikiki,* take H-1 West and continue as it merges with H-78 West, toward Aiea. *For Moanalua Gardens,* take Exit 3. Go up the off-ramp and turn right on a road that hairpins back down and into the gardens. *For Moanalua Valley,* stay on H-78 West and take Exit 2-Moanalua-Red Hill. Go right on Ala Aolani and continue 1.5 miles to Moanalua Valley Neighborhood Park. Leave the car outside the gates, on the street near the bridge. *If Eastbound on H-78,* take Exit 2 also, and follow signs to Moanalua Valley, heading up Ala Aolani. *To the* *gardens from H-78 Eastbound*, take Exit 3, go left on Jarett White Rd., over the freeway. Then make your first left, at Mahiole, and hook left to the road that leads to the gardens.

HIKE: Moanalua Valley to: Seven Bridges and petroglyph rock (2 mi., 100 ft.), or valley view (3.5 mi., 350 ft.), or head of valley (6.75 mi., 700 ft.); Moanalua Gardens (.25-mi.)

Talk Story: Upon her death in 1884, Princess Bernice Pauahi Bishop willed most of the Moanalua Valley to Samuel M. Damon, who had been the trusted business partner of Charles Reed Bishop, husband of the princess. Friends of the monarchy made out in those days. Damon's children built homes in the valley. The H-3 freeway was once slated for this locale, and nowadays subsequent generations are tempted by real estate developers. Local preservationists are at work to keep the valley as it is. *Be Aware:* Posted signs say that permission to enter the valley is required. Locals have used the trail without expressed permission for many years. Use your own judgment. State law exempts landowners from liability for persons using their land for recreational purposes. On certain weekends, pig hunters are up the valley, and additional signs are temporarily posted across the entry gate. Stay out on these occasions.

For all **Moanalua Valley hikes**, head up through the middle of the park and proceed through an opening in the fence on an unpaved road. When the stream is flowing and sunlight filters down through the treetops, this is one of the most beautifully sylvan walks on God's green earth. At the beginning, near a monkeypod tree and marker 3, a short driveway leads to the former home site of Douglas Damon, Samuel's son. (The interpretive marker refers to a historical pamphlet that is available at Moanalua Gardens.) As the old road weaves through a tropical forest, you pass by **seven bridges** in quick succession, each with a curving rock underside mirrored by streamside pools. The road also runs through the stream, bypassing the turn-of-the-century spans and giving you a nice vantage point. The vines, ferns, palms, bananas, and subtropical overstory boggle the eyes. Bring your field guide.

May Damon's fireplace, Pohaku Ka Luahine petroglyphs

Moanalua Valley, one of the bridges

Just after bridge seven, at marker 10, on the right is Pohaku Ka Luahine (stone of the old woman), a 10-foot, egg-shaped stone etched with ancient figures, or petroglyphs. On the right lower side you'll also find a 90-dot konane board, a checkerslike game played by the ancients. One of the petroglyphs is a type unique to this valley. The stone is considered sacred. Many petroglyphs found on Hawaii predated the knowledge of even the first Polynesians. A couple hundred feet past the stone, look for marker 11, and head up the trail to the right. You'll find the ruins of the smaller home of May Damon, Samuel's daughter. Ferns grow from a fireplace that's ready to give in to gravity. Continue past these ruins; the trail loops out to the main road. (A spur trail gives you a chance to scamper up for a view up the valley.)

Continue on the main road, passing kukui trees and beginning what will be numerous crossings of the streambed. After a third crossing and slight descent alongside slopes of uluhe ferns, you reach marker 13, at a wide grassy area that could be used as a vehicle turnaround. A spur trail leads up and to the right to a commanding **valley view**. Then the main road drops again to stream level, a green tunnel of ferns and towering trees filled with birdsong. You'll notice more native vegetation, unlike the exotic flora nearer the bridges. You cross the stream four or five more times, and then the road goes right around a formation that separates the upper valley into two watersheds.

The road turns to a grassy trail. Wild pigs root around up here, particularly liking the small forest of ginger. Now, nearing the **head of the valley**, the trail becomes rocky and harder to follow. Pink plastic ribbons help, but you will soon be zigzagging through a tangle of rocks and trees. *Be Aware:* Passage is manageable for the sure-footed in the

Moanalua Valley

upper valley, but following the trail on the way back will be more difficult. Keep taking your bearings. The ridge at the top of the valley connects with the Stairway to Heaven; (see TH30, page 122) but there is no easy-to-follow trail.

Moanalua Gardens are not among Oahu's most spectacular, but they're worth seeing if you're in the neighborhood. Some 17 acres of rolling lawn support magnificent monkeypod trees, one of which is the world's most beautiful tree, according to Ripley's *Believe It or Not*. A Buddha tree from Ceylon has historic roots, but the real crowd pleaser is the 'Hitachi Tree,' at least among Japanese tourists. The subject of a popular TV commercial, it's the one they flock to for photos upon filing out of tour buses. Also on the grounds are a serene taro patch and koi pond, next to the summer cottage used by Kamehameha V in 1867, before Damon was bequeathed the property. Large stands of golden bamboo are next to Chinese Hall, which dates from 1904. Moanalua Gardens is a popular wedding venue; it's free.

12. BISHOP MUSEUM   HIKE

WHAT'S BEST: This museum surpasses its solid-gold reputation. As entertaining and easy on the eyes as it is educational, Bishop Museum can absorb visitors for a day, and then some. Close by is a forested ridge trail beginning at an obscure neighborhood trailhead.

PARKING: *From Waikiki,* take H-1 West to Exit 20A-Likelike Hwy. 63. Go mauka on Hwy. 63, turn right on the first street, Bernice, and continue one block to the free museum parking lot. *Note:* City bus #2, and the Waikiki Trolley Redline also serve the museum. *From H-1 Eastbound*, take Exit 20A-Likelike Hwy. 63 and follow directions above. *Note:* Admission is $16 for adults. After a several-year restoration, the Hawaiian Hall reopened in the summer of 2009. Hours are daily, 9 to 5.

HIKE: **Bishop Museum (up to .5-mi.); Kahili Ridge (up to 4.5 mi., 1,300 ft.)**

Talk Story: **Bishop Museum** grew from the personal collection of Princess Bernice Pauahi Bishop, many of the items handed down through the generations even preceding the lifetime of her great-grandfather, King Kamehameha I. She was the Great One's last living descendant. Five years after her death, her husband Charles Reed Bishop in 1889 founded the museum in her honor. The museum's main buildings date from that time. Funded by one of the richest endowments in the world, the collection has been enriched to include millions of Hawaiian and Pacific Island artifacts and heirlooms, as well insects, marine life, plants, and mammal specimens that are the envy of natural history curators worldwide. But the Bishop doesn't overwhelm visitors with volume.

You enter through Shop Pacifica, a trove of artful Hawaiiana, and emerge into an acre of lawn and garden, with the look of a venerabel universtiy campus. To the right is the main event, the three-story, stone-block Hawaiian and Polynesian Hall. (Behind the hall are the museum archives and Hawaiian Sports Hall of Fame, both open to the public.) The entrance building also includes Bishop Café, and observation deck, and a Planetarium, featuring films that are included the admission price. To the left of the central lawn is the Science Learning Center, a modernistic sweep of a building that compliments the towers of Honolulu that can be seen in the background beside it. Completed in the fall of 2005, the center offers hands-on amusement for kids and families, with interests that range from the ocean's depth to deep space and include volcanoes and all the earthly stuff in between.

The grand Hawaiian and Polynesian Hall is the place to start. You can become engrossed wandering the ornate stairways and the three-level open balconies of Hawaiian Hall. But don't forget to get involved in the series of programs taking place throughout the day, as archival specialists lead walking talks of the exhibits and gardens. There's also story telling, revealing the drama from ancient Polynesia right up to Queen Liliuokalani, the last monarch. Best of all, an authentic music and dance performance takes place on the stage beside recreated village structures.

Anyone familiar with Hawaiian culture will be slack-jawed at some of the items: The feather mask of the war god, Ku, that was given to a young Kamehameha; a pipe with a bowl the size of a baby fist that was held by the great king in his later years; the large bone Maui's Fishhook, called Manaiakalani, that predates Western contact by many centuries—the item by which the demigod Maui was able to "pull the islands from the sea"; the chipped Puapualenalena Shell from the Waipio Valley on the Big Island

Polynesian Hawaiian Hall, King Kamehameha

that was handed from chief to chief for a thousand years. Handcrafted bowls, tools, and weapons demonstrate how the Polynesians grew their culture from the land and sea, and thrived for centuries on the world's most remote landmass.

In the Polynesian Hall is the world's largest collection of items from Pacific Island nations, a world most people don't know exists. The more-modern periods of Hawaii are also amply represented—Captain Cook and the arrival of the West, missionaries and whalers, the sugar industry, and the last days of the monarchy before annexation when the Hawaiians, in spite of having lost 90 percent of their population due to the introduction of Western diseases, became one of the more literate cultures in the world. (Kamehameha Schools remains a crowning achievement of the Bishop Foundation.)

The **Kahili Ridge** trailhead is up Highway 63 from the museum. Just before a pedestrian overpass, turn right on Nalanieha, drive to its end, and make a left. Then make your first right on Manaiki Place. The unmarked trailhead is at the end of Manaiki, a set of concrete stairs that are to the left of address 1801. (You'll think you're going into someone's yard.) Double-back and park on the street; on weekends you may wind up parking a block or more away. This trailhead features a greenhouse of flora, with views of the Ko'olaus and earful of the traffic noise on Highway 63. Part of the Honolulu watershed, the trail is virtually unmaintained and gets knarly higher up. Turn around where it suits you.

The initial 175 lava-rock-and-concrete stairs take you past a modest Buddhist retreat and then proceed among ironwoods past a water tank and up the ridgeline. You get friendly with the flora, as barking dogs and roosters act as cheerleaders. About .75-mile into the hike, you'll reach the top of a pu'u that affords a mauka view and is planted with native ohia and koa. Guava and even sandalwood add to the mix as the trail continues over pu'u and saddles. It gets steep, with a rope provided in one spot near the trail's high point. *Be Aware:* Some sections of the trail are narrow with drop-offs, a hazard disguised by uluhe fern and other thick growth.

13. NU'UANU VALLEY   HIKE

WHAT'S BEST: In ancient times Nu'uanu was the valley of Hawaiian royalty. You can pick up threads of the past today, starting with a garden stroll and ending with a mountainous hike—with a queenly palace and the resting place of kings and queens in between.

PARKING: This trailhead covers a 3-mile stretch along Nu'uanu Ave., starting at Foster Gardens and heading mauka. *From Waikiki*, take Beretania west, pass Punchbowl, and turn right on Nu'uanu. Then turn left on Vineyard and drive along the garden's boundary for a block and turn into the parking lot. *From H-1 Eastbound* take exit 20B-Vineyard Proceed several blocks and hang a U-turn at Nu'uanu to reach the garden parking lot. *Note:* Further directions continue in the activity descriptions.

HIKE: **Foster Botanical Gardens (up to .5-mi); Royal Mausoleum (.25-mi.); Queen Emma's Summer Palace (.25-mi.); Judd Trail loop (.75-mi., 200 ft., with an option for farther and higher)**

Talk Story: Foster Botanical Garden can trace its roots to 1853, when Queen Kalama leased some of the property to a young German doctor and botanist, William Hillebrand, who planted many of the humongous trees that tower today. Thomas and Mary Foster later bought the property and continued to expand the plantings. The Fosters gave the property to the city, which expanded it again to its present 14 acres. It opened as a public park in 1931, Honolulu's first botanical garden. *Note:* A $5 admission is charged. Open 9 to 4 daily.

Just blocks from downtown Honolulu, **Foster Botanical Garden** is a pleasing green space, although the bordering freeway detracts considerably. Birds don't seem to mind. You'll find a full menu of Pacific trees, most of them giants, like the Mindanao Gum and Bo Tree, a sacred Buddhist tree that was propagated from its famous ancestor in Sri Lanka. *More Stuff:* The 7.5-acre Liliuokalani Botanical Garden, devoted to native Hawaiian plants, is up Nu'uanu Avenue—turn left on N. Kuakini. The queen's former picnic ground is open daily from 7 to 5.

For students of Hawaii and history freaks, the **Royal Mausoleum** is the sanctum sanctorum. To get there, go up Nu'uanu Avenue for several blocks and just past the Nu'uanu Cemetery—heads up—hang a right through the mausoleum's stone pillars. The Royal Mausoleum, or Mauna 'Ala, is the resting place for a few dozen high chiefs and historic figures, including all but two Hawaiian monarchs: Kamehameha the Great, whose remains were taken to a still-secret burial spot on the Big Island; and William Charles Lunalilo, the last male in the Kamehameha line, whose mausoleum is across from Iolani Palace. The Royal Mausoleum grounds are the only place where the Hawaiian sovereign flag flies unaccompanied by the American flag.

The real joy of the Royal Mausoleum is curator William Kaihe'ekai Maioho, an articulate man, whose ancestors have presided over the royal remains since the secret burial of Kamehameha the Great. If he's available, William will let you see the interior of the main mausoleum, now a chapel with koa paneling and pews. The Gothic chapel's original coral-block walls from 1862 are now plastered over, one of several restorations to preserve the building. Next to the mausoleum is the Kalakaua Crypt, constructed in 1907 for King David Kalakaua, Queen Liliuokalani, Prince Jonah Kuhio and others. You can walk down a flight of stairs and peek in.

More Stuff: Next to the Royal Mausoleum, in the back of the Nu'uanu Cemetery, is a 5-minute hike to Kapena Falls, a 15-foot cataract under a canopy of trees. Park in the lower lot and take an unsigned trail to the left of the large building and to the right of a lava-stone building. *Be Aware:* Mosquitoes can be pesky.

Another quick respite can be found at the **Queen Emma Summer Palace**, sitting on two idyllic acres that adjoin the larger streamside lands of Nu'uanu Valley Park. To get there, continue mauka on Nu'uanu as it merges with Highway 61, the Pali Highway toward Kailua. Stay to the right, since the palace is less than .5-mile after

Queen Emma Summer Palace, Royal Mausoleum

the merge, just past Lomi Road. *Talk Story:* In the mid-1800s, the palace was a country escape for Queen Emma, wife of Kamehameha IV. The frame home was shipped from Boston in 1848. When Emma died in 1885, plans were hatched to destroy the palace to make room for a park, but the nonprofit Daughters of Hawaii came to the rescue. What grabs you are the palace's original portraits and furnishings, like the little porcelain-and-koa bathtub stand for Prince Albert Edward, who died at the age of four. A sense of humanity shines through in every room. *Note:* Admission is $6.

The woodsy, wet **Judd Trail** is a quick loop that you can turn into a 1,000-foot climb by taking the Nu'uanu Trail on the backside of the loop; or, on a hot day, make it a short hop to the Jackass Ginger swimming pool, which awaits downstream of the trailhead. The Judd Trail begins along Nu'uanu Pali Drive. To get there, veer right from the Pali Highway less than .5-mile mauka Queen Emma Summer Palace. After nearly a mile, and not long after Polihiwa Place, park at unimproved turnouts at a concrete bridge. You should see a Na Ala Hele sign. *Be Aware:* Plan for mud and mosquitos.

From the road, descend under banyans to the stream, which you have to cross immediately. The best place is to the left of a sign that points in both directions (indicating a loop). From a bamboo grove, head left, away from the stream initially. Then contour to the right on this clockwise direction of the loop. After rising through a fine stand of Norfolk pine, you reach the signed Nu'uanu Trail junction, on your left. Exercise fiends can ascend on a dozen or more forested switchbacks, rising the better part of 1,000 feet. You reach Pauoa Flat and a viewpoint of Nu'uanu Valley. The Nu'uanu Trail connects with the Tantalus Trails. To continue the Judd Loop, truck on by the trail junction.

The trail descends at the edge of the pines, and gets moister as you drop. Ferns and mossy swamp mahogany trunks rise through a tangle of hau trees and guava. You'll contour right, heading upstream on the hillside. About one-eighth mile from the trailhead, look for a stake and an unsigned trail leading down to the Jackass Ginger pool. You'll hear the cascade, and on sunny days, you might hear people leaping from boulders into the chilly waters.

WHAT'S BEST: A 10-mile loop road tunnels through greenery, passing a half-dozen tropical trailheads and popping out to reveal vistas of Honolulu. Nearby Punchbowl, formally called the National Memorial Cemetery of the Pacific, is a place to reflect, in the green bowl of a dormant crater.

PARKING: *From Waikiki*, go west on Beretania and turn right on Punahou. Cross over H-1 and make your first left, on Wilder. Then make your third right, heading mauka on Makiki St. At little Barker Park, veer left on Makiki Heights Dr. At the first hairpin left, continue straight, toward the Makiki Forest Reserve Area. Use the assigned lot on the left. *From H-1 Eastbound*, take Exit 23-Punahou St. and go left. Then turn left on Wilder, as per the directions above. *Notes:* The Tantalus directions continue below, in a clockwise circle, starting at this parking spot. Additional directions for Punchbowl are given below.

HIKE: Tantalus Trails hikes: Makiki Valley loop (2.5 mi., 625 ft.); Manoa Cliff Trail car-shuttle (3.75 mi., 400 ft.); Pu'u Ohia Trail to: Tantalus Summit (1 mi., 375 ft.), or Manoa Valley view (2.25 mi., 475 ft.); Moleka Trail to Herring Springs (.75 mi., 100 ft.); Pu'u Ualaka'a State Park lookout (.25-mi.); Punchbowl-National Memorial Cemetery of the Pacific (up to .75-mi.)

Talk Story: The **Tantalus trails**, part of more than a dozen that make up the Honolulu Mauka Trail System, can be cobbled together to make any number of longer hikes that connect Nu'uanu Valley with Manoa Valley. To get a better handle, stop by the Department of Land and Natural Resources Visitors Center, a five-minute walk up the road from the parking. They'll provide free maps. (Darn, the visitors center is closed on weekends and holidays.) Then double back a short distance to the trailhead, which is behind the new Hawaii Nature Center. The center puts on outdoor programs for local kids and visitors.

For the **Makiki Valley loop**, cross the bridge behind the center and proceed a short distance to a trail junction. Go right on the Maunalaha Trail, a steady ascent of a dry, forested ridge for .75-mile. At a nice resting bench, you reach a trail junction, where you want to go left on the Makiki Trail. You descend a ferny embankment and cross a few lush gullies on footbridges, amid gardens of ti, banana, ginger. Nearly a mile later is the **Kanealole Trail** junction. Go left on the homeward leg. This trail drops through jungle forest alongside the stream, at times nearing bedrock cascades and then passing a decrepit dam. The last pretty part of the trail, includes footbridges and a streamside garden. *More Stuff:* For a quickie at Makiki, visit this new gardenscape: From the trailhead behind the nature center, keep left on the Kanealole Trail.

To continue to other Tantalus trailheads, drive back from the Makiki trailhead to the main road (Makiki Heights) and turn right, thus beginning a clockwise, 10-mile Tantalus loop drive. After a short distance, a turnout gives up a big Honolulu view, and after .5-mile you pass the The Contemporary Museum, good for a rainy

Manoa Cliff Trail

day sojourn. After .75-mile, turn right on Tantalus Drive. Over the next few miles the road twists upward, revealing more turnouts with views toward Waikiki and Diamond Head, and passing the short trail at the Tantalus Arboretum.

The **Manoa Cliff Trail car-shuttle** hike begins about 4 miles along. On the left is a sign for Kalawahine Trail, noting that the Cliff Trail junction is about a mile away, up a forested ramp. The pick-up for this car-shuttle hike is farther along on Tantalus Drive; see directions below to the Moleka Trail. The Manoa Cliff Trail contours high above Nu'uanu Valley and climbs to the right over a saddle above Pauoa Flat. At a junction, stay right on the switchbacks rather than continuing straight on the shortcut to Pauoa Flats. After topping out, the trail contours high above Manoa Valley and comes to an end on Round Top Drive (the conintuation of Tantalus Drive). You do get views, but much of the walk is in mysterious thickets of bamboo, ohia, and other native trees.

The **Pu'u Ohia Trail** begins about 4.5 miles along, at the summit of Tantalus Drive. You'll see the green pipes of a large paved lot on your right. **For both hikes**, cross the road and begin up dirt steps. Guava and passion fruit line a leafy upward traverse. You then penetrate a bamboo grove and come to a short staircase that leads to a paved service road—about 15 minutes from the trailhead. For the **Tantalus Summit**—one of the prime short walks on Oahu—go hard left at this road, up a steep concrete ramp that leads to telecommunications tower. *Be Aware:* Signs note that this road is off limits. People make the walk frequently. At the top of the ramp, go through a fence opening, between the tower and a building, and follow block steps to Tantalus. A 5-foot-square concrete platform is the prime spot to behold a view of the Waikiki coast.

To continue to the **Manoa Valley view**, go right on the paved service road. Bamboo borders the road on the quick ascent to a concrete block building. Go to the left of the building and pick up the trail. You'll descend with a view of the windward side. After a few minutes you reach the Manoa Cliff Trail. Go right for .25-mile and you'll begin to get views of Manoa Valley. Pick your own turnaround spot and retrace back to the Pu'u Ohia Trailhead. *Be Aware:* Vegetation disguises dangerous drop-offs on the Cliff Trail.

From Tantalus Summit

Puu Ualakaa State Park lookout

Just beyond the Puʻu Ohia parking lot, Tantalus Drive becomes Round Top Drive. The charming **Moleka Trail to Herring Springs** is on the right, almost 5.5 miles along the loop drive. (The Manoa Cliff Trail junction is across the road.) The Moleka Trail immediately enters a rain forest and streambed. You could continue 1.5 miles and reach the visitors center, but this hike is about getting in there to go gaga at the greenery.

To reach **Puʻu Ualakaʻa State Park lookout**, take a signed right turn, up a stately treed drive about 7 miles along on the loop drive. The lookout parking lot is a .5-mile, winding drive into the 50-acre park. A 200-foot long path leads to a covered viewing area, with a 3-D model of Diamond Head, Waikiki, and Honolulu lying below a green buffer in the foreground. This park makes the driving tour A-list, for sure.

To visit **Punchbowl-National Memorial Cemetery of the Pacific**—maybe the most underrated among Oahu's well-known attractions—continue on Round Top Drive, passing the entrance to the Makiki Forest Reserve. At Tantalus Drive, go left. After .75-mile, veer left on Puowaina and follow it for almost .5-mile. Park on the right at the visitors center. The cemetery is within the extinct Puowaina Crater, translated as "Hill of Sacrifice." In ancient times, chiefs were buried in secret places, and violators of the kapu (laws) were, er, sacrificed. *Note:* To get from Waikiki to Punchbowl, take Beretania west past Punchbowl Street and turn right on Queen Emma (opposite Alakea). Follow Queen Emma over the freeway, and, at the lights at School Street, veer left on Lusitana. Good job. Now veer right on Puowaina, as it curves around the right and enters Punchbowl. Hours are from 8 to 5:30 daily.

Inside the small visitors center are photographs of the Medal of Honor recipients who are among the 33,000 servicemen interred at Punchbowl, including Ernie Pyle, the distinguished war correspondent. Also buried here is Hawaii's Ellison Onizuka, the astronaut who died aboard Space Shuttle Challenger in 1986. From the center, walk up the middle lane, past a 120-acre lawn now covered to capacity with markers, most flush to the ground. At the head of Punchbowl is the grand Honolulu Memorial, its tall curving walls decorated with colorful stone mosaics that schematically detail the epic

Honolulu Memorial at Punchbowl

Pacific campaign, including Iwo Jima, Midway, and Battle of the Coral Sea. War buffs can spend hours. Leading to the memorial are seven flights of stairs that pass the Courts of the Missing, a series of walls etched with the names of nearly 30,000 soldiers missing in action in wars from WWII to Vietnam. Going to the left from the Honolulu Memorial, as you face it, is the Memorial Walk, which ascends to an overlook at Punchbowl's rim to see that life goes on in Honolulu.

15. MANOA VALLEY   HIKE

WHAT'S BEST: Yes, there's the prime waterfall walk and a view hike to a pu'u. But the jewel of Manoa is Lyon Arboretum, with its exotic garden paths and tropical trails.

PARKING: *From Waikiki,* take Ala Wai Blvd. west, turn right on McCully, and then go left on Beretania. From Beretania, turn right on Punahou, which becomes Manoa Rd. after you cross over the freeway. *From H-1 Eastbound,* take Exit 23-Punahou and go left. Punahou becomes Manoa Rd. *For Lyon Arboretum and Manoa Falls,* continue mauka on Manoa Rd. for about 3 mi. The road narrows at an overpass for Treetop Restaurant. *For Manoa Falls,* the parking will be on your right. A $5 fee is charged; pay attendent or purchase a ticket at the restaurant. The trailhead is .25.-mi. farther down the road. *For Lyon Arboretum,* pass the pay lot, turn left on a signed road, and drive up about .5-mile to a large parking lot. A $5 donation is suggested; they plans are to be open daily 9 to 4, although in recent years have operated Monday through Friday. *For Pu'u Pia,* veer right from Manoa Rd. onto E. Manoa Rd. Continue past the cemetery and turn left on Alani Dr. Park where Alani makes a sharp right, at Woodlawn Dr.

HIKE: Lyon Arboretum to: garden paths (about .75-mi, 150 ft.), or Aihualama Falls (1.75 mi., 225 ft.); Manoa Falls (1.5 mi., 800 ft.); Pu'u Pia (2 mi., 375 ft.)

Talk Story: The patio behind the gift shop and visitors center at **Lyon Arboretum** is a perfect elevation above the floor of Manoa Valley—high enough so that gardens slope downward in the foreground, while the jagged green ridge of the Ko'olaus rise above in the distance. Lyon is unquestionably among Hawaii's best gardens, whether you want to hike, stroll, or find a place to veg-out. Plantings date from 1918, and, besides being nearly 200 acres of enchantment, the arboretum is a research facility for the University of Hawaii, which took over care in 1953.

Garden paths radiate below the visitors center, leading to a spice garden, flowering tropicals, Hawaiian ecosystem plants, an enormous fig tree, and a stream viewpoint. The Young Memorial Garden is one particularly sublime place to sit down and let nature do her work. Mauka from the parking is the trailhead for **Aihualama Falls**. Strolling paths veer left up the hillside from the main trail, leading to floral wonder (really, it is amazing) that is close by. A bronze Buddha rests near a shelter, and short trails lead to Fern Valley and a grassy opening at Inspiration Point, tucked within the towering monkeypods. Some of these trunks are several feet in diameter, their upper boughs forming a ceiling for many levels of biodiversity. These nearer paths loop down to the cobblestone road that leads to the falls.

Manoa Falls Trail

Fern Trail, Lyon Arboretum

The falls hike is more about going rather than getting there. Although the greenery becomes less manicured, it's still a gardenscape, yielding botanical marvels like a forest of heliconia with leaves the size of surfboards. Along the way, short spur paths lead to special gardens, such as a Hawaiian area. The wider path narrows to a trail near Aihualama Falls, which is often a mere trickle through a jumble of rocks.

The popular **Manoa Falls** trail often hosts to parade of students, paying customers of low-budget hiking tours, and foreign-speaking tourists for whom the short walk is an adventure into the wild. A footbridge leads to an elfin land of ferns and streamside shrubbery, lit by sunbeams filtering through from leafy heights. The fantasy continues as you climb over a bamboo staircase and under the arches of large banyans. The falls is a tropical classic, sheeting some 200 feet down a vertical face to large oval pool. *Be Aware:* A large rockslide occurred in 2002, demonstrating the danger of being in the pool. Swimming is prohibited. *More Stuff:* Beginning at a junction just before the falls, the Aihualama Trail switchbacks up from Manoa Valley—over 1.25 miles and 1,200 feet—to join the Pauoa Flats trail that is part of the Tantalus systems. You go left on the Pauoa Trail to reach the Pu'u Ohia trailhead. A partway, up-and-back trip will enter a forest that includes bamboo and cinnamon trees.

Primarily a locals' exercise jaunt, the trail to 900-foot **Pu'u Pia** ends above Manoa Valley's rain forest, with a view that extends from the Ko'olau Range to the blue waters of Waikiki. From the street parking area, walk past a few homes on a cul-de-sac off Alani Drive. The trail begins in a green tunnel, up a rooty grade. After only five minutes you reach a picnic shelter where the Kolowalu Trail goes to the right. This trail, a mile long, ascends over 1,000 feet to join the Wa'ahila Ridge Trail, on the way to Mt. Olympus.

Keep plugging up the grade. You'll cross a flash-flood gully as the trail curves around to the left, joining a shoulder that spurs from Wa'ahila Ridge. The last part of the walk is along the spine, with small koa trees and uluhe ferns bordering the trail. The green bench of the pu'u is a satisfying spot to take in the view.

16. WA'AHILA RIDGE STATE RECREATION AREA   HIKE

WHAT'S BEST: Mount Olympus gets nominated for Best View Hike on Oahu. Take a run at the peak, or stop short at other panoramas that are less of a challenge.

PARKING: *From Waikiki*, take Ala Wai Blvd. to Kalakaua Ave. and turn right. Then make an immediate right on Kapiolani Blvd. and continue until crossing under the freeway. You veer right as Kapiolani becomes Waialae Ave. Just after First Ave., go left on St. Louis. Continue up and keep straight on Bertram, as St. Louis turns sharply right. After 1.6 mi., go left when Bertram ends at Peter St. Then make a left on Ruth Pl. that leads into the recreation area. *From H-1 Eastbound*, take Exit 25A-King St. Make your first left, under the freeway on Kapiolani, which then becomes Waialae Ave. Turn left on St. Louis and follow the directions above.

Mt. Olympus

HIKE: Wa'ahila Ridge Recreation area to: park stroll (up to .5-mi.), or Manoa Valley overlook (3.75 mi., 600 ft.), or Mt. Olympus (6.5 mi., 1,900 ft.)

The densely packed homes along St. Louis Drive transition to wild lands in an eye-blink upon entering the 50-acre pine forest of the **Waʻahila Ridge State Recreation Area**. Trails lead around the Cook, Norfolk, and ironwood evergreens that envelope the parking lot, but you will most likely want to begin the **park stroll** by approaching the railed overlook toward Manoa Valley. The prime spot is a picnic table downhill to the left, perched over the valley facing Honolulu.

For the hikes, head through the parking lot past the Na Ala Hele trailhead sign on an easy grade through ironwoods, the beginnings of the Waʻahila Ridge. *Be Aware:* Bring water, and prepare for wind, sun, and rain. The final stage, an unmaintained trail, requires handholds in places and presents a drop-off hazard, although it is not dangerous to the careful hiker. Roots, rocks, and slick mud make a slip-and-sit likely. Wear dark shorts.

About .25-mile into the hike, at an arrow sign, the trail descends to a narrower ridgeline section, the first of many on this upward rollercoaster over puʻus and across adjoining saddles. Guava, grasses, and ferns accent the trail. You'll start to pick up tree-filtered Waikiki views as you climb, but keep going to the prime spot, a grassy patch, the **Manoa Valley overlook**, which will be the end point for less-energetic hikes. The big blue water view of Honolulu is an engrossing backdrop for a picnic. Continuing from the overlook, the trail drops into trees and reaches the signed junction with the Kolowalu Trail, which drops 1,000 feet to the left, to the Puʻu Pia trailhead in Manoa Valley.

For Mt. Olympus, keep to the right at the Kolowalu Trail junction, beginning the ungraded trail. Tree ferns, ohia, and koa grace a route now dominated by native vegetation. This trail is easy to follow and better than okay, but watch your step. One spot has a rope to help out, and branches extend welcome handholds in many places. About .5-mile past the trail junction you reach a 20-foot grassy oval atop a puʻu surrounded by uluhe ferns. If the weather is clear, most adventure seekers will want to press on toward the summit of Mt. Olympus (a.k.a Awaʻawaloa). Shade is scarce on the last, steep parts of the journey, with only dwarf ohia (with red, bottle-brush flowers) clustered in nooks as you scramble up eroded, red-dirt slopes and skirt near-vertical faces. At last, you run out of up, at a little grass patch that looks 2,500 feet down the pali at the Maunawili Valley and the entire Windward Coast. Inland, to your left, you also get a look at green Kaʻau Crater. This vantage point is actually the false peak—the broader summit of Mt. Olympus is still a few hundred feet to the right.

17. MAUʻUMAE RIDGE TRAIL   HIKE

WHAT'S BEST: An obscure trailhead and arduous trail lead to a fantastic spot on the Koʻolau Ridge: Adventure hikers have a green light.

PARKING: *From Waikiki*, take Kalakaua Ave. east and turn left on Kapahulu Ave. Follow Kapahulu all the way to where it crosses under H-1, and make your first right, on Waialae Ave.

Continue past 10th Ave. and turn left on Sierra Dr. Follow twisting Sierra for 2.25 mi. and turn left on Maunalani Circle. Go about .25-mi. and look for the trailhead on the left, near a gated road with a chain-link fence and water tank. The trailhead is a signed public access between the tank fence and a fence at a residence. *From H-1 Eastbound*, take Exit 25A-King St. Go left on Kapiolani and then go right on Waialae Ave. Follow the directions above.

HIKE: Mau'umae Trail to: view knoll (3.25 mi., 1,000 ft.), or Kainawa'a Summit (7 mi., 2,300 ft.), or Lanipo Summit (7.5 mi., 2,400 ft.)

Equip your pack for serious trekking on the **Mau'umae Trail**, and plan on averaging a mile or so per hour. The route is not dangerous for the cautious hiker, but your hands and butt will contact the ground in steep places. After a few miles you'll get a great look at the green Ka'au Crater, whose white waterfall belies its volcanic origins. For all hikes, make your way over the grassy trail beside a home, in the shade of ironwoods. You break into the open, with the homes of Palolo Valley down to the left and green Waialaenui Gulch down to the right. You descend nearly 200 feet on a narrowing ridge over rock outcroppings, a beginning that gives fair warning of the trail ahead.

The ridge broadens as you climb up the other side of the saddle, passing a utility pole and heading deeper into the koa trees of the Honolulu Forest Reserve. The route levels somewhat, in a grove of ironwoods, but then it's up time again, on an eroded section of the trail. You'll level out again, among the bushy ohia trees and sharp-leafed koas before making the final pitch to a **view knoll**. A circular grassy area invites a sit-down to enjoy the view back toward the city. *Be Aware:* Look mauka, to see if the weather will cooperate. Aside from eliminating views, rain makes the trail treacherous.

The trail passes ferns and Norfolk pines, and traverses below the ridgeline on an up-and-down ascent. To the left rests the Ka'au Crater, which blew out of the Ko'olaus as a last gasp of Oahu's active volcanic period. Vegetation becomes sparser as you climb higher. One view spot well below the ridge will be an opportunity to wuss out. The hearty will continue down from this viewpoint, and then over a last knob, a hands-on exposed area that requires both resolve and skills. Finally, the last ascent of **Kainawa'a Summit** lies ahead. From this summit, at 2,500 feet, **Lanipo Summit** lies to the right, on the Ko'olau so-called trail. Watch out for slips as you make the last .25 mile and 100 feet of upping. Some hikers will call it a day and enjoy the windward view from Kainawa'a. *Be Aware:* Take care to stay on your feet on the homeward journey since fatigue and gravity make accidents more likely going down.

18. WILIWILINUI RIDGE   HIKE, SURF

WHAT'S BEST: A graded road and high-elevation trailhead jump-start a (relatively) easy ascent of the Ko'olau Ridge. This is a winner. Wiliwilinui's sister ridge, Hawaiiloa, gets more publicity and locals' footprints—but it is especially tough on tourists.

PARKING: *For Wiliwilinui Ridge,* head east from Waikiki on H-1. The freeway becomes Hwy. 72. Continue for about .5-mile and turn mauka on Laukahi. Follow the road up for 1.75 mi. to a security guard station. You will be asked for identification and directed to trailhead parking lot that is .75-mi. farther, on Okoa. *For Hawaiiloa Ridge,* follow the above directions, only continue east on Hwy. 72 past Laukahi. After about 1.75 mi., opposite Kawaikui Beach Park, you want to turn left on Puʻuikena Dr. To do so (no left is allowed from the Hwy. 72) pass Puʻuikena and make a U-turn. Hikers must check in a guard station at the bottom of the road. *Be Aware:* Someone in your party needs a Hawaiian driver's license or military ID to use this trail.

HIKE: Wiliwilinui Ridge Trail to: Five Poles Puʻu (3.75 mi., 1,100 ft.), or Koʻolau Ridge (6 mi., 1,650 ft.); Hawaiiloa Ridge Trail to Koʻolau Ridge (6.5 mi., 1,700 ft.)

The **Wiliwilinui Ridge Trail** begins on a paved road amid high-end homes perched at 1,000 feet. The road becomes red-dirt, nicely graded as you ascend through a tree tunnel of ironwoods, formosa, and guava. Open portions reveal looks at the Koʻolau Ridge. Utility lines follow the road, and a large antenna awaits at hike's end, but the trail is free of traffic noise (leaving bird chirps as a soundtrack). About .75-mile into the walk, over and down a hillock of Norfolk pines, the route enters a world of ferns and koa, and occasional mud bogs. As with all the ridge hikes, the trail flattens and even drops in places. You'll contour around a steep hillside of uluhe fern and reach a vehicle turnaround spot, where the route becomes a trail. This is about 1.5 miles in.

Head up steps through ferns, gain another 150 feet, and you'll reach **Five Poles Puʻu**, which gives up a fine seaward look at Diamond Head and Koko Head. The second part of the hike is mostly open, in dwarf vegetation. A second puʻu, this one with four poles and scads of guy wires, is another 10 minutes along on the ridge trail. After the second puʻu, begins the last, most difficult 800 feet of the ascent. *Be Aware:* Although doable for fit hikers, handholds and ropes aid in steep sections and dangerous drop-offs border narrow trail sections. Don't step into any greenery. The last trail section ascends more gradually. You pass a relay installation, and reach the **Koʻolau Ridge** at an elevation of about 2,500 feet. Over the ridge is the Waimanalo coastline.

The **Hawaiiloa Ridge Trail** has received some good press—enough to attract tourists who later learn that a mainland ID won't be accepted to access the trail. (The state's Na Ala Hele trails office welcomes incessant complaints from all visitors, especially from irate land-use attorneys.) About three-fourths of the hike is a romp through dry forest of guava and native shrubbery. It begins as a dirt road that passes over a rocky section and becomes a trail.

As with the Wiliwilinui Trail, the route gets wetter and steeper as the Koʻolau Ridge draws nearer. You'll reach a view knob, about 900 feet below the summit, a place to do a weather check. A short descent and fairly flat section follows the view knob, but—big surprise—the last part of the hike is very steep, with steps and ropes that help out in places.

SURF: With shallow waters, **Kawaikui Beach Park** is more for wading than swimming or snorkeling. Try splashing out and enjoying the view of Koko Head. It's a four-star picnic park, with a nice lawn and tables under spreading palms, kiawe, and koa trees. Kawaikui Beach Park is across from Puʻuikena Street, about 2 miles west of Hawaii Kai. The reef offshore draws surfers, as well as windsurfers, to two breaks, **Toes** and **Secrets**. Toes is to the left of the beach park; Secrets is offshore right.

19. HAWAII KAI   HIKE, SURF

WHAT'S BEST: Most people (who aren't into jet skis, parasailing, or shopping) drive by on the way to Hanauma Bay. But behind Hawaii Kai is one of the island's exciting ridge hikes, and in front is the intriguing Portlock coastline on Koko Head's lesser known shore.

PARKING: Take H-1 East from Waikiki and continue as it merges to become Hwy. 72. Continue for almost 3 mi., to Paiko Dr., on the right. *Note:* Directions continue below.

Wiliwilinui Ridge Trail

HIKE: Kuliouou Trail to: Kuliouou Valley (2.25 mi., 325 feet), or Koʻolau Ridge (5 mi., 1,900 ft.); Portlock coast (up to .75-mi., 100 ft.)

For both **Kuliouou Trail** hikes, pass Paiko Drive and make a left at the light on Kuliouou Rd. After .25-mile, the road makes a left and then an immediate right. Follow it up, turn right on Kalaʻau Place, and park near the end. The trailhead is off the cul-de-sac. *Be Aware:* This is a hunting area on weekends. Wear bright clothes and don't make snorting sounds. The trail has steep sections with drop-off hazards.

Less than .25-mile after entering this shaded crease in the Koʻolaus, you reach a trail junction. For the **Kuliouou Valley**, keep straight. This exercise walk through forest follows an often-dry stream to the head of the valley. Birdwatchers and botanists will enjoy the easily achieved solitude. After rains, the end of the trail is at a modest waterfall, which normally is a trickle.

To challenge the **Koʻolau Ridge**, take a right up the trail junction, beginning an immediate upward traverse in an open copse of koas. After a few minutes you'll hit switchbacks that afford valley as well as seaward views. After a half-dozen of these zigzags, the trail goes more directly toward the ridge in an ironwood grove. About 1.5 miles into the hike take a break at a picnic shelter to get ready for a steep part. Near the top, you punch out of the guava and ironwood cover and into the open. Steps help on eroded steeper sections on last part of the journey. On top is a sweeping view of the island—even though the ridge here has tapered down 500 feet from the highest elevations on the range. *Be Aware:* Stay oriented by looking back occasionally as you wind up the ridge, as side trails and turns might get you confused on the way down.

The oddball **Portlock coast** has several right-of-way accesses in a ritzy neighborhood, some leading to small, sandy beaches, others to deep-water rocky shelves. To take a look at this hidden side of Koko Head, pass the beach parks of Hawaii Kai and the traffic signal at Keahole Road, and then veer right on Portlock Road. The first two right-of-ways, at addresses 255 and 277, lead to the nicest beach, in the back yards of choice homes. You'll see several other access points, but the best is at the end of the road. Between gated mansions, take a path along a wall that quickly pops out at Kokeʻe Place. Go right at the cul-de-sac to explore Kokeʻe Beach Park. A grassy trail drops to smooth rock shelves. Go right to a scenic fishermans hangout.

You can also get to Kawaihoa Point, the tip of Koko Head, where large waves smack an overhanging shelf, resulting in blasts of white water. To catch the drama, drive back on Portlock Drive, and make three quick rights—on Lawai, then Makaweli, and then on Poipu Drive. From Poipu, go left on Moloaʻa and, finally, right on Lumahai. At the end of Lumahai is a steep trail. The undercut cliffs repel waves in thunderous eruptions. Be careful at water's edge, to avoid becoming part of the seascape. Getting here isn't as difficult as it sounds, but the subdivision, the brainchild of 1960s developer Henry J. Kaiser, is pocketed with cul-de-sacs that dissuade looky-loos.

SURF: Keep right on Paiko Drive to find a beach access used by board fiends, a reef break called (take a guess) **Paiko Drive**. The right-of-way is just before the end of the road. (People aren't allowed into the wildlife sanctuary and lagoon at the end of this peninsula.) At Kuliouou Beach Park—between Kuliouou Road and Keahole Drive, are several spots: **Turtles**, **Tunas**, and **Manhattans**, all of which are a paddle out. This beach is a put in for kayakers who stay within the calmer waters of Maunalua Bay.

Surfers with cajones like several breaks off Portlock. Near address 370 is access to **Seconds**. From the cliffy shelves of Koke'e Beach Park, surfers dare the waters of **Pillars**. For the real derring-do—and an excellent place to watch surfers—head to little Koko Kai Beach Park. To get there, follow Poipu Drive and take a right on Hanapepe Loop. The access is at the end, off a cul-de-sac, but parking is prohibited so you need to walk down. **China Walls**, **Fingers**, and **Point** all break offshore of this tricky bit of coast. In calm waters, this is also a prime divers spot, but strong currents are dangerous for snorkeling. Be watchful of waves breaking at the shore.

Hanauma Bay

10. HANAUMA BAY   HIKE, SNORKEL

WHAT'S BEST: An extinct volcanic crater, now at sea level, has become Hawaii's most popular snorkeling destination and the crowds can be a hassle if you don't play it right. Across the highway, stairs lure hikers 1,000 feet skyward to the rim of a sister volcano.

PARKING: *For Hanauma Bay Nature Preserve snorkeling*, go east on H-1 from Honolulu. H-1 merges to become Hwy. 72. Continue for a few miles past Hawaii Kai. At the top of the hill, turn right at signs and drive down to a large parking lot. By bus, from Waikiki, take #22 on Kuhio Ave. *Notes:* Parking is $1 per car; admission to the park for snorkeling is $5 per person, free if you have a Hawaiian or military identification. The park is *closed Tuesdays*. Hours are 6 to 6, an hour later during the summer. Night snorkeling until 10 on Saturdays—but only on the second Saturday of the month during the winter.

For Koko Crater Stairs hike, follow the above directions to Hawaii Kai. After Keahole Dr., turn left on Lunalilo Home Rd. Then turn right on Kaumakani, follow it around, and turn right again on Anapalau toward Koko Head District Park. Park at the far lot, at Mike Goss Field.

HIKE: Koko Crater stairs (1.25 mi., 1,200 ft.)

Talk Story: Koko Crater is inland from Koko Head, which rises directly above Hanauma Bay at the coast. You must know that the Hawaiian name for Koko Crater is Koheleple, meaning 'fringed vagina,' a reference to the mythical flying vagina of Kapo, the sister of volcano goddess Pele. It's a long story. Regardless, Koko is the tallest cone in Hawaii, and probably Oahu's most recent active site, having had fresh flows only 7,000 years ago.

Make sure to begin the **Koko Crater stairs** hike with plenty of water and sun protection, since this one is a cooker. The trail ends with an astonishing vista of this end of the island, including a vertigo view 1,000 feet down into the arid garden floor of the crater. From the parking area, walk toward four upright pipes and across a weed

patch that leads to a road. Jog left on the road and then go right to reach the bottom of more than 1,000 railroad ties that staircase to the top—part of a tramway that transported workers to a WWII-era radar installation.

The staircase gets steeper as you near the summit, but it never becomes a ladder. Adventure trainers make it up in about 30 minutes, but normal people take an hour to 90 minutes. *Be Aware:* One 70-step section about midway is a bridge span that may give acrophobics a twinge. Some hikers may use their hands going up and choose to butt-slide on the way down. Look back down as you make the climb, to make

Platform atop Koko Crater   sure the angle of descent will be

Koko Crater

okay. Dwarf kiawe trees provide welcome pockets of shade in places, including the top of the stairs, which ends at the tramway's pulley system. Don't stop there. Take a short trail to the true top—Pu'u Mai at 1,208 feet—where the old concrete powerhouse and a steel-grated platform provide the ultimate view. On the way down, be extra careful since fatigued muscles may betray you.

More Stuff: To see ironic Pahua Heiau, continue on Lunalilo Home Road past the district park turnoff and make a left on Hawaii Kai Drive. Then make a quick right on Waioli and a quick left on Makahuena Place. Built in the 1400s, the heiau stands as a fixer-upper next to neighbors in a suburban cul-de-sac.

SNORKEL: Several thousand fish freaks descend daily to **Hanauma Bay Nature Preserve**, about one-third the number in the 1980s when it got out of hand, but still a crowd to be reckoned with. (This is a far cry from 1795, when Kamehameha the Great, having conquered Oahu, staked out these sands as his kingly fishing ground.) *Be Aware:* When the parking lot fills, arrivals are turned away. Peak times are mid-morning on weekends and holidays, since locals are off work-school, and they are allowed in free. So, to play it safe, try the early morning (it opens at six), or early afternoon when the initial throngs have departed. If the lot is full, you probably don't want to swim anyway but … you can also park the Koko Head District Park (see Koko Crater hike above), which is a mile or two drive away; from there, a road closed to traffic leads up to the highway directly across from Hanauma Bay—only a ten-minute walk. Signs in the upper Koko lot say parking is prohibited for snorkelers but the lower lot has no such signs. Additionally, a shuttle service operates from Hawaii Kai, see *Resource Links*.

After getting past the bay's ticket booth, notice that your color-coded ticket is stamped with an entry time, since you may have to wait up to an hour when Hanauma is crowded. Use the time to wander the multi-million dollar, bermed-over visitors center, or check out the enticing view of the aquamarine waters awaiting below. When the magic time arrives, you are herded into a safety and informational video, before being allowed to walk the short, steep road to the park. (Second-time visitors can forego the video.) A shuttle bus is available to the beach—50 cents down and a buck to ride up. Lockers, at $5 a pop, are available at the beach, and snorkel equipment rents for under $10.

Okay, time to get in the water. Snorkelers who have experienced the colorful knobs and sprays of coral in other Hawaiian waters may be disappointed at the flat, grey reef of Hanauma. Though algae make it not dead, technically, it looks lifeless. (Coral is comprised of living organisms; don't step on it.) Most snorkeling is done near shore; only experienced divers should try the deeper spots of Toilet Bowl and Witches Brew at the mouth of the bay. In the middle of Hanauma is Keyhole Lagoon, a shallow swimming area encircled by reef. Sandman's Patch is a flipper-around zone on the right side of the beach, one of the prime spots to drop a beach towel. Two channels lead out from the beach. Back Door Lagoon is at the far left, and Cable Channel is about midway in the bay, in front of a lifeguard tower. Both channels are man-made. Cable Channel, 200-feet wide, was blasted out in 1956 for telephone lines. Although low tide makes getting out chancy, you'll normally find the clearest water and best fish along the outside of these channels, that is, along the outside edge of the reef closest to the beach. *Be Aware:* Rip current may be present in the channels. Check with lifeguards.

A shade umbrella is a good idea at Hanauma Bay, since the backshore's treed areas are few. Avoid this issue by trying the nighttime snorkel. Aside from the rental shack and beleaguered rest room, the backshore also includes an interpretive center staffed by volunteers of the nonprofit Friends of Hanauma Bay. At the end of the day, visitors to Hanauma may feel like they've been to a Hollywood blockbuster that got the hype and drew crowds but didn't quite deliver the payoff.

21. SANDY BEACH   HIKE, SNORKEL, SURF

WHAT'S BEST: Local bodysurfers swarm long, sunny Sandy. A cliffy coast nearby offers a blowhole, whale viewpoints, and a little beach with a movie starlet's reputation. Best of all, a nearby trail wanders into the botanical garden inside of Koko Crater.

PARKING: Go east on H-1 from Honolulu. H-1 merges to become Hwy. 72. Continue for a few miles past Hawaii Kai and Hanauma Bay. Directions continue below.

HIKE: Blowhole stroll (up to .75-mi., 200 ft.); Koko Crater Botanical Garden loop (2 mi., 225 ft.)

Eternity Beach

The **Blowhole stroll** is a tour of roadside attractions. The first stop is about .5-mile past Hanauma, at the Lanai Lookout. From here, three of Hawaii's main chain of islands will be in view on clear days, all grouped together: Lanai is the one to the right of Molokai, and rising behind them is the larger, taller island of Maui. During the winter months, humpback whales will be spotted. An unofficial trail leads from the right side of the lookout. Be watchful of waves that want to sweep people from the rocks. The cheap-thrill hike from here is the drainage tunnel path. Walk down to where a guardrail begins. Step over it and enter the narrow tunnel which goes under the highway and comes out on a rocky point.

About .75-mile past Lanai Lookout, and before the next paved turnout, pull out at a guardrail, beyond which is a rock monument for the Honolulu Japanese Casting Club. Walk the rocky head toward Halona Point, *the* prime view spot that is visited by few people. Across and down is the Halona Blowhole Lookout, the magnet for most tourists, and your next stop. The blowhole, on the shelf below the closed-off portion of the viewing area, is an opening in the reef through which pressurized waves erupt with sprays of white water. This particular blowhole is often a blowhard, all talk and no action. To the right as you face the water is the darling of this coast, Halona Cove, better known as Eternity Beach. Even those who don't remember Pearl Harbor know the scene in *From Here to Eternity*, where wave-foam washes over the intertwined bodies of Burt Lancaster and Deborah Kerr. A well-worn trail leads down.

More Stuff: From the Halona Blowhole parking is an alternate trail to the top of Koko Crater. You need to walk up the highway to the end of the guardrail and start up a toe of land, beginning parallel to the road. The route then goes right, up the face of the slope, and then follows the rim to the left. Only attempt this unofficial trail if you can confidently read the route standing at the bottom. It's about 2 miles and more than 1,000 feet. Steep, rocky slopes make this a fairly difficult and dangerous route.

Koko Crater Botanical Gardens

The **Koko Crater Botanical Gardens** are one of Oahu's pleasant surprises, especially in the morning hours when sunlight bathes the 1,000-foot inner crater walls and throngs of birds are atwitter. To get there, go past Halona Blowhole and Sandy Beach and turn left at the light on Kealahou Street. After less than .5-mile, turn left on Kokonani Street toward the stables, at a low sign announcing the gardens. *Note:* A guard watches the parking area. Admission is free; hours are sunrise to sunset daily.

Head up the dirt road past a large grove of plumeria and bougainvilleas, a heavenly start when these babies are in bloom in March, but unspectacular when they're not. Stay right as you reach a sign for Loop Trail of the Americas, thus beginning a counterclockwise spin around the 60-acre floor of the crater. The cactus garden, which lies ahead, would impress Disney animators, with its barrels and spires and twisting fingers, some like a giant squid that has done a nose dive into these arid soils. The route continues past a dry land zone of native wiliwili and kiawe with vines hanging as bird perches. Just past this zone, take a seat in the Hawaiian section, featuring loulu palms, the only ones native to the islands. The homeward downslope passes through exotics from Africa and Madagascar, and you finish the loop in an array of dry-land palms, some bushy and fernlike, others with fanned out fronds, all clattering in the slightest breeze.

SNORKEL: This coastline is generally unfriendly or downright dangerous to swimmers. Experienced scuba divers get in at the drainage tunnel below **Lanai Lookout**. The terraces below **Halona Blowhole Lookout** also attract divers, but these waters are almost always too rough for snorkeling. When the surf is low, snorkelers can get in at **Eternity Beach**, but moderate-to-high surf will bring rip current. Turtles like the inshore waters. If the shoreline is not gentle, stay close in. Midway along **Sandy Beach,** where young palms are making a go of it, is a spot to take a dip, before the lava reef interrupts the sandy shore. The tide pools and reefs at **Irma's** can be a good snorkeling venue, but most often the seas are too rough. To get to Irma's, pass the entrance and Sandy Beach and the traffic signal at Kealahou. Then veer right on a dirt road to unimproved Wawamalu Beach. When the wave action cooperates, you should be able to observe marine life without getting in the water.

SURF: Sunny **Sandy Beach** (visible down the grade from Halona Lookout) is one of the four-or-five happening beaches on Oahu, luring the frisky youth from metro Honolulu to bodyboard, hook up, and trumpet car stereo systems. When competitions take place, the scene amps to da' max. The park extends for .5-mile along the shore, and the far, grassy end is quieter. Rest rooms are not normally the big draw at a beach park, but the murals, including one of Duke, are worth a mention. Sandy's shore break draws bodysurfers, boogie boards, and skim boards. *Be Aware:* It looks like fun, but many a tourist has suffered spinal injuries in these bone crushers. Beginners, stay out. Farther down the shore (heading north) shortboarders ride the quick south swell at **Half Point** and **Full Point**. Beyond that, at the far end of the park, is **Pipe Littles**, a left-breaking tube. The shallow break at **Irma's** (see *Snorkel* above) also attracts shortboarders, but the break is not reliable.

Sandy Beach

Windward Pali

Toward Koolau Pali from Olomana Ridge

Other Hawaiian Islands have sea cliffs, like Kauai's notorious Napali coast and the dramatic north shore of Molokai. But on Oahu a boat isn't needed to see them. A toe of land, rather than an expanse of ocean, extends from the eastern base of the Ko'olau Pali, enticing hikers into rain-forest valleys, botanical gardens, and hidden waterfalls.

The ridgeline of the Ko'olaus, only a foot or two wide in many places, squiggles for about 50 miles on a rollercoaster ranging from 1,500-feet to 3,000-feet in height. On the west side, the mountains descend relatively gently to the rift zone above Honolulu and to the Wahiawa Plateau farther north. But on the east side the drop is as straight as a falling coconut, a continuous rampart of fissured greenery that astounds first-time visitors and keeps everyone else coming back for more.

The majestic Ko'olaus today are only a remnant of their former greatness, the eroded crags of a volcano millions years old that once reached another 10,000-feet above the sea. Wind, rain, and time have artfully chiseled them down, leaving not only the pali, but also serrated fingers that radiate from it, razorback ridges that stand alone near the coast, and a series of small islands that are seabird sanctuaries. Some are within swimming distance. All this adds up to what many feel is the most visually captivating coastline in Hawaii.

The love-at-first-sight look at the windward side is from Makapu'u Point, the southern tip of the Ko'olaus, which is also Oahu's most easterly land. A hike to the top overlooks Rabbit Island and several sweet beaches, including Makapu'u Beach Park, a bodyboarders' special, and Makai Research Pier, where underwater explorers ready their intrepid submarines and snorkelers will find some of the fishiest coral on the island. Next up the coast from Makapu'u is Waimanalo, the birthplace of slack-key guitar music, no doubt inspired by several miles of sandy shore that is accented by a long forest of ironwood trees. Inland is a lush upcountry, land of flowers and fruits, and also a trailhead for the 10-mile-long Maunawili Trail that contours the base of the pali.

Midway on the Maunawili Trail is the mini-adventure to Maunawili Falls, a stream-crossing jaunt through a rain forest rich in archeological sites. At the gateway to the falls trail is Oahu's glamour hike for daredevils only, Olomana Ridge, with its three pointed peaks. The first peak can be reached by fit hikers who aren't acrophobics, but the remaining two require climbing skills and a high-tolerance for risk. Olomana overlooks the Ulupo Heiau, now a state monument, which in turn lords over the Kawainui Marsh, with elaborate fishponds and agricultural terraces that were the spiritual center for the canoe-going ancient Hawaiians.

For many modern Hawaiians, the center of life is the side-by-side beachfront of Kailua Bay and Lanikai, kissing cousins that were each named America's best by

Makapuu Beach Park, Kailua kayakers

a well-known travel magazine. The seabird sanctuaries of Mokulua Islands and Flat Island (destinations for kayakers as well as flipper-flailing swimmers) are beauty marks offshore, and Kawai Ridge hangs above them inland as an opportunity for hikers to get a foldout view. Not as well trod is the north end of Kailua Bay, a beachcomber's delight that extends to the off-limits Kaneohe Marine Corps Base on the Mokapu Peninsula.

West of Kailua is a notch in the Ko'olau Range, the infamous Nu'uanu Pali Lookout, where in 1795 the invading forces of Kamehameha the Great used both cannon and club to push several hundred defending Oahu warriors on a freefall to their deaths. Nowadays, every 15 minutes, several hundred tourists gather to gaze from the windy gap that is a state park. The Old Pali Highway is a scenic, instant-getaway hike that can be extended to an all-day trek on the Maunawili Trail that snakes through the jungle to Waimanalo. The Nu'uanu Pali also can be viewed from below at the fabulous Ko'olau Golf Club, where the Likeke Pali Trail embarks on a little known contour through an arboretum of tropical flora to a waterfall—a top contender for Oahu's sleeper-spectacular hike.

North of Kailua, the peaks remain lofty, but the Ko'olau Range begins a slow curl away from the coast and opens up to inspiring valleys. Ho'omaluhia Botanical Gardens, covering 400 acres below the brooding rim of the pali, is reachable via a rain forest drive. On the grounds are a half-dozen separate gardens. In the Haiku Valley is the Stairway to Heaven, sets of interconnected ladders that ascend 3,000 feet—an astounding journey that will, may, should be re-opened to hikers one day, any day, someday, whenever. The Valley of the Temples, on the other hand, is a sure thing, a place where even the cynical may find religion at the Byodo-In Buddhist Temple. North of this sancturary, at Waihe'e and Waikane, are rain forest valleys that the county has set aside for nature parks.

Byodo-In Buddhist Temple

Koolau Pali

The coastline north of Kaneohe is viewed via a two-lane blacktop, a portion of the Kamehameha Highway that reveals the natural features that sustained the agrarian-and-seagoing life of the ancient Hawaiians for 10 centuries or more. First up is He'eia State Park, a view knoll that overlooks historic fishponds, today cared for by community volunteers. Then, at the other end of wide Kaneohe Bay, is Kualoa Regional Park, the setting to view Mokoli'i Island, better known by what it looks like, Chinaman's Hat. The jagged Ko'olaus are a backdrop for the park's open, sunny acres. Snorkeling and kayaking are supreme. The parklands in ancient times were a kind of prep school for the children of the royalty, where they learned the ways of nature and about the cultivation of living things—skills most revered in Hawaii. The inland valleys vie to steal the show at historic Kualoa Ranch, site for adventure activities and location for many jungle-themed movies.

Around the point from Kualoa, is the island's showpiece, Ahupua'a O Kahana State Park. A forested beach and sandy bay are cleaved by a wide stream and accented by historic Huilua Fishpond. Short hikes lead to a fishing shrine and lookout. A longer trail follows the stream inland past agricultural terraces and loops into a forest showered by a few hundred inches of rain each year. All these physical ingredients make up an ahupua'a, the division of land around which all ancient villages were structured. Native Hawaiians live in the state park today, a model, perhaps, of how the laws of the state can be compatible with the ways of Hawaii.

Likeke Falls Trail

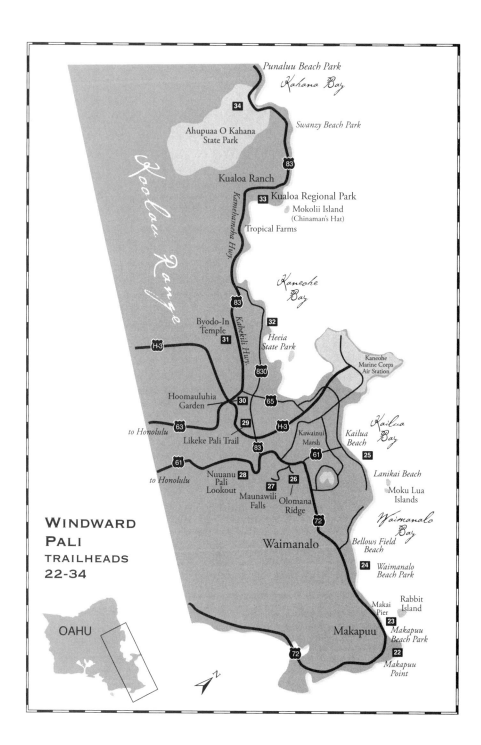

Punaluu Beach Park
Kahana Bay

34

Ahupuaa O Kahana
State Park

Swanzy Beach Park

83

Koolau Range

Kualoa Ranch

Kamehameha Hwy

33 Kualoa Regional Park
Mokolii Island
(Chinaman's Hat)
Tropical Farms

Kaneohe Bay

83

Byodo-In
Temple

H-3

31

32

Heeia State Park

Kahekili Hwy

830

Kaneohe
Marine Corps
Air Station

Hoomauluhia
Garden

30

65

Kailua Bay

to Honolulu **63**

29

H-3

Kailua
Beach

Likeke Pali Trail

83

Kawainui
Marsh

61

25

61

to Honolulu

Nuuanu
Pali
Lookout

28

Lanikai Beach

Moku Lua
Islands

27

26

Maunawili
Falls

Olomana
Ridge

Waimanalo Bay

72

Waimanalo

Bellows Field
Beach

**WINDWARD
PALI
TRAILHEADS
22-34**

24 Waimanalo
Beach Park

Makai
Pier

Rabbit
Island

23

OAHU

Makapuu

*Makapuu
Beach Park*

22

72

*Makapuu
Point*

N

WINDWARD PALI
TRAILHEADS 22-34

PLEASE NOTE:
All hiking distances in parentheses are ROUND TRIP. Elevation gains of 100 feet or more are noted.
See *Resource Links* page 232 for telephone numbers for all attractions and public agencies.
Admission prices listed are for full-price adults. Leave your car free of valuables at EVERY parking spot.

22. MAKAPU'U POINT STATE WAYSIDE   HIKE, SNORKEL

WHAT'S BEST: From a lighthouse knoll is a love-at-first-sight look at Oahu's windward pali and seabird islands—evoking the romance of the South Pacific. Or, get this same view with a shorter lookout stroll. Adventure hikers can navigate a wild coast to swimable tide pools.

PARKING: Go east on H-1 from Honolulu. H-1 merges to become Hwy. 72. Continue for a few miles past and Hanauma Bay, Sandy Beach, and the light at Kealahou St. Continue for a mile. *For Makapu'u Lighthouse and Tide Pools*, on the uphill grade look for a right-turn lane that leads to paved lot. *For Makapu'u Lookout*, continue to the top of the hill and pull off at a second right-turn lane that leads to another paved lot. *Note:* A restored section of the ancient Kings Road, a path parallel to the highway, connects the two lots.

HIKE: Makapu'u Lighthouse Road (2.25 mi., 475 ft.); Ka Iwi Scenic Shoreline-Makapu'u Tide Pools loop (2.5 mi., 500 ft.); Makapu'u Lookout (.25-mi.)

Makapu'u Point is the most-easterly land on Oahu. **Makapu'u Lighthouse Road** doesn't got to the lighthouse but rather to a railed lookout above it. Local exercise walkers favor this jaunt, which begins as a traverse up an easy grade (Lighthouse Road) with green Kealakipapa Valley down to the right. Viewing rocks invite a short side-trip as the road makes a left at the top of the grade and continues up Makapu'u Head. Then, about three-quarters of the way to the lookout, you'll pass a signed whale-watching spot, a hot-ticket during winter migrations. *More Stuff:* Near the sign is where a rough footpath descends to tide pools and two blowholes, the return leg of the loop is described below. Some people go down here and skip the coastal route.

Makapuu Beach Park

Not long after the whale viewing area, a road veers right, passing a square concrete building; this road leads to the lighthouse, but it is fenced off with plenty of warning signs. Cacti and succulents mix with the low vegetation over the last bit of ascent. The view from the railed lookouts is why people come to Hawaii. Rabbit Island lies below, and several other seabird islands lie offshore an undulating coastline, all of it in the shadow of the 3,000-foot green wall that is east side of the Ko'olau Range. *More Stuff:* An easy scramble up another 150 feet gets you to the scraggly ironwoods and bunkers atop Makapu'u Head—and trailblazers can head right over the top and drop down to the Makapu'u Lookout.

Only adventure hikers game to get muddy, ruddy, and perhaps a tad bloody will want to try the **Ka Iwi Scenic Shoreline-Makapu'u Tide Pools loop**. No, it's not *that* bad, the hike requires minor rock climbing and trail-finding skills along the coast, as well as an ascent up a rough trail on the return leg. Local conservationists have plans for the area, so conditions may improve. Begin by backtracking a short distance from Lighthouse Road and taking a lower ranch road across the Kealakipapa Valley toward the sea. This is the muddy part. Near the coast you'll reach a prominent stack of rock, an archeological site known as Pele's Chair, where the goddess of volcanoes left Oahu to begin her work farther south in the islands. Round Pele's Chair and then begin the coastal scramble, where your hands may get nicked on sharp rocks. About .25-mile along the slow-going coast, look for a rock face with a circular eroded pattern, below which is a tidal pool big enough to dunk in. This pool is about halfway to the main cluster of pools. Continue toward the cliffs ahead, with the lighthouse visible.

Some of the tide pools are just birdbaths, but some are wading pool-sized. Some fill only at high tide through wave action, while others are filled through sea channels. The blowholes, which don't always blow their holes, are on the mauka side of a main cluster of pools. The 400-foot climb to Lighthouse Road begins here. You should see white-painted rocks and be able to follow the foot-worn route of previous hikers. The

Rabbit Island

rough trail tops out at the whale-viewing spot on Lighthouse Road. To the left is a nicely graded, .75-mile descent to the highway. *Be Aware:* Don't attempt this hike during high surf. Stay back from the edges and don't turn your back on the ocean.

You really don't have to hike at all from the **Makapu'u Lookout**. Just get out of the car and behold a vista very similar to the Lighthouse Road lookout. But even a short walk up the face of Makapu'u reaps big scenic dividends and may just lure you all the way to the top. Make sure to stay back from the north-facing cliffs as you pick a weaving route of ascent.

SNORKEL: No one with a straight face can say the **Makapu'u Tide Pools** are a sure-thing snorkeling destination. But on the right day—high surf is the big deterrent—you'll be as happy as a dipping dolphin. Lots of people take the plunge.

23. RABBIT ISLAND BEACHES   HIKE, SNORKEL, SURF

WHAT'S BEST: The alluring seabird sanctuary of Rabbit (Manana) Island lies offshore, hypnotizing surfers and snorkelers at several choice beaches. Then snap out of it for a visit to Makai Research Pier, where today's argonauts prepare for expeditions to the depths of the Pacific.

PARKING: Go east on H-1 from Honolulu. H-1 merges to become Hwy. 72. Continue past Hanauma Bay, Sandy Beach, and Makapu'u Point.

HIKE: Rabbit Island coastal stroll (up to 2.25 mi., 150 ft.)

Talk Story: Highway 72 rounds Makapuʻu Point to reveal one of Hawaii's most enchanting vistas, Manana Island—known **Rabbit Island**. It does looks like Bugs with his ears laid back, but the island was nicknamed after being used as a breeding ground in the 1970s. Now, the seabird sanctuary is off-limits to rabbits and humans alike, although kayak landings are allowed at Kaohikaipu Island, a smaller island sanctuary close by. The windward pali rises steeply on this coastline, which is dotted with a half-dozen other islands and pointed landforms that appear as islands in the grand vista.

You'll probably do the **Rabbit Island coastal stroll** as part of a stop-and-go drive, but you could park the wheels and do it all from Makapuʻu Beach Park, on the right at a guardrail opening opposite Sea Life Park. From the parking area, a trail winds down to an ample scoop of sand that is maybe the best bodyboard break on Oahu. Makapuʻu Lighthouse clings to the cliffs on the far side of beach and the mountains paint a pretty picture at the backshore. But bring your own shade. Backtrack from this beach (there are several routes) and hug the coast along the volcanic rock tide pools that form the upper section of the beach park. Across this stumpy peninsula is the road into unimproved Kaupo Beach Park. From there, drop to the sands of a board surfing beach known most commonly as Cockroach Bay. As you reach the water, look

University of Hawaii Underwater Research Lab

right to see the tide-washed rock called Pohaku Paʻakiki; farmers of ancient times left offerings to the shark gods on the tabletop to ward off attacks. Damned if it hasn't worked.

At the far end of the beach is Makai Research Pier, a T-shaped dock supporting the boathouse used by HURL—Hawaii Underwater Research Laboratory. There are no official tours, but the rule at HURL is, when the boathouse's sliding door is raised, it's okay to check into their friendly and fascinating world. Regardless, take a walk out the pier for the offshore views and a dry-land look at

Makai Research Pier

colorful fish and coral. *Talk Story:* Under the auspices of the University of Hawaii and federal agencies, these guys not only maintain their own yellow submarines, but also pilot them to ocean depths offshore Hawaii and around the world. A recent voyage was to floor of the undersea active volcano, Loihi, 20 miles offshore of the Big Island. They wanted to see the effects of a 1996 earthquake that collapsed the dome of that emerging island into a deeper crater. Gulp. *More Stuff:* Sea Life Park, is an old-school theme park featuring performing dolphins, barking sea lions, waddling penguins, and the like, spread over 9 acres. Admission is pricey at about $26 per adult, with another $3 nick to park. Turn left across from the beach park.

SNORKEL: Makai Research Pier ranks right up there on the short list of Oahu's best snorkeling sites. Park at a dirt turnout to the left of the pier and enter there, or swim over from the beach area on this end of Cockroach Bay. Before getting in, you may wish to take a look by walking the pier to its end. The coral is lively and you should see lotsa fish. *Be Aware:* Low budget outfitters occasionally discharge vanloads here, and the parking area has seen break-ins. Also, be mindful of fishermen's lines.

The **Makapu'u Keiki Ponds,** although not a flipper-around spot, provide a safe and scenic dip into clear water. Park at the Kaupo Beach Park, on the right past the turn into Makapu'u Beach. The ponds are along the lava reef between the two beaches.

SURF: Makapu'u Beach Park is bodysurf central, home to Oahu's first-ever championships that began in the 1950s. A rock abuts the surf about midway in the bay, at **Middles**, providing a grandstand for onlookers. Bodyboards join in the fun, but longer boards are kapu. The right break closer to the cliff is called **Baby Makapu'u** and the site closer to the trail coming down is known as **Generals**. Board surfers head to Kaupo Beach Park for a right-break toward Cockroach Bay called **Suicides**, since the sharp, shallow reef makes for risky business. The adventuresome wave riders in these parts paddle the .75-mile out to the northwest side of **Rabbit Island**—on surfboards or using wave-riding kayaks.

24. WAIMANALO   HIKE, SNORKEL, SURF

WHAT'S BEST: Head mauka to see rural upcountry, either driving or hiking beneath the 2,500-foot pinnacles of the Ko'olaus. Or, stay makai and go barefoot along several miles of scenic beach that are backed by an ironwood forest.

PARKING: *For the beach hike,* take H-1 east from Waikiki and stay with it as it becomes Hwy. 72. Continue past Hanamua, Makapu'u Point, and Makai Pier. Continue past Hull St. and the two entrances to Waimanalo Beach Park, and turn right on Wailea. Then turn left on Laumilo and park near the fourth right-of-way at Manana. *Alternate route if driving directly here from Waikiki:* Take Hwy. 61 (the Pali Hwy.) toward Kailua. Turn right at the junction with Hwy. 72. Drive through the business district and go left at the McDonalds on Aloiloi, which takes you to Laumilo. *For the Upcountry and Maunawili Trail,* turn mauka at the light on Kumuhau, which is on the Kailua end of Waimanalo. Continue for .75-mi. to a stop sign and turn right on Waikupanaha. Mahiku Pl. is on the right, and immediately following on the right is the gated, signed trailhead.

Waimanalo Beach

HIKE: Waimanalo Beach hike (up to 5.5 mi.); Upcountry and Maunawili Trail to: Aniani Nui Ridge (1.75 mi., 350 ft.), or The Whole Banana (9.5 mi., and about 1,100 ft.)

Talk Story: The fertile slopes beneath the Ko'olau Range yielded sugar from the late 1800s until World War II, when John Cummins' Waimanalo Sugar Plantation closed for good. His father, Thomas, was a missionary who married a Hawaiian high chiefess, allowing young John to school with the future kings, William Lunalilo and David Kalakaua. Those associations, along with acumen for real estate development, were parlayed into a fortune by John later in life—a story that can be retold, plugging in different missionary offspring, throughout Hawaii. Midway in that history, in 1919, Prince Jonah Kuhio, the islands' first congressional representative, helped establish the Hawaiian Homelands Act that set aside acreage for native people. Waimanalo remains a rural community. In recent decades it has become known for slack-key guitar music, like Nashville is for country. The coast has been home turf to legendary performers such as Gabby Pahanui and members of Sons of Hawaii.

The **Waimanalo Beach hike** begins in the middle of the longest run of sand on Oahu. Each direction is described in the next paragraphs. Along Laumilo are beach cottages and B&Bs, and right-of-ways at each of a half-dozen intersecting lanes. This beach strip rivals well-publicized Kailua-Lanikai, but with a fraction of the visitors. There are other parking options, which are used mainly by locals: At the Kailua end of town (before the McDonalds) you can drive in on Walker Road for .5-mile to the large, forested Waimanalo Bay State Recreation Area. Or, at the other end of Waimanalo are the two parking lots for the Waimanalo Bay Beach Park and the small lot for Kaiona Beach Park (see *Snorkel*). Tourists will like the Laumilo spots best.

From the right-of-way at Manana, walk out the short path and do a 360 to take in the long strip of sand, the offshore islands, and the pali that seems to wrap around the bay. Okay, take off your shoes and go. To the right on the beach takes you by the grassy slopes and family picnic grounds of Waimanalo Beach Park. After nearly a mile from the start, you reach Kaiona Beach Park, where you might have to wade around a bulkhead. You quickly reach Pahonu Pond, a large, rectangular rock enclosure that in ancient times was a pen for turtles, a delicacy that only royalty could enjoy.

Going to the left from the Manana access, you immediately pass an old sugar plantation landing. A quarter-mile later begins the sloping beachfront of Waimanalo Bay State Recreation Area. The large ironwood grove is known also as Sherwood Forest, a Robin Hood reference derived from the rip-and-run activities of a local band of youth who would strip cars of the 'rich' and give the ill-gotten booty to their poor ol' selves. Authorities have cracked down on these practices, for the most part. After .5-mile, you'll reach Puha Stream, on the far banks of which the sands continue along Bellows Field Air Force Base. You can drive into Bellows on weekends.

The **Maunawili Trail** extends from Waimanalo on an undulating contour at the curving base of the Ko'olau Pali, ending at the Highway 61; see TH28, page 118. Midway, you can access the trail from Maunawili Falls, described in TH27, page 115.

The Waimanalo side of the trail ranks third in popularity among the three trailheads, and is more often used as a pick-up point for car-shuttle hikes. Before embarking on a hike, you may wish to drive the **upcountry**, along Waikupanaha, which runs for about 3 miles along the pali, heading in the opposite direction from the trail. A few dead-end streets along the way (Kakaina, Mahailua, Kaulukanu) provide opportunities to drive deeper into the creases of the Ko'olaus. Though this is not a tourist area (heed kapu and no trespassing signs), you will see pastoral lands that are a reminder of days gone by, complete with old-timey fruit and flower stands.

For **Aniani Nui Ridge**, or any bite from **The Whole Banana**, head up the road at the gated trailhead. You'll be in an ascending tunnel of tropical greenery. At a junction, pass the Maunawili Ditch Trail on the right, which is 2.75-mile spur heading makai. The road reaches the Aniani Nui Ridge, an offshoot of the Ko'olaus that forms part of the bowl-shaped Maunawili Valley. Take a left fork here to continue on the Maunawili Trail. The connector trail to Maunawili Falls is about halfway along the 9-mile run, but first timers will probably want to walk in a ways and sample a lush forest—uluhe ferns, koa, ohia, rose apples, and many more, all tangled together. Dozens of gulches and streams intrude on this so-called contour, providing interest as well as minor undulation. *Be Aware*: Bring rain gear. A hiking pole will help with foot placement.

SNORKEL: Kaiona Beach Park and **Pahonu Pond** are the best bet for snorkeling and swimming in Waimanalo, and for a family picnic. In fact, the pond snorkeling is very good, with clear waters protected by an offshore reef and featuring an alluring view of Rabbit Island. It can be shallow at low tide. Look for facilities and parking lot near address 41-564 on Highway 72 leaving Waimanalo toward Makapu'u—just next to the large, pink Shriners Club. The sands of **Waimanalo Beach Park** get high marks for a day of sunning and swimming. Same goes for the beach at **Waimanalo Bay State Recreation Area**, but the winning choices for visitors are the **right-of-ways along Laumilo**. *Be Aware:* Waimanalo Beaches are known as habitat for stinging jellyfish, the Portuguese man-o-war. The painful sting lasts about 15 minutes. For treatment, gently rub with sand and then hustle to a fresh water spigot to rinse off.

SURF: A sandbar runs along the shore of **Waimanalo Bay State Recreation Area**, creating a gentle wave for bodysurfing and wave play, a good place for novices to give it a try. Just down the road, **Bellows Field Beach Park** is known for bodysurfing and bodyboarding, although short boarders also take to the waters. Bellows is open to the public on weekends, when it can be a zoo. Turn makai on Tinker Road, between the Waimanalo business area and the state recreation area.

25. KAILUA   HIKE, SNORKEL, SURF

WHAT'S BEST: Kailua and Lanikai beaches are hailed as America's best by national travel magazines. Snorkeling, fine-sand beaches, and kayaking to an island all factor in. But to appreciate the intangibles, begin the visit with a hike to a stand-alone ridge above the coast.

PARKING: *From Waikiki*, take Hwy. 61 (the Pali Hwy.) toward Kailua. Pass all junctions. The route becomes Kailua Rd. Keep straight on Ku'ulei Rd. at a light, where Kailua Rd. goes right. Ku'ulei ends at a stop sign, where you go right on S. Kalaheo Ave., which becomes Kawailoa Rd. *For the west end of the beach*, turn left at Kalapawai Market on Lihiwai Rd. *For main area of Kailua Beach Park*, continue on Kawailoa over the bridge and turn into the large parking lot. *For the Kaiwa Ridge hike and Lanikai Beach directly*, pass Kailua Beach Park and go left at a stop sign on A'alapapa. Round the turn. *For the hike only*, turn right toward a Mid-Pacific Country Club on Kaelepulu. Pass the country club and park on the right or a chain-link fence, across from a private drive sign at address 269. *To Lanikai Beach*, continue on one-way A'alapapa to its end and turn left on Mokulua Dr., a one-way the other direction. Beach access described in *Snorkel*.

HIKE: Kawai Ridge (1.25 mi., 600 ft.); Kailua Beach to Lanikai Beach hike (up to 2.25 mi.); Kalama Beach to Kawainu Canal (2.5 mi.)

No signs note that **Kawai Ridge** is an official State Na Ala Hele trail, and the hike's beginning is up what looks like a driveway to some residences. But at the top of the drive, on the right, is an opening in a chain-link fence that leads to the eroded, red-dirt path. The initial steep section breaks out to a crumbly rock slope that supports dry grasses and scrub, habitat for small birds. The view knobs on top of the ridge come into sight; you'll reach the first, marked by a bunker, after about 20 minutes. Continue along the ridge to a larger bunker at the top. The prime view is from the roof reachable via a ladder. You get a romantic look at the coast, extending from Kaneohe to Makapu'u Point. Rabbit Island is far right, while Lanikai's sweet twins, Mokulua islands, are straight offshore. Also note Flat Island, to the left, offshore Kailua Beach Park. But don't forget to spin around. Inland is the vertical wall of the Ko'olau Range, and to the right is the triple-peaked, stand-alone ridge of Olomana.

Even on a perfect day you might get motivated to rise from the towel and do a people-watching, wade-walk from **Kailua Beach** to **Lanikai Beach**. In the late 1990s *Conde Nast* magazine dubbed each of these beaches as America's best—you decide. Kailua Beach Park's 35 acres of rolling green backshore draw picnickers and its calm shoreline invites windsurfers and small sailboats, along with a flotilla of kayakers who make the short paddle (less than .25-mile) out to Flat Island, a.k.a Popoia Island. Begin by looping west (left as you face the water) to the far end of the developed park. At Kalapawai Market, circa 1932, you can soak in some charm, and pick up a turkey pepper wrap or feta veggie as a later reward at journey's end. Then head to the right, across the sloping sands of Kailua. At the far end of the beach you'll need to pop up to a pedestrian path that passes the stone obelisk at Alala Point. Take the first right-of-way off sleepy Mokulua Drive out to Lanikai Beach. With the twin cones of the seabird islands of Mokulua in view (the larger is Moku Nui, the smaller Moku Iki) you will be able to walk another .5-mile or more, until reaching a point where the sea laps up to the bulkheads of beachside homes. Denizens of Lanikai spill out from a quiet grid of cottages and estates, some of which date from the 1920s.

The **Kalama Beach hike** takes in a more solitary seascape, since it covers a length of beach with little access due to gated McMansions of one of Kailua's tony neighborhoods. To drive to Kalama Beach Park, go right as you leave Kailua Park's main lot, toward Kaneohe. Kawailoa becomes Kalaheo Avenue. The park is about a mile down the road in a modest neighborhood. Walk through the gardens of the small beach park and hang a left. Mokapu Peninsula rises from the water ahead and two seabird sanctuaries, Mokolea and Moku Manu, add drama to the offshore views. The homes get statelier as you approach Kawainu Canal, an area called Castle Beach. It's named for Harold Kainalu Castle and his predecessors, the Kings of Development from the late 1800s onward. Across the canal is reefy Kapoho Point, and around that is the Kaneohe Marine Corps Base, where entry is verboten.

SNORKEL: Kailua Beach Park has excellent conditions for novice snorkelers: Calm water, sandy entry, and a shallow, sprawling coral reef that extends out to Flat Island. Start at the beach in front of the large parking area, between the lifeguard towers where the island is directly offshore—less than .25-mile away. You should be

Kailua Beach, Lanikai Beach, Heliconia, Kawai Ridge

able to make your way through sandy channels within the spreading reef. *Be Aware*: Windsurfers, kayakers, and small craft (a boat ramp is to the right, toward Alala Point) present potential hazards. Average-to-strong swimmers will be able to swim all the way to Flat Island, in depths seldom over five feet. Don't be shy about seeking advice from lifeguards. Stay in assigned areas when you reach this bird sanctuary.

Lanikai Beach may get the edge in a snorkel-off competitions between these two rival beaches. You'll see about ten right-of-ways all along Mokulua Drive. But the short paths don't lead to nice beach areas until you reach the right-of-way between Kualima and Haokea drives, which is about .75-mile along Mokulua. Fine white sand and turquoise water shout, 'snorkel me.' A gradual entry slopes to coral reefs offshore, with depths of 10 to15 feet, although coral heads may peek above water during low tide. Current is not usually a problem. *Be Aware:* Don't stand on the living coral. Be mindful of windsurfers and small sailboats. Bring sunblock, since shade is scarce. And, believe it or not, thieves roam the quiet street parking so leave the car empty.

SURF: Trade winds beckon kiteboarders and windsurfers to the shallow waters off **Kailua Beach Park**, but his coast is not known for primo surfing. Beginning surfers do ride a break off the reef at **Flat Island**, as well as other minor breaks along the outer reef.

26. OLOMANA RIDGE   HIKE

WHAT'S BEST: Adventure hikers need to psyche up to scale the awesome triple peaks of this razorback ridge. Fit hikers can get a thrill from the first peak, after just one sweaty-palmed climb. Then everyone can descend, relax, and enjoy one of the largest heiaus in Hawaii.

PARKING: Take Hwy. 61 (the Pali Hwy.) toward Kailua from Waikiki. Pass the junction of Hwy. 83, which is across from first Auloa Rd. Then pass the traffic light at Kapaʻa Quarry Road. *For Olomana Ridge*, turn right at the second Auloa Rd. and make an immediate left (on Auloa), toward Luana Hills Country Club. After less than .25-mi., and just before a bridge, hang a U-turn and park at a dirt turnout alongside a chain-link fence. *For Ulupo Heiau*, continue on Hwy. 61 (now Kailua Rd.) past the junction with Hwy. 72. After passing Kailua Community Methodist Church on the left, hang a U-turn, at Hanalei Pl. Drive back up Kailua Rd, pass the Methodist church, and park at a dirt turnout that is just beyond a bus stop and at the beginning of a guardrail. (This parking is easier than the monument's main lot—right on Uluoa, and right again on Manualoha at the Baptist Church.)

HIKE: Olomana Peak (4.25 mi., 1,575 ft.); Ulupo Heiau State Monument (.25-mi.)

Talk Story: To appreciate what you're in for, take a look at Olomana Ridge from the road into Maunawili Falls (see next trailhead), or from Highway 72 as you drive from Waimanalo toward Kailua. The scalloped, thin ridge is a poster child for Oahu hikes, and has been featured in national press, such as *New York Times*, and others. *Be Aware:*

Olomana is your normal, steep, hands-on hike until the last 20 feet, when a climb is required. Vertigo may set in after that. The second peak is doable for daredevils, but the third peak is dangerous, even for technical climbers. Remember, Olomana is the eroded lip of a volcano that began about 10,000 feet higher eons ago. Some rocks are as stable as peanuts stuck in chocolate.

Begin the **Olomana Peak** hike by walking the road past the hiker-friendly security guard station, and, about .5-mile later, look to the left for the trailhead. (A sign will say that continuing on the road is prohibited.) The trail starts innocently enough, by crossing a luau area and under a dome of banyans and other trees. You'll climb gradually to the left and then hook right, beginning the ascent of the ridge at a stand of ironwoods growing from red dirt. From here is a view mauka of the pali, as well as the shark fin that is Olomana Peak. The trail gets steeper and narrows—big surprise—as you

Olomana Ridge

continue up the rooty, rocky spine, and you may zip up sections that will give pause for thought on the way down. Limbs of dwarf trees offer a helping hand, and a flat section provides a breather, just below the last push to the top.

Be sure to test the rope that dangles from the 20-foot-high rock pile that stands between you and the big view from Olomana Peak. Take your time going up, visualizing how you will soon back down. After this brief jungle gym, you top out on the outcrop and get a view toward the middle peak, called Pakui. The far end of the ridge is anchored by Ahiki. A few hikers make for a crowd on top of Olomana, just a narrow ledge. Intrepid hikers can use ropes and caution to make it to Pakui, but only experienced daredevils should go for Ahiki.

To see **Ulupo Heiau State Monument**, take a path at an opening in a low Cyclone fence that leads to the 8 acres of trees and gardens bordered by the busy street and modest homes. *Talk Story:* Now a rather forlorn setting for kids after-school powwows, the heiau was the spiritual center of the region from the 1400s to around 1800. Initial construction was by the diminutive Menehunes, the earliest Polynesian arrivals from the Marquesas. Around the heiau were several hundred prime acres of fishponds and agricultural terraces. Unlike many heiaus in Hawaii, visitors are free to explore, with care, the 120- by 180-foot platform. The heiau's down-slope walls are about 30 feet high. About 200 years ago, what is now a marsh was a large fishpond call Kawai Nui, which itself had been built by the earliest Polynesians in an area that had a large lagoon with favorable canoe landings. Two other heiaus were on the edge of Kawai Nui, located to the left as you face the sea at Ulupo Heiau. Pahukini Heiau, now partially restored, sits virtually in the city landfill off Kapaʻa Quarry Road—a setting emblematic of the disregard developers had for cultural sites in the mid-1900s. The other heiau is gone completely.

More Stuff: Joggers needing a fix, and people staying on the windward side, might enjoy a 1.25-mile path that runs along Kawainui Marsh. You can access the path most easily by taking Kailua Road toward town from the heiau; hang a left at Kainehe Road, and backtrack up Kailua Road about .25-mile, to near the Lutheran Church. You get a photographer's view across the marsh toward Olomana and the curving wall of the Koʻolau Pali.

27. MAUNAWILI FALLS   HIKE

WHAT'S BEST: Lace up the mud shoes and head into a jungle valley on a mini-adventure to a waterfall with a swimming pool.

PARKING: Take Hwy. 61 (the Pali Hwy.) toward Kailua from Waikiki. Pass the junction of Hwy. 83, across from the first Auloa Rd. Then pass the traffic light at Kapaʻa Quarry

Road. Turn right at the second Auloa Rd. Keep right *just* after the turn, but then veer left on Maunawili Rd. Follow for 1.5 mi. and turn right on Kelewina. Park on Kelewina where indicated by signs.

HIKE: Maunawili Falls (3 mi., 425 ft.)

Begin the journey to **Maunawili Falls** by backtracking on Kelewina and going right at a signed gate. The real trailhead is on the right, a few minutes away. *Be Aware:* The Maunawili Falls hike is a winner and therefore can get hammered with hikers on pretty weekends and holidays. Though not difficult, it's not a turkey trot either, since rocks, roots, and four stream crossings create an obstacle course for the feet. Sometimes crossings can be made over rocks; otherwise you're better off wading.

Maunawili Falls trail

The trail begins through a garden of tropical flora, complimented by a birdsong symphony. These terraces surround the site of the ancient Kukapoki Heiau. Less than .5-mile from the trailhead, railroad-tie steps lead down to the right to the first stream crossing. *Be Aware:* During heavy rains, watch out for rising water. If you get caught on the other side, wait it out. Bananas join the greenery on the other side of the stream, as you ascend gently over roots the size of pythons. The second stream crossing is only ten minutes farther, under a large banyan, after which you'll walk an imbedded-rock road through a clearing that reveals a big view of the pali. A third stream crossing soon follows. Then begins the hike's primary ascent, made easier by long flights of steps that top out on a finger of a ridge coming from the Ko'olaus.

Here, at the trail's most scenic point, is a junction. A straight-ahead trail leads to the Maunawili Trail, joining it midway between the Waimanalo and Pali Highway trailheads. For Maunawili Falls, go left from this junction, losing most of what you just climbed as you descend on a nicely built staircase. At the bottom, the trail reaches the stream. Do not go right on a nowhere trail up a tributary to the main stream. Cross the tributary and hug the right bank of the larger stream for a couple hundred feet and you'll pick up the trail again. The falls are not far ahead, a 25-foot cataract tumbling into a rock cavern. People swim in the oval, but many like the pool just above it that can be reached via a short rock climb to the left of the falls.

28. NU'UANU PALI   HIKE

WHAT'S BEST: Busloads of visitors learn why the east shore is called the *wind*ward side as they admire the view from on high. Take a short hike to lose the crowd and gain an appreciation of what the losing side saw when Kamehameha's invading forces drove them over the edge. Or embark on a jungle trek past many streams on the Maunawili Trail.

PARKING: Take Hwy. 61, the Pali Hwy. from Waikiki. If Westbound on H-1, use Exit 21-B, Pali-61 North. For the scenic route from Waikiki take Beretania west to Nu'uanu Ave., turn right and follow the activities in TH13, page 72. From Hwy. 61, look for the Nu'uanu Pali Lookout exit, as the highway crests. *For Maunawili Trail,* continue on Hwy. 61 past the lookout. Continue through the two tunnels and past a truck runaway ramp. As the road makes a big bend to the left, pull out to the right at a scenic point.

HIKE: Old Pali Highway to: **Kahanaiki Stream Bridge (.75-mi., 150 ft.), or Maunawili Trailhead car-shuttle (.75-mi., minus 350 ft.); Maunawili Trail (up to 9.5 mi., one way, 1,100 ft.)**

Talk Story: Trade winds often whistle through the 1,200-foot-high **Nu'uanu Pali Lookout**, at an opening that is about half as high as the 50-mile ridge of the Ko'olau Mountains. The three-acre state park sees swarms of tourists. In 1795, the invading army of Kamehameha the Great used newly acquired cannons to push the defending Oahu forces up the Nu'uanu Valley. Among the defenders was High Chief Kaiana,

Old Pali Highway

said to be Kamehameha's match in both size and intelligence, but you've never heard of him since he was among the 500 warriors who were killed or driven over the edge. Weapons used were spears, rocks, and clubs. A century later in 1897 when the first Pali Highway was built, engineer John Wilson and his crew found some 300 skulls.

The **Old Pali Highway** hugs the cliff to the right from below the lookout railings. Tropical flora is quickly reclaiming the old pavement with encroaching ferns, overhanging vines, and banyan bark slowly crawling the concrete railing like The Blob. Watch your step, as runoff makes for slippery footing in places. From the **Kahanaiki Stream Bridge** you'll get a good look back at the pali and the windward vista. Look below the stream's fall and past the modern highway to an old road, where adventure hikers can join the Likeke Pali Trail; see *More Stuff*, below.

To continue on to the **Maunawili Trailhead car-shuttle**, keep on trekkin' the old road. In some places greenery shuts the route to a one-lane path, with ferns and ginger tickling your shins. The route lowers to the elevation of the real highway and continues alongside a fence. A nice pandanus grove, from which hats and baskets are woven, is in this area. When you reach a trail junction, go left down a cobbled slope and you'll be out at the trailhead parking in a minute or two. Hopefully someone drove down to pick you up.

More Stuff: A quirky, fun 'trail' connects the Old Pali Highway to the Likeke Pali Trail, which is described in TH29, page 120. Hikers can use this route for a longer car-shuttle that ends at the Likeke Pali trailhead. Or try it as an add-on to the Old Pali Highway. As the old road reaches the level of the new—and before the chain-link, boulder fence—you'll see a slide area and old wall. Go left and back, down toward the highway. Descend a short set of rickety stairs. Duck under the first roadway and walk under the second. Keep left on an overgrown concrete road (a closed section of Auloa), and continue on a gradual downhill for about 10 minutes. You'll reach the now-closed Kionaole Road, where you go left a short distance to a low, concrete wall on your left at a stream. The Likeke Trail begins to the right of that wall, climbing into the greenery, before contouring right to the Likeke Trailhead.

The **Maunawili Trail** is an easy way to take a long walk in the rain forest. It is basically a contour along the curving foot of the Ko'olau Pali, although dozens of little gulches and ridge ripples add elevation as well as interest to the trail. Botanists and birders will go bonkers. Most hikers will want to do an out-and-back of varying lengths. Long-distance walkers can do a car-shuttle that ends at either Maunawili Falls trailhead, page 115, or in Waimanalo, page 107. After a few minutes, keep left at a junction, where the Old Pali Highway trail is to the right. The Maunawili Trail, aside from being a wonderland of water-washed flora, gives up fine seaward vistas along with neck-straining mauka views.

29. LIKEKE PALI TRAIL   HIKE

WHAT'S BEST: One of Oahu's best-kept hiking secrets. Seriously. A waterfall, wild arboretum and gardens, and a view of Nu'uanu Pali are close but faraway.

PARKING: From Waikiki, take H-1 West to Exit 20A-Hwy. 63, the Likelike Hwy., toward Kaneohe. (If using H-3, take Exit 9- Hwy. 63 toward Kaneohe.) On the windward side, pass under H-3 and pass by Hwy. 83, Kahekili Hwy. to the North Shore. At the light in Kaneohe, turn right on Kamehameha Hwy. 83 toward Kailua. Just before passing under H-3, turn right on Kionaole Rd. Then turn right into Ko'olau Golf Club and park in the upper lot to the left as you face mauka. *Alternate trailhead parking:* Should the golf course parking become unavailable, by-pass the entry and park where Kionaole Rd. is closed at a fence. Walk the road a short distance to a bridge, inscribed '1919.' On the downhill side of the bridge a short trail leads to the right up to the Ko'olau parking lot; just across the bridge, a trail leads up to the right and joins the Likeke Trail.

HIKE: Likeke Pali Trail to: Likeke Falls (1 mi., 200 ft.), or Likeke arboretum (about 2.5 mi. 350 ft.); Likeke Trail-Kionaole Rd. loop (2.5 mi., 450 ft.)

Likeke Pali

Ko'olau Golf Club rests below the towering pali, a setting that is second to none among the windward side vistas. The club's elegant interior features an atrium and waterfall, and a wrap around patio shows off an inspiring view.

For all hikes, head up a road that angles to the right from the parking lot. Just before the water tank, go left on an unsigned trail that immediately penetrates a ferny gardenscape, with birds whistling above in a canopy of monkeypods. Pass a trail coming from the left, which goes down to Kionaole Road. After a hau thicket and frock of heliconia, the trail breaks into the open on a cobblestone pathway. **For the Likeke Waterfall and arboretum,** go right on an unsigned trail, as the cobblestone road continues its ascent. You'll cross a boardwalk section and get a pali view before

Likeke Falls

coming upon the 50-foot-high cascade. A bench under a kukui tree frames the falls, and a flowered view knob affords a seaward view.

From the falls, the Likeke Trail continues on an undulating contour for almost 2 miles to the makai side of the Wilson Tunnel on Highway 63. About .25-mile from the falls is a clearing with a dramatic look up to the Nuʻuanu Pali and the Kahanaiki Stream Bridge. A huge grove of mangos, red ginger, ti, and strawberry guava are among the multitude of flora decorating the trail as it weaves in and out of gulches. It's easy walking. Pick your own turnaround. *Note:* After getting back to the cobblestone section keep an eye peeled for the left junction of the trail that goes back to the water tank road. If you miss it, no biggie. You'll drop down to old Kionaole Road, where you cross the bridge and go immediately left on a short trail back to the parking lot.

For the **Likeke Trail-Kionaole Road loop**, keep going up the cobblestone road, passing the right-hand junction of the Likeke Trail to the falls. As you ascend, the rocks peter out and the route becomes a trail. You follow an old ditch up steeply, and then the trail loops left around a gorge that sports a mammoth monkeypod. You top out at a finger ridge of the pali, at a four-way trail junction. Go straight, down steps toward the road that is visible ahead. You come out at the bridge that is accessed via the Old Pali Highway. Go left at this point, through the tree tunnel that is a closed section of Kionaole Road, a route often used by cyclists. You'll reach an old bridge with '1919' etched in concrete. Cross the bridge and go left up a trail on a two-minute walk to the golf club parking lot.

30. HOʻOMALUHIA BOTANICAL GARDEN   HIKE

WHAT'S BEST: Wander by car or on foot streamside gardens with tropical plantings from around the world, all of them in the shadow of the spectacular Koʻolau Pali. A nearby 'Stairway to Heaven' would be a marquee attraction, if it ever opens to the public.

Hoomaluhie Botanical Garden

PARKING. From Waikiki, take H-1 West to Exit 20A Hwy. 63, the Likelike Hwy., toward Kaneohe. (If using H-3, take the Likelike Hwy. exit toward Kaneohe.) Pass the junction with Hwy. 83 (the Kahekili Hwy.) to the North Shore and turn right on Anoi. From Anoi, turn right on Luluku and follow uphill to enter the garden. *Notes:* Directions continue below. Hours are from 9 to 4 daily. Admission is free. *For the Stairway to Heaven,* see the description below.

HIKE: Hoʻomaluhia Botanical Garden (various trails, up to 7 mi., 300 ft.); Stairway to Heaven, a.k.a. Haiku Stairs (2.5 mi., 2,300 ft.)

Six distinct garden areas are planted within 400 rolling acres, putting **Hoʻomaluhia Botanical Garden** in the running not only for Oahu's best, but right up there with any garden in Hawaii. The nearly 3,000-foot-high Koʻolau Pali broods above, a scenic asset for sure, but also drawing frequent showers—the main demerit for the parkland. Closed-off Luluku Road winds for 2.5 miles through the mauka edge of the gardens, a choice for exercise walkers and joggers.

You may have already snapped a few images on the scenic drive to the visitors center. Pull in there to visit the gift shop and get current trail information, as well as a free map. As you continue on the main park road, six spur roads go left into various gardens. First up is Pa Luana, featuring tropical American plants and the Lake Trail, leading about .5-mile to the garden's 32-acre reservoir, Loko Waimaluhia. The shores are popular among catch-and-release fishermen. About .25-mile later on the main road is Kahua Kuou, planted with exotics from India and Sri Lanka. From here you can also reach the reservoir by going left, or hooking right to the Stream Trail.

Hoʻomaluhia's highpoint, both in elevation and scenic amplitude, is the Kilonani Mauka Overlook, which is on the right about a.5-mile from the visitors center. A wide concrete path climbs a fern-covered hillock to a view made for painters and wide-angle shutterbugs. Just after the overlook hillock is a spur road to Kahua Lehua, a garden of some 1,000 native Hawaiian plants, many of which are endangered. The Stream Trail leads from the Hawaiian garden to the reservoir, giving you a good look at the island Moku Moʻo, and loops back via the stream.

Off the main road past the Hawaiian garden is the Polynesian, Kahua Kuku, and the garden of hau trees, Kahua Hau. A short path connects the two. The Polynesian plants are bananas, ti, breadfruit, coco palms, and others that most visitors associate with Hawaii, but were actually brought by the first South Pacific voyagers, beginning in the first or second century AD. After these stops, you come to the garden's wide-open spaces at the Kahua Nui gardens, a large field used by campers on weekends.

Talk Story: The fabled **Stairway to Heaven**, or **Haiku Stairs**—all 3,900 of them connected in a series of railed segments—rent skyward from Haiku Valley beside the H-3 freeway to the 2,720-foot Puʻu Keahi. Some sections are sweaty-palms vertical, others nearly flat, and most climb at about a 45-degree angle. Why? Good question. The Haiku Stairs were installed by the Navy in 1942 in order to hoist a mile-long cable antenna across the valley to facilitate the low-frequency, long-wavelength needed for extra-long-distance transmission. The copper antenna alone weighed in at 6,000 pounds, a small fraction of the construction materials that were hoisted up. Nowadays, any adolescent can accomplish the same communication with a two-ounce cell phone. The present metal stairs replaced the original wooden ones in 1957. The Coast Guard took over in 1971, and the Haiku Stairs were Oahu's most-thrilling hike, until they were closed in 1987. By 1998 a group had organized to have them re-opened, and managed to get the city to pony up $875,000 to have the stairs repaired in 2003. Alas, "closed indefinitely," may still be the response from the mayor's office; they sincerely hope that people like you and all your friends call twice every day to inquire.

Accessing the Stairway to Heaven: People still make the ascent, but access is a problem and trespassing arrests have been made. The most probable lawful trailhead will be at the Hope Chapel parking lot. From Highway 63, makai of H-3, turn left, or north, on Highway 83, the Kahekili Highway. Then go left on Kea'ahala and turn left on Po'okela, before Windward Community College and the Hawaii State Hospital. The chapel is to the right, at the end of Po'okela. You'll see a set of steps at the back of the lot that lead to a frontage road used in the H-3 construction; go right on this road. *Be Aware:* Obey posted signs.

Stairway to Heaven

31. VALLEY OF THE TEMPLES   HIKE

WHAT'S BEST: Even agnostics may see the light as sunbeams streak down the green cliffs and land upon idyllic Byodo-In Buddhist temple. Afterwards, independent travelers can explore other windward valleys that are slated to be nature parks.

PARKING: From Waikiki, take H-1 Westbound and merge with H-78 Westbound. Then take H-3 toward Kaneohe. Take Exit 9-Kaneohe, Hwy. 63. From Hwy. 63 go left on Hwy. 83 (the Kahekili Hwy.) northbound. After about 3 mi. and a long straightaway, turn left at the first light on E. Hui Iwa Dr. at a sign for Valley of the Temples Memorial Park. Continue up the valley and keep left at Holy Cross Blvd. to the parking lot for Byodo-In Temple. *Notes:* An admission of about $2 is charged to visit Byodo-In Temple. Directions heading north continue in *More Stuff.*

HIKE: Byodo-In Temple (.5-mi.)

Okay, the Valley of the Temples is a vast cemetery. But with the Koʻolau Pali jutting above rolling parklike acres, the place is anything but morbid, and, when lit by sunlight, it is downright inspiring. From the parking lot, pay the man his money and walk over a footbridge to absorb the instant curb appeal of the **Byodo-In Temple**. The view is across a large koi pond, home to swans and ducks. *Talk Story:* The ornate Japanese temple is a replica of a 900-year-old temple in Kyoto whose architecture reflects an image of a Phoenix rising from the ashes. Byodo-In was built in 1968 as a centennial memorial to Hawaii's first Japanese immigrants.

Valley of the Temples, Amida Buddha

You are free to roam about the 10-acre gardens around the temple. To the left as you approach is the hut for a seven-foot bronze bell, the gonging of which, accompanied by a small donation, is said to rid the mind of evil temptations. Ah, were it that simple. Inside the main room of the temple is 18-foot-tall Amida, the Buddha of the Western Paradise, gold-lacquered and seated in a lotus position. A Buddhist priest is normally on hand at the rear of the temple to greet followers of this Eastern religion. To the right of the temple is the Tea House and Gift Shop, an opportunity to sip and behold an impressive array of Buddhaiana. On the way out from Byodo-In, you might want to go right up Chapel Road for an ethereal view from near large mausoleums that the Dillinghams and other well-off Hawaiian families have built for themselves.

WHAT'S BEST: Take a scenic byway along the coast of ancient fishponds and stop for the serene views at a small state park with a big sense of community.

PARKING: From Waikiki, take H-1 West and merge with H-78 West. Then take H-3 toward Kaneohe. Take Exit 9-Kaneohe, Hwy. 63. Go north on the Hwy. 83, (the Kahekili Hwy.) and turn right at the light on Kahuhipa, which is the street past Kea‘ahala. Take Kahuhipa down to Hwy. 830, Kamehameha Hwy., and turn left, or north. Directions continue below. *Note:* If going north from Byodo-In, you'll have to backtrack a mile on Hwy. 83 and turn left on Kahuhipa.

HIKE: He‘eia State Park (up to .5-mi.)

The 1.5-mile drive on Highway 830 from the Windward Mall to **He‘eia State Park** gets you centuries into the past. From the park's 19-acre peninsula jutting into Kaneohe Bay are views north and south of seabird islands and the tufted spur ridges of the Ko‘olau Range. Inland and towards Kaneohe from the park grounds is He‘eia Fishpond, a centuries-old rock enclosure that kept the Polynesian arrivals supplied with mullet and other fish. The 90-acre pond used to have four observation towers and was still in use until the 1950s.

At the state park, a path leads from below the community visitors center to the site of Kalaeulaula Heiau, which was destroyed in the 1800s but remains a sacred spot. The park is under the care of The Friends of He‘eia, a nonprofit association of locals who volunteer to keep the place maintained and also offer guided tours. Give them a call if you're looking for a rewarding experience. Visit on Sundays from 9 to 3, and you'll be treated to the Windward Open Market, where locals gather to present arts, veggies, flowers, fruits, and healthy doses of aloha.

Continuing north on Highway 830, you drop down to the Kaneohe Fishing Pier, a chance to see the comings-and-goings of smaller boats, and snatch some fries at a dockside eatery. The scenic blacktop hugs the coast for another 2.5 miles before popping out to join Highway 83 in Kahalu‘u. On the right at the junction is Kahalu‘u Pond, another 'fish store' built in ancient times by early Hawaiians. A curving 1,000-foot-long wall planted with coco palms is pleasing to the eye. A heiau on the point was destroyed by pineapple growers in the 1800s, a time of disregard for Hawaiian antiquities. Kahalu‘u Beach Park is just past the junction of the highways.

33. KUALOA REGIONAL PARK   HIKE, SNORKEL, SURF

WHAT'S BEST: The beach along this sacred shoreline invites a walk to Secret Island, or a hike-swim to Mokoli‘i Island, better known as Chinaman's Hat. Inland are adventures on huge Kualoa Ranch, 'Hollywood of the Pacific,' and nearby are the gardens of Tropical Farms, a family tradition.

Puu Kanehoalani at Kualoa Ranch

PARKING: From Waikiki, take H-1 West and merge with H-78 West. Then take H-3 toward Kaneohe. Take Exit 9-Kaneohe, Hwy. 63. Go north on Hwy. 83, the Kahekili Hwy. Continue about 8 mi., passing Johnson Rd., near address 49-200.

HIKE: Tropical Farms (up to .25-mi.); Kualoa Regional Park shoreline to Secret Island and Moli'i Fishpond (up to 2.5 mi.); Kualoa Ranch (various activities)

Tropical Farms is one of a disappearing genre of family tourist places, where hospitality is genuine. It's on the right, less than a mile from a sign announcing that the Kualoa visitors center is 2 miles ahead. Steve and Chrissy Paty, and brother Randy, have carried on their parents' tradition, offering a variety of made-in-Hawaii pleasures, including a generous sampling cup of Kona coffee and bowls of flavored of

Macadamia nuts. All the fragrant flowers and fruits of the islands are presented amid family pictures and memorabilia. The gift shop sits not far from the historic Moli'i Fishpond. On the grounds, is the Ali'i Tour, run by Chief Sielu Avea—a music-and-dance-filled, hour-long introduction to the many uses of Hawaiian plants. The tour includes a boat ride on the pond. *Note:* Call the amiable Chief for reservations; admission is around $12.

About a mile farther north, is **Kualoa Regional Park**, 150-plus grassy acres, sparsely planted with large beach trees. *Talk Story:* The green parklands spread from the towering Ko'olaus toward the turquoise waters of Chinaman's Hat, a sunny expanse that escapes many of the frequent mauka showers of the Windward Coast. The entire park is revered in Hawaiian culture and designated as National Historic Area. In ancient times, perhaps around 1100 AD, Chief Kahai and his crew completed a round-trip canoe sail from their South Pacific homeland, bringing back breadfruit and numerous seeds that were to establish the region's valleys as fertile growing areas. Centuries later, even Kamehameha the Great's vessels would lower their sails as a sign of respect when passing Mokoli'i Island. Kualoa was associated with the makahiki season, from fall to spring, when the god Lono was thanked for providing fertility and abundance. Kualoa was used as a kind of prep school for the children of the ali'i (royalty), where they learned about the ways of nature and the hard work that was required to perpetuate the Hawaiian way of life.

Mokolii Island (Chinaman's Hat)

For the **shoreline hike to Secret Island and Moli'i Fishpond**, you could park in the huge lot to the left and then walk to your right around the point. But the better bet is to take the rougher road on the right from the roundabout and continue about .25-mile to the park's woodsy camping area. From there, a short walk to the left takes you to Kualoa Point, and the pleasing view of Chinaman's Hat, or Papale Pake, a name assigned by Hawaiians after observing the head gear of the newly arrived sugar cane workers in the 1800s. Back then, it wasn't a derogatory name. Royal palms add charm to the point. Hidden inland is 3.5-acre Apua Pond, where you might see an endangered Hawaiian stilt hanging out and feeling good about life.

Then backtrack from the sandy point and head inland along the shore. The rising mountains frame this far end of Ko'olau Bay, which is a nook of Kaneohe Bay. You'll

On Kualoa Ranch

be walking a strip of sand bordered by a thick hedge of hau, which hides the 125 acres of the Moliʻi Fishpond. You can fight the flora, or see the pond via a road that veers from the coast at the end of the campground. As is the case with many fishponds throughout Hawaii, this one was constructed by the mythical Menehunes, the smaller Polynesians from the Marquesas who arrived as early as 200 AD, centuries before the Tahitians arrived and displaced them. About .75-mile down the beach is a bulge in the strip of land known as Secret Island, destination for tour groups that arrive via a boat ride over the pond or a hike from the private property that connects the 'island' to the shore. You'll see a covered picnic area.

Kualoa Ranch is mauka the highway, about a quarter-mile past the park entrance. The ranch's visitors center has a lanai with a blue-water view, a great place to enjoy one of their local-style sandwiches or a plate from their Asian buffet. The gift shop is expansive, and you are free to roam the stable area out back to say howdy to horsies. The ranch's 4,000 acres are cleaved by the jagged ridgeline of Puʻu Kanehoalani, which juts seaward from the Koʻolaus, forming the photogenic Kaʻaʻawa Valley on its north side. The valley's environs have been the site for many movies, including *Godzilla, Mighty Joe Young, Windtalkers,* and *Jurassic Park.* (Every place on Oahu

has been a location for either *Hawaii Five-O* or *Jurassic Park.*) You can tour the ranch via horseback, ATV, open-air jungle vehicles, or small bus. Prices range from $15 to $100. Another tour takes you on a hike through tropical gardens to Secret Island. The pick for adventure seekers will be the kayak-snorkeling trip to Chinaman's Hat.

Talk Story: The ranch got its start in 1850 when Dr. Jerrit Judd, consultant to Kamehameha III, purchased some 600 acres from the king for a whopping $1,300. After a period in the sugar business (the ruins just north of the ranch road on the highway date from 1864), the family got into cattle ranching and subsequent generations expanded the lands to their current size.

Sugar plantation ruins, Kualoa

Secret Island

SNORKEL: The waters offshore **Secret Island** are usually millpond, perfect for taking a dip and then retreating to a shaded nook inside the hau grove. You have a portrait-quality look across the water toward the ramparts of the Koʻolau Range. Another perfect day-at-the-beach spot is **Kualoa Point**, where Chinaman's Hat factors into the view and the palms and flora of Apua Pond add interest to the backshore.

The pick for adventurous flipper fiends will be the snorkel-hike, snike if you will, to **Chinaman's Hat**, or Mokoliʻi Island. For this one, park in the open lot directly ashore the island. You might want to pace off 550 yards on the beach to get a handle on how far away the island is. Depths range from 5 to 10 feet, depending on the tide. Booties or a surf shoe that fits your fins is a good idea, or strap on some Tevas to explore the shores when you get there. Since Mokoliʻi is not a seabird sanctuary, you are free to look around. A 'trail' leads to the 200-foot top of the Hat, but the last part is near-vertical and crumbly. *Be Aware:* Current is not generally a problem, but avoid this adventure during periods of high surf. Once you get offshore, float and check the bottom to see if you drift.

About 2 miles north of the ranch are **Kalaeoio** and **Kaʻaʻawa beach parks**, both close to the road, but with nice palms and ironwoods along the shore. A reef offshore provides coral and a decent swimming area, but watch out for rip current, especially in moderate-to-high surf.

SURF: Around the point north of Kualoa Ranch, about 1.25 miles away, is **Kanenelu Beach**. Park at a turnout after the guardrail. It's a long paddle out to a break known as **Rainbows**. Across the highway is the private road leading to Kaʻaʻawa Valley, used by the tours from the ranch.

34. AHUPUA'A O KAHANA STATE PARK   HIKE, SNORKEL

WHAT'S BEST: King Kong would feel at home in these tropical wildlands along a verdant stream valley below 2,000-foot-high ridges. Embark on a jungle trek, select shorter view hike, or walk alluring Kahana Bay with its historic fishpond. Then follow up the hike with a snorkel at either of two nearby beach parks.

PARKING: From Waikiki, take H-1 West and merge with H-78 West. Then take H-3 toward Kaneohe. Take Exit 9-Kaneohe, Hwy. 63. Then go north on the Hwy. 83, Kahekili Hwy. Continue past Kualoa Regional Park and Crouching Lion Inn, which is near mm27. Directions continue below.

HIKE: Huilua Fishpond (.5-mi.); Kahana Bay stroll (.75-mi.); Ahupua'a O Kahana State Park to: Keaniani Kilo lookout (1.25 mi., 200 ft.), or Kahana Valley loop (4.25 mi., 425 ft.)

Talk Story: An ahupua'a, all five syllables of it, is the wedge-shaped division of land consisting of a beach and fishing area, a stream that irrigates agricultural terraces, and forests extending inland to the ridgeline. The life of the ahupua'a sustained the life of the people. And vice versa. Though the concept of an ahupua'a is essential for all human beings everywhere, pronunciation was easier for tourists a number of years ago when these 5,300 acres were called Kahana Valley State Park.

For the short **Huilua Fishpond** hike, look for a chained, grassy road on the right, after you have rounded the point from Crouching Lion and are descending toward the bay. Park at the shoulder. (By the way, the Crouching Lion Restaurant is a tour bus stop, where you can sidle up and eavesdrop as a driver points out the ridgetop

Huilua Fishpond

formation, which is the visage of a male lying down and facing mauka.) Heliotropes, palms, and other beach trees surround the fishpond. At low tide you can walk out the rock wall that shields the pond from Kahana Stream and bag a terrific valley view. On the makai side is a prime spot to kick back and call it a day. The pond dates back centuries, to Menehune times, but it was in use until the 1920s. For the leg-stretcher stroll along the classic crescent of **Kahana Bay**, pass the pond turnout pull off to the right on the inside turn at Kahana Beach Park. A forest of ironwoods rims the shore. To the right on the beach is a lagoon formed by slack stream waters. Farther away to the left is a boat landing where you can hop up and view the peaks rising about the bay. Not too shabby.

For all Ahupua'a O Kahana State Park hikes, turn mauka across from the beach park. Drive in about .25-mile to the (probably) rundown Orientation Center, where can pick up a trail guide and interpretive flyers from upbeat park people. **For the Keaniani Koko lookout**, go to the right of a tin-roofed restroom and stay on a weedy road that runs parallel to the highway. (Avoid side trails to the left, leading to some ancient walled sites.) You'll pass banana plants, and, after about 10 minutes of walking, go left at an arrow sign. The trail traverses up under a leafy dome. You soon break out to a bay view, where decrepit wooden handrails border the trail, and then drop into a ferny forest in a gully with a bedrock streambed. *More Stuff:* An unofficial trail leads to the left from this gully, ascending 1,500 feet in just 1.5 miles to the top of Pu'u Piei. A sign says that the trail is not recommended. The trail is visible all the way, but you get personal with brush and some sections are very steep, requiring all four limbs.

Just past the gully, the main trail reaches the rock fishing shrine of Kapaele'ele, where ancient fishermen made offerings to give thanks and assure bountiful fishing in years to come. It may not be much, but those rocks were piled centuries ago. From the shrine, the trail curls left through grasses and reaches a junction. Go left up the eroded hillside among ironwoods to the lookout. *Talk Story:* The skilled eyes of Hawaiian fishermen could spot fish, commonly the silver akule, in the bay from this lookout. They'd then signal canoes, directing them to surround the schools with nets, which would be pulled ashore by all able-bodied people in the village. The whole shebang was called a hukilau, and was common throughout Hawaii until the 1950s. You can climb the hillside above the lookout and achieve excellent bay and valley view. *More Stuff:* The right bearing trail descends to the highway, so you can make a loop hike along the highway or beach bacl to the parking spot.

For the **Kahana Valley loop**, drive past the Orientation Center and park where signs indicate, about .6-mile from the highway. *Be Aware:* Bring rain gear. Inland gets 300 inches per year, about 4 times the amount at the bay. Mosquito repellant is also a good idea. Bring mud shoes, since the trail makes a number of stream crossings. The going is slow, so allow several hours of daylight. Avoid this hike during heavy rain, and on weekends when hunters may be present.

Keaniani Koko lookout trail

You begin with a walk through the log homes of a community that existed generations before the valley became a state park. Kahana is a model, of sorts, for how public lands and native Hawaiian ways can be preserved together. At the end of the homes are a gate and the beginning ascent on a paved lane. Palms, ti, pandanus, and other Polynesian plants let you know this will be a moist hike. A concrete portion of the road tops out at a clearing where a gravel road goes left, and you will see the trailhead a few hundred feet ahead. (The road to the left descends to taro fields, a side trip to note the agrarian vibe of Kahana Valley.) After continuing to the trailhead, go left (the road to the right ends at gate). Then go right shortly thereafter on the Nakoa Trail. The road continues down to Kahana Stream, which will be the homeward leg of the 2.5-mile loop portion of the hike.

Over the next mile, the Nakoa Trail makes a wiggling contour above the valley, crossing gulches and two streams—more if it's been raining. Keep an eye out for koa trees, which have curved pointed leaves. You descend to a small clearing at a four-way

Kahana Bay from Keaniani Koko lookout

trail junction. You want to go left on the Nakoa Trail, dropping down to Kahana Stream. *More Stuff:* The straight-ahead option at this four-way junction leads farther into the valley on another 1.75-mile loop. A popular stream pool is less than .25-mile ahead on this farther loop. After making the 200-foot gradual descent to the stream, you've got to cross and climb back up the other side. Near the top of the shoulder, the trail curves up the valley a bit. At a signed junction hang a left, heading back down the ridge and into the valley. Cross the stream one more time at the bottom—where a small dam creates a popular swimming hole—before ascending an eroded road back to the hunter's check-in station, only about .25-mile away.

More Stuff: As you drive north and round the turn from the state park, pull in at the boat launch area for a scenic look at the bay.

SNORKEL: If conditions are right for a freshwater dip, try the **Kahana Stream Swimming Hole**. Follow directions for the Kahana Valley loop, only stay left on the road at the trailhead rather than going right on the Nakoa Trail. For saltwater dips, the beaches on this coast aren't the greatest for snorkeling. South of the state park in Ka'a'awa is **Swanzy Beach Park**, an interesting place to check out the weekend family scene. Steps lead down from a breakwall at the edge of the park's lawn, but conditions are normally too turbulent. The park was donated by Julie Judd Swanzy, from one of the island's founding families, who dedicated herself to preserving nature.

Swimming is safe at **Kahana Beach Park**, and can be ideal during summer months and dry periods. Often, stream runoff clouds the bay. The best bet for snorkeling is **Punalu'u Beach Park**, 1.5 miles north on Highway 83 from the state park. The

Punaluu Beach Park

beach park's several acres lie close to the road, but palms, pandanus, and heliotropes paint a nice tropical postcard. And a strip sand fronts some healthy coral—punalu'u means, 'to swim for coral.' *Be Aware:* Low tide causes shallow conditions, and high surf will bring rip current. Toss a stick in and see if it goes anywhere.

North Shore

Ehukai Beach Park

Every island has a north shore. But *the* North Shore can only be one place, and that's on Oahu, where a prow-shaped coastline greets a northern swell to create monster waves ridden by big-boy surfers from around the world. Foaming avalanches 30 feet and higher come rolling in, and winter wave heights of 10 to 15 feet are ho-hum. Board riders from all the Hawaiian islands make their mark on the North Shore, joined by an international surfing set—Australia, Brazil, France, Japan, the mainland—and watched by thousands of camera lenses held both by a cadre of professionals and gaggles of tourists who step out of shuttle buses with shutters clicking.

Even with all the hoopla of the pro surfing circuit and a host of other events, the North Shore so far has managed to shun boutique tourism and high-end timeshares typical of other Hawaiian resort areas. Here, miles of sand- and coral-reef beaches are backed by a rural, funky nonchalance that is *so* North Shore. Surfers have named about 50 different breaks along an 8-mile run from Haleiwa to north of Sunset Beach, which, more accurately, is the northwest coast of Oahu.

Unlike many spots in Hawaii—where surfing was the sport of kings and waves have been ridden for centuries—the boarding history on the North Shore began mainly in the 1940s when some of the Waikiki beach boys came up to give it a whirl. The surfer-Joe movies of the 1960s, by California director Bruce Brown and others, gave the scene a boost. Fueled today by sponsorships from companies that are big into surf wear, energy bars, and sports drinks, a whole new generation of surfers brave the waters at competitions, mainly at the North Shore's big-four: Sunset Beach, Banzai Pipeline, Waimea Bay, and Haleiwa.

The northeast shore is not without its surfing waves, but hikes and other attractions hog the attention. Foremost is the Polynesian Cultural Center. Hawaii's most popular paid attraction, PCC welcomes tourists by the busload and comes with a healthy admission fee—the ingredients for a tourist trap. But it's far from it. The nonprofit wing of the Mormon Church is staffed by students from around the Pacific who attend nearby Brigham Young University. Polynesian culture and arts are faithfully represented at a number of village recreations set around a large lagoon. Visitors both view and take part in a non-stop extravaganza of dance, crafts, I-max movies, torch-lit luaus, and genuine good cheer. The college town of Laie is a breath of fresh air and the Mormon Temple is an interesting counterpoint to the Byodo-In Buddhist Temple down the coast. Hukilau and Kokololo beach parks are among Oahu's charmers, and Laie Point provides scenic punch, a limestone finger that points toward two, wave-bashed seabird islands.

Just south of Laie, the Hau'ula Forest Reserve is a chance to take two forested view hikes that help visitors get over the closure of nearby Sacred Falls State Park, site of a tragic landslide a few years back. Koloa Ridge is another view hike at the south edge of Laie, while just north is the dark-horse contender for best waterfall hike, to Laie

Pipeline, Turtle Bay Resort, Polynesian Cultural Center

Falls. Also on the outskirts of Laie is the big forest and beach at Malaekahana State Recreation Area. The beach is more than enough, but the bonus here is Goat Island off the sandy point, a hike-swim that makes adventure seekers drool.

North of Malaekahana are the shrimp shacks, marshlands, and plantations cottages of Kahuku, a chance for independent travelers to see a bit of old Hawaii. Then, north of Kahuku at the true north of Oahu, is a chance to see a lot of new Hawaii. The Turtle Bay Resort, with more than 400 rooms, is not exactly quaint, but it is surrounded by wild lands and open coast—an area considerably larger than all of Waikiki. You'll find forested paths and a hike to the island's wildest beach, the windswept shores of Hanakailio. At the south end of the resort's property is Kawela Bay, the kind of palm-lined crescent that causes daydreams in cubicles across America.

South of Turtle Bay begins a several-mile stretch, from Sunset Beach to Waimea Bay, where many of the top surfing contests are held. A quiet lane and a bike path run between the highway and the sand, allowing cyclists and hikers to weave in and out of the scene. Midway on this run is the daddy of surfing beaches, the Banzai Pipeline, which is a block south of Ehukai Beach Park. The giant tubes at Pipe either propel surfers to glory or, more commonly, dash pride, bodies, and boards on the reef.

At Pupukea, just south of Pipe, snorkeling takes over, especially in the summer when Shark's Cove and Three Tables provide pristine, shimmering water. Inland from Pupukea is Pu'u O

Hauula Forest Reserve, North Shore waterman

Pipeline, Haleiwa Beach Park

Mahuka Heiau State Monument, a prime spot to pay respects to the ancients, as well as cop a view of Waimea. Mauka the heiau is the forested Kaunala Trail, where a loop hike rises above salt air in the northern Ko'olau Range. Waimea Bay, around the bend from Pupukea, is home to epic waves and surfing competitions, including the prestigious memorial to favorite son, the late Eddie Aikau. Lagoons extend inland from the bay to the Waimea Valley, a Hawaiian-run, nonprofit garden rich in both flora and history. Many visitors, especially nature freaks, will choose Waimea Valley as Oahu's don't-miss attraction.

Haleiwa is officially the Surfing Capitol of the World, although it isn't clear who bestows such a title. Oahu's best walk-around beach town, Haleiwa also can brag about a varied coastline that offers snorkeling, outrigger canoes, sailboats, fishing charters, and surfing galore. The town itself is strung along the Kamehameha Highway, made up of vintage buildings and a mixed bag of small malls. The sandy-footed set mixes with tourists and the more well-heeled residents in shops, eateries, and quirky galleries. Poke around Haleiwa and the unexpected is guaranteed.

The Mokuleia Coast stretches for about 8 miles due west of Haleiwa. Many visitors, intent of circling back to Honolulu, make the mistake of missing this beauty. The

sleepy Farrington Highway runs between a wild-and-scenic coast and the encroaching Waianae Range, a zone chocked, yes chocked, full of adventure-sport opportunities. Two trails—the Kealia and the Mokuleia Access Road—launch hikers into the Wainanae Mountains and Pahole Natural Area Reserve. Coastal access includes Makaleha Beach Park, the environ for the TV program *Lost*, and Mokuleia Beach Park, where snorkelers can dip their flippers on days when kiteboarders aren't putting on colorful displays of derring-do.

A few miles of sandy beach connect Mokuleia Beach Park with Camp Erdman, farther down the road. Dillingham Field, a former military site, now hosts gliders, skydivers, and hang gliders, an invitation to thrill seekers who tire of the earth and ocean. At the end of Farrington Highway is a prime spot to space out watching for whales and rogue waves, or to take the hike out the Kaena Point, the natural area that is land's end on western Oahu. Give this hike extra points for the tide pools along the way.

Kamehameha Highway, Waimea Bay

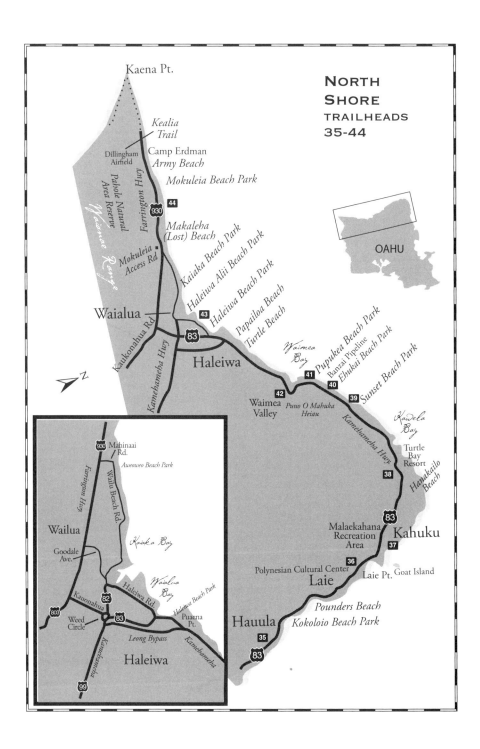

Kaena Pt.

Kealia Trail

Dillingham Airfield

Camp Erdman Army Beach

Mokuleia Beach Park

Pahole Natural Area Reserve

Waianae Range

Farrington Hwy

930

44

Makaleha (Lost) Beach

Mokuleia Access Rd.

Kaiaka Beach Park

Haleiwa Alii Beach Park

Haleiwa Beach Park

Waialua

Kaukonahua Rd.

43

Kamehameha Hwy

83

Papailoa Beach

Turtle Beach

Haleiwa

Waimea Bay

Pupukea Beach Park

Banzai Pipeline

Ehukai Beach Park

Sunset Beach Park

41

40

39

42

Waimea Valley

Puuo O Mahuka Heiau

Kamehameha Hwy

Kawela Bay

Turtle Bay Resort

Hanakailo Beach

38

83

Malaekahana Recreation Area

Kahuku

37

Polynesian Cultural Center

36

Laie

Laie Pt. Goat Island

Pounders Beach

Kokoloio Beach Park

Hauula

35

83

OAHU

N

Mahinaai Rd.

930

Wailu Beach Rd.

Aweoweo Beach Park

Farrington Hwy

Wailua

Kaiaka Bay

Goodale Ave.

Haleiwa Rd.

Waialua Bay

Haleiwa Beach Park

82

Kauonahua

803

Weed Circle

83

Puaena Pt.

Leong Bypass

Kamehameha

Haleiwa

99

TH:	TRAILHEAD
HIKE:	ALL WALKING, FROM SHORT STROLLS TO FULL-FLEDGED DAY HIKES
SNORKEL:	BOTH FISH-VIEWING WITH MASK AND FINS, AND PLACES TO SWIM
SURF:	BOARD, BODYSURF, BODYBOARD, WINDSURFING, KITEBOARDING
MAKAI:	TOWARD THE OCEAN
MAUKA:	INLAND, TOWARD THE MOUNTAINS
MM:	MILE MARKER, CORRESPONDS TO HIGHWAY SIGNS

PLEASE NOTE:

All hiking distances in parentheses are ROUND TRIP. Elevation gains of 100 feet or more are noted. See *Resource Links* page 232 for telephone numbers for all attractions and public agencies. Admission prices listed are for full-price adults. Leave your car free of valuables at EVERY parking spot.

35. HAU'ULA FOREST RESERVE   HIKE, SURF

WHAT'S BEST: Take an exercise break on either of two, nicely constructed loop trails. You get far away fast in this forest with a view.

PARKING: From Waikiki, take H-1 West and merge with H-78 West. Then take H-3 toward Kaneohe. Take Exit 9-Kaneohe, Hwy. 63. Then go north on the Hwy. 83, Kahekili Hwy. Continue past mm22. (Numbers descend as you drive north.) In Hau'ula, turn mauka in town at the (second) Hau'ula Homestead Rd. Go .25-mi. park at a dirt shoulder on the right, where Ma'akua Rd. veers to the right. The neighborhood is Hawaiian Homelands; ask someone if you are unsure of where to park.

HIKE: Hau'ula Trail loop (2.75 mi., 700 ft.); Ma'akua Ridge Trail loop (2.75 mi., 800 ft.)

At **Hau'ula Forest Reserve**, the Ko'olau Range begins to curl away from the coast, and radiating eastward from the range are smaller gulches and finger ridgelines—giving hikers many topographic ripples and a variety of flora over a short distance. These are two get-out-and-boogie trails with good scenic values. If you can only hike one, the Hau'ula Trails gets a slight edge, but, hey, flip a coin and go with it. **For both hikes**, walk up Ma'akua Road to the hunters check-in station and the state Na Ala Hele signs. Proceed on a paved lane. *Be Aware:* Hunters may be present on weekends. Bright-colored clothing is recommended.

For the Hau'ula Trail loop, go right at a trailhead after walking only a few minutes. You cross a stream, ascend rooty switchbacks in ironwood trees, and then reach a

Hauula Trail

junction that is the trail's loop portion. Go right. Easy switchbacks go through a ferny forest of tall Norfolk and Cook pines. The trail then crosses a bedrock stream that could be in any number of mainland forests. Sit a spell. Then begin more upping, to where the trail hooks left, or mauka, along an eroded ridge. Steps make the going easy. The ridge tops out with great views into Kaipapau Gulch to the right and a blue-water look at the coast—the scenic high point of the loop. From the ridgetop the trail goes left, across an intervening gulch, and then rises to a shoulder that is the hike's highest elevation. An unofficial trail leads up the ridge. Your route is down on a contour through ironwoods, koa, and noni trees. Bird lovers will especially like the homeward descent into Waipilopilo Gulch.

Ma'akua Ridge Trail begins on the left, a two-minute walk past the Hau'ula Trail. You immediately cross Ma'akua Stream and climb 250 feet on switchbacks in a hau grove, which gives way to an open shoulder. A Boy Scout picnic shelter and well-placed benches beckon daydreamers to enjoy a blue-water view. Above the benches, the trail begins its loop portion. Go to the right, as the trail begins a traverse on the south side of Ma'akua Gulch and reaches a saddle. You then drop down to the stream that feeds the next gulch to the south called Papali. You climb again, briefly, as the trail begins to swing makai on the return leg. The trail does another dip before beginning a high contour; to the south is a view of Pu'u Waiahilahila, which lords above the entrance to Sacred Falls.

More Stuff: If you pass both these trailheads, the paved lane reaches a fenced pumping station less than .5-mile from the hunters check-in. The Ma'akua Gulch Trail begins to the left—between a wall and a fence—where the road continues on a switchback to the right. The trail continues for about 2 miles, climbing about 800 feet alongside the stream, and crossing it several times until the ever-narrowing valley ends at a waterfall. The bad news: This trail has been closed because of falling-rock and flash-flood hazards.

The indefinite closure of the Ma'akua Gulch Trail took place as a reaction to a tragedy on Mother's Day of 1999, when 8 hikers were killed by a landslide in Sacred Falls State Park. Until then, the waterfall's pool was among the most popular hikes on Oahu. The state park has been closed since, and you should not try to enter. To look in from the highway, go south from Hau'ula just past the Hawaiian Church, near address 53-800 and between mm22 and mm23.

SURF: Hau'ula Beach Park has a break that's good for beginners, though not a big draw. Take a look at the shallow reef on the north, Laie-side, of the park.

36. LAIE POINT-POLYNESIAN CULTURAL CENTER
HIKE, SNORKEL, SURF

WHAT'S BEST: The Polynesian Cultural Center deserves its standing as the number-one paid attraction in Hawaii. But don't miss nearby Kokololio Beach Park and a scenic Laie Point, which also will rank high among sightseers.

PARKING: From Waikiki, take H-1 West and merge with H-78 West. Then take H-3 toward Kaneohe. Take Exit 9-Kaneohe, Hwy. 63. Then go north on the Hwy. 83, Kahekili Hwy. Continue past Kahana and Hau'ula. Directions for each activity continue below.

Polynesian Cultural Center

HIKE: Polynesian Cultural Center (up to .75-mi.); Mormon Temple (up to .5-mi.); Laie Point State Wayside (.25-mi.); Koloa Ridge (1.5 mi., 400 ft.); Pounders Beach to Kokololio Beach (up to 1.5 mi., 100 ft.)

Talk Story: In spite of a pricey admission and average crowds of several thousand per day, the Polynesian Cultural Center delivers an entertaining, personalized experience that few visitors will find lacking. You'll see the large parking lot for the center on the left as you enter Laie, after mm20.

The center is open daily (except Sunday) from 12 until 6. Tickets may be purchased beginning at 11. The luau begins at 5. A Horizons evening performance is from 7:30 to 9. Economy admission is about $43, which doesn't include meals or the evening show. Luau and evening-show packages range around $100. Buses transport guests from Waikiki: some $15 for the large bus, picking up at 9 major hotels; and $25 for the shuttle bus, with more pickup locations. Ask for details when you make reservations. On-site parking is $5. No reservations are required for general admission.

Visiting strategies: The Polynesian Cultural Center, or PCC as it is known locally, is a nonprofit, dedicating itself to promoting authentic Polynesian traditions and also providing jobs and scholarships for students at Brigham Young University, which operates the center. Many of students are from the South Pacific. Independent travelers will appreciate the economy admission, which gets you to all the attractions, including the afternoon Rainbow of Paradise canoe pageant that is a substitute for the Horizons evening show—minus the tiki torches and replica of a fiery volcano.

If you're staying for the luau and evening show, the bus transportation options save a 35-mile drive across Oahu at night. Your hotel or car rental agency may offer admission discounts. Ask around. Snack bars and restaurants on the grounds provide lunch and dinner options for non-luau folks, but then you miss the show at the luau, which is a replica of the ancient Hawaiian feasts.

The 42-acre grounds of the **Polynesian Cultural Center** are a seven-island circus, where a large lagoon meanders between village recreations of Tahiti, Tonga, the Marquesas, Fiji, Hawaii, Samoa, and Aotearoa-Maori (New Zealand). Waterfalls and tropical gardens mold the sites together, and a wealth of native-clad performers, guides, and artisans keep the place humming. Performances or cultural presentations take place every half hour at each village, which can keep you hopping all day, especially if you add in the Mission Settlement, Migration Museum, Halau Wa'a (authentic saliing canoe), and Rapa Nui exhibits. The place is a constant swirl of quilt making, fire starting, dance and chants, and traditional games and crafts—recreating in detail traditions from antiquity. Visitors take part in much of the stuff. Never sit in the front row of a performance if you have a phobia about being dragged on stage.

All the hoopla comes together, usually at 2:30, at the Rainbow of Paradise canoe pageant down the center of the lagoon. Dancers and drummers representing all the islands crew a parade of double-hulled canoes in a swaying- and foot-stomping extravaganza. Throughout the day, canoe rides are also available for visitors seeking a serene break. At the far end of the grounds is the 3,000-seat Pacific Center, where I-max (ultra-wide-angle) movies show five times daily. The movies vary, but you're sure to be immersed in the coral reef, living sea, and lives of the Polynesians. This theater is also the venue for the nightly Horizons show, a free-for-all of 100 performers who interweave the music and dance of their Polynesian heritage.

Shuttle buses run from PCC to the **Mormon Temple**, but you are free to visit on your own. No admission is charged. Go north from the center, pass the shopping center, and turn left on Hale La'a Boulevard. Royal palms line a royal entrance to the luminous temple, which rests above and beyond garden terraces and fountains. In 1865, Mormons began their largest settlement outside of Salt Lake in Laie, and in 1955 BYU-Hawaii was founded. They've succeeded in creating a friendly college town, sans coffee shops and brewpubs. One of the Mormon sisters will guide you around the grounds, finishing with a stop at a visitors center that opened in 2005. Inside the door, a statue of Christ, his arms outstretched beneath a twilight of the heavens, evokes a spiritual, non-suffering view of Christianity.

For the stunning seascape at **Laie Point State Wayside**, turn makai at a traffic light on Anemoku, across from the Laie Village Shopping Center. Then turn right. Laie Point is a wave-bashed limestone finger, popular among fishermen and loco mocos who leap from ledges near the south base of the point. Two seabird sanctuaries lie off the point, Kukuiho'olua Islet (with a sea arch) is closer and to the left, while small Mokualai Islet is straight out. Farther north, or left, is Goat Island. Don't forget the mauka view of coastal beaches and the nuanced valleys of the Ko'olaus.

The **Koloa Ridge hike** takes you to a view high above the Polynesian Cultural Center—and can be extended to a longer ridge hike, or a get-wet gulch trek to a waterfall. The trailhead is south of Laie: About .25-mile north of Kokololio Beach Park's second entrance, you cross a bridge with guardrail and turn mauka on a dirt road. The road is at mm20, across from address 55-147. Take this road in for one-tenth mile, to where a chain blocks entry. *Note:* Although people hike this trail frequently, a sign notes that permission is required from Hawaii Reserves, Inc., which oversees property for BYU. Use your own judgment.

After a few minutes walking you'll reach a memorial for Jonathan Taylor, a Boy Scout who in 1994 died in a Koloa Gulch flash flood. The trail begins from this gravel area and enters a shade tunnel, before breaking out and curving right in a sponge-grass meadow. You then hook left and begin an ascent of the red-dirt ridge held together by ironwood roots. Koloa Ridge is a minor landform, a finger off the larger Kaipapau

Pounders Beach

Ridge that abuts the Ko'olaus. *More Stuff:* After the view area and a brief descent, the main trail peels off the right into Koloa Gulch. A pink ribbon should mark the spot. This rock-hoppers' special crosses the stream numerous times and climbs more than 500 feet over about 2 more miles. The reward is a waterfall and pool, but only experienced hikers should attempt this hike—and only on clear days when flash flood threat is minimal. At the junction of the gulch trail, the ridge trail continues to 1,200-foot Kaipapau Ridge, but it is used less frequently and harder to follow.

Of course, you can drive from **Pounders Beach to Kokololio Beach Park**, but a semi-tough coastal stroll gives a ringside seat at some righteous bodysurfing and bodyboarding. Pounders—more properly Laie Beach Park—is just north of mm20, about .5-mile south of PCC. Begin on the north (left) end of the beach at the remains of Laie Landing, a stopover for coastal steamers until the early 1900s. Then walk to the right along the treed backshore at Pounders, and step up to the low limestone cliff, called Pali Kiloia (an ancient fish-observation spot). From the cliff is a point-blank look at the expert bodyboarders who ride the bone-crushing shore break, veering away from a low wall on at the last instant. The trail across the cliff gets pesky with brush as you approach Kokololio Beach Park. You have to climb down about 15 feet. The first part of the sand, in front of condos, is Mahakea Beach, whose sands blend with the lovely beach park. Wave action, eastern light, and 16 acres of sloping parkland make Kokololio one of Oahu's most scenic beach parks.

SNORKEL: Wave action, especially during the winter, makes for iffy swimming and poor snorkeling. Even so, on many days you'll be able to take a dip at **Kokololio Beach Park**—about a mile south of PCC and just south of mm20. The rolling bluffs of the beach park can't be beat for a picnic spot. Another sweet swim is at **Laniola Beach**, across the highway from PCC and accessed via a right-of-way near address 55-470. Laie Point juts to the north side of this strip of fine sand. Onshore reef fragments protect the shore, but wave action brings rip current, so be cautious. If swimming doesn't look good try **Temple Beach**, which is at the base of the point on the north side. Look for access from the highway, opposite of where Hale La'a Boulevard leads to the temple. The beach is protected by a reef from the point, and the grassy inland area invites idle thought.

SURF: The shore break at **Pounders**, Laie Beach Park, is among Oahu's best, but definitely not for beginners. As noted in the hike above, the cliff above the beach is a prime view spot. At **PCC**, off Laniola Beach, you won't find hoards of shortboarders, even though the site's long left-break has a good rep.

37. MALAEKAHANA STATE RECREATION AREA
HIKE, SNORKEL, SURF

WHAT'S BEST: Goat Island beckons just offshore forested acres. Laie Falls calls from a hidden nook in the Ko'olaus. Adventure seekers will have to sit on a gorgeous beach and decide what to do first. Then, on the way north, nose around the shrimp shacks and curios of Kahuku.

PARKING: From Waikiki, take H-1 West and merge with H-78 West. Then take H-3 toward Kaneohe. Take Exit 9-Kaneohe, Hwy. 63. Then go north on the Hwy. 83, Kahekili Hwy. Continue past mm20 and the Laie Village Shopping Center.

For Laie Falls, pass Hale La'a Blvd., turn mauka on (second) Naniloa Loop, across from the beach park. On the backside of the roundabout, turn mauka on Po'ohaili. Pass through a first gate (noting that it closes at 3:30 on Saturdays and Sundays). Continue .1-mi. to park at a chain-link fence, where a sign notes the trailhead. *For Hukilau Beach Park*, just past Naniloa Loop turn right into parking lot next to the highway. *For Goat Island-Malaekahana Recreation Area*, pass Hukilau Beach, continue for .5-mi. and turn makai at a signed entrance. Drive in .5-mi. and park in the dirt lot to the right. *For the Kahuku Section of the Recreation Area*, go north .6-mi. after the main entrance to Malaekahana. *For Kahuku town* directions, see below.

HIKE: Laie Falls (5.5 mi., 1,400 ft.); Malaekahana beach-and-forest loop (**up to 2.75 mi.**); Kahuku-Tanika Plantation Complex (car-hop outing)

The **Laie Falls Trail** climbs to a majestic copse of Norfolk pines, traverses a gulch through a long tunnel of strawberry guava, and then makes a ragged drop to a jungle nook that is below one falls and above a second. Laie is right up there among Oahu's best waterfall hikes. *Note:* Although people hike this trail frequently, permission may

Laie Falls trail, Malaekahana Beach, Laie Falls pool

be required from Hawaii Reserves, Inc., which oversees property for BYU. Use your own judgment. Landowners are not responsible for injuries to persons using their property for recreational purposes.

You begin on a road through a leafy birdland, and veer right at a fork after .25-mile. A few minutes after this fork, go left at a trailhead sign. Thus begins the long, gradual ascent up a red-dirt ridgeline, with open grassy spots and ironwood groves, along with koas that shade a fern ground cover. Footing is made for speed. The trail hooks right and follows an old fence line to a grassy view knob, above which the Norfolk pines are lofted. When you get there, notice that a few bushy-bowed Cook pines mingle with the Norfolks. The trail weaves through them along a spine, and then drops left. You then begin a traverse high above the gulch, which is barely visible through the multitude of smooth-barked strawberry guava saplings.

The guava tunnel continues as you climb grasping the young trees for a helping hand for about .75-mile—long enough so you may suspect you've missed the cutoff trail. But after a couple view openings (watch out for drop-offs) you'll reach the trail junction on the right, at a notch in the ridge that is obvious, and the only such opening since leaving the pine forest. Head through the notch and begin a 200-foot, steep descent, where ropes help in places. You'll hear white water and then come upon the bedrock bowl. Laie Falls sheets 30 feet into a good-sized pool and the outflow passes by sitting rocks, before tumbling into a cataract to another pool below. *More Stuff:* The trail continues up the ridge from the falls junction—add on 6 miles round-trip, plus another 800 feet of elevation. The trail is hiked less often and is partly overgrown—not the kind of hike to attempt without planning.

Hukilau Beach Park is a good place to begin the **Malaekahana beach-and-forest loop**. Walk the green space from the parking lot across the dune area and work your way along the sandy shore to the left. Sandy Kalanai Point, directly ashore of Goat Island, is about .5-mile away along a strip of sand that is fringed by false kamani and other beach trees. You can continue even farther around the point, as the land dips to form a bay fronted by the private Malaekahana Campground, and then continues along the Kahuku Section of the State Recreation Area. This more northerly section ends before the low-lying Makahoa Point. Then double-back along the beach past the private campground and cut inland through some of the nicely forested, 110-acre parkland. The picnic areas and campground are choice. Of course, you could also drive into the main Malaekahana parking area and do your own darned loop, combining a segment of this scenic beach with a loop back through the forest.

Highway 83 curves away from the coast just north of Malaekahana, at the former sugar town of **Kahuku**, noted today for shrimp shacks along the road and wetlands that extend northwesterly to the coast. Tourists are not solicited, but you can quietly see a bit of Old Hawaii by turning makai at the light on Pu'uluana and making your way along the margins of Kahuku Golf Course to Kahuku Beach. Continuing

north on the highway, you'll pass the Mill Marketplace (with the big, painted gears) that looks better driving by than up close. About a half-mile north of this landmark, just after a second highway bridge, is a makai turn for a unit of the James Campbell National Wildlife Area. Visitors must gain permission (see *Resource Links*) to enter the 164 acres of marshlands. Birders rank the windy, open grasslands as second best on Oahu, right behind the seabird islands.

The best reason to stop in Kahuku is the farthest north, at the outskirts of town. Pass the red shrimp shack (Rory's) and near mm14 pull right into **Tanika Plantation Complex**. Shrimp shacks and the S. Tanika Store, built in 1908, combine to create a quirky enclave. Inside the old store is a junk-

Tanika Plantation Complex, shrimp shack

and-antique shop extraordinaire, called The Only Show In Town—beads, costume jewelry, fishing floats, license plates—piles of stuff sure to fixate browseaholics. .

SNORKEL: The snike (snorkel-hike) to **Goat Island** is on Oahu's short list of bona-fide-fun adventures. Drive to the Malaekahana Recreation Area and walk through the campground to the sandy point directly ashore the flat seabird sanctuary, a.k.a. Mokuauia. It's some 350 yards offshore. Waves ripple around either side of the island, coming together across the shallow reef that connects the island to shore. Much of the time you can walk out, although low tide is optimum. But it may be easier swim.

You choose—that's why they call it a snike. Try the area just to the right of where the waves come together, in depths from 3 to 5 feet. Surf shoes or booties that fit in the fins are a good idea. Or start out with the flippers and figure a way to carry Tevas, or some other get-wet shoes. Fins and a mask are a good idea, since, if you wind up swimming, equipment greatly enhances your power and therefore safety. A sign welcomes arrivals. A shore-side trail is open to people, but most of the island is for birds only. To the left on the trail are the sandy shores of Mokuauia Beach, a place that will fondle your memory months after your return to the workaday world. Swim around pockets in the lava reef and keep the mask peeled for octopi and lobster amidst the fish. *Be Aware:* Be wary of high surf days and rip currents.

Hukilau Beach Park, operated by the Mormons, gets high aesthetic marks, and during low surf is a good place—one of the best—to take dips in between logging some towel time. Community net fishing, a hukilau, was popular here until the 1970s. **Malaekahana Beach** is also a scenic beauty. Drive to the recreation area and go to the left from Kalanai Point, where you can normally pick out a calmer spot. At the **Kahuku Section**, you'll find a nice swimming and decent snorkeling, to the left where the beach curls out to Makahoa Pont. *Be Aware*: Shore break is a potential hazard for swimmers. Lower wave action also means less current offshore.

SURF: Bodyboarding and bodysurfing are the thing at both **Hukilau Beach Park** and the **Kahuku Section of Malaekahana Recreation Area**—with the latter the best spot for novices. Shortboard surfers ride a left break off the south shore of **Goat Island**. A harder spot to get to is offshore the golf course in Kahuku, called **7th Hole** (guess where it is) or **Kahuku Beach**.

38. TURTLE BAY   HIKE, SNORKEL, SURF

WHAT'S BEST: Miles of coastal trails surround the North Shore's only destination resort. Beachcomb to remote Hanakailio Beach, beyond Oahu's most-northerly point. Or spend the day at a classic beer-commericial bay with good snorkeling.

PARKING: From Waikiki, follow H-1 West. Take Exit 8A-H-2 to North Shore. From H-2, take Exit 8, Wahiawa, Hwy 80. Follow Hwy. 80 through town, past Whitmore Ave., and then veer right on Hwy. 99. Near the coast, keep right on the Leong Hwy. (Haleiwa by-pass) which merges with Hwy. 83, the Kamehameha Hwy. Follow Hwy. 83 north for about 11 mi. *For the Turtle Bay Resort*, turn makai toward the Turtle Bay Resort on Kulima Dr. At the entrance station, request a Shoreline Public Access permit. The resort has about free 40 public access spots but they may not be forthcoming in telling you about them and may try to direct you to pay/validated parking. If the free spots are taken, ask for a permit to visit a restaurant; or park on the highway and walk in the .5-mi. *For Kawela Bay*, go 1 mi. south from the resort. Park at a turnout, where the low chain-link fence ends. A communications road is across the highway. A sign may indicate tresspassing, but the resort directs people here and the trail is in constant use by the public.

Kulima Cove at Turtle Bay Resort

HIKE: Turtle Bay Resort to: Kahuku Point (2 mi.), or Hanakailio Beach (up to 4 mi.); Kawela Bay to Turtle Bay Resort (2.5 mi.)

Talk Story: **Turtle Bay Resort** is the only fancy place on the North Shore, sporting 400-plus rooms and two championship golf courses, not overkill really, since its 880-acre grounds are 220 more than all of Waikiki. The architecture is austere—three, six-story concrete shoe boxes arranged end-to-end like spokes of a wheel—but the dramatic seascape, beaches, and forested trails should draw raves. Grandiose development plans have been in the works, but so far the locals have put up enough of a protest, and the state is trying to convert much of the acreage to official parklands.

For both hikes, make your way around to the right of the resort and down to the cabana at sweet Kulima Cove, a.k.a. Bay View Beach. Stay to the shore and pass the new beach bungalows. After about .25-mile you can cut inland and pick up a path that becomes paved, skirting the Arnold Palmer Golf Course. Stay left on the dirt path through ironwoods, where the paved path hooks mauka. Not far ahead, about midway along what is called Kaihalulu Beach, is a tiny opening in the reef and a sandy beach—the Kaihalulu Keiki Pool. Vegetation drops away as you veer seaward across dunes at the far end of the beach toward **Kahuku Point**. Stay to the left on the low-slung lava shelf, passing tide pools and reaching the farthest-north spout of land on Oahu. From Kahuku Point you can look right across the .75-mile run of sand and reef that is **Hanakailio Beach**. At the far end of the windswept sands is blunt Kaleuila Point. Bring sunscreen and water for this beach hike into wide-open spaces. Although questionable access can be gained via Marconi Road, not many people, not even surfers, make it to this true-north shore.

From the highway parking, a dirt path leads a short distance through dense tropical flora and past an enormous banyan before reaching the sands of **Kawela Bay**. A sign lays out the resort's color-coded trail system, but it is confusing and you're better off with directional wandering. **To the Turtle Bay Resort**, walk under the coco palms and ironwoods along the beach to your right. At the far end, hop up to a coastal path. (Of course, you could begin this hike at the resort, but you'll probably want to chill at Kawela Bay once you've seen it.) The trail penetrates tree-climbing cacti, and then loops seaward to the sandy grasses of Protection Point, site of a WWII bunker. From the point you can see the resort at the far end of Turtle Bay, a mile or so of sand and on-shore reef, backed by ironwoods. A shoreline footpath provides a scenic route. In front of the resort portico is where a radar installation picked up Japanese zeros an hour before the attack on the Day of Infamy, but their signal was misidentified as incoming American B-17s. After casting a solemn gaze skyward, skirt the wild shore on a path makai the resort to Kulima Point. A prime contemplation bench awaits.

SNORKEL: Waves pound this north-north coast, but you can find several snorkeling spots that can be good-to-excellent. **Kulima Cove**, at Bay View Beach to the right of the resort, is protected by two limestone points. An area is usuallly cordoned off for swimming. A snack shack and tidy rest rooms cater to lounging resort guests. Wave action can decrease visibility, but the swimming is good. The **Kaihalulu Keiki Pool** is less than a half-mile walk north up the beach. You'll spot a reef opening that creates a cute, sandy pool. Though small for snorkeling, it's one to write postcards about.

Kawela Bay (use the directions in *Parking*) is a place to drag all the stuff and spend the day. You'll may be lured both left and right at the beach. A gardenscaped path rings the backshore of the bay. You won't find tons of coral in Kawela Bay, but fish swim among submerged rocks. Although a reef protects the mouth of the bay, high surf can bring current farther out.

Kawela Bay

Backshore at Kawela Bay

Snorkeling on most winter days would be suicide at **Waiale'e Beach Park**, but on calm days the swim to close-by Kukaimanini Island—which is smaller than its name—is a mini-adventure. Sit out there and think up stranded-on-an-island cartoons. The attractive park is on the highway south of Turtle Bay Resort, just north of mm10.

SURF: Off **Kulima Point** in front of the resort, surfers ride a right break toward reefy Turtle Bay. A bench at the point is ringside for spectators. **Wild Beach** is a willy-nilly break in the middle of the bay. Surfers also try the point break at **Kawela Bay**, but more popular is the offshore reef break at Waiale'e Beach Park, called **Bongs**. **Revelations** (which, of course, follows Bongs) is at a near-shore reef just to the south, at Waiale'e Beach right-of-way. Go makai for .25-mile on a dirt road toward the U of H Livestock Center, just south of the old Crawford Convalescent Hospital.

39. SUNSET BEACH   HIKE, SNORKEL, SURF

WHAT'S BEST: Sunset Beach marks the northern end of the North Shore's run of world-famous waves—and also the takeoff point for some long, foamy beach hikes.

PARKING: From Waikiki, follow H-1 West. Take Exit 8A-H-2 to North Shore. From H-2, take Exit 8, Wahiawa, Hwy 80. Follow Hwy. 80 through town, past Whitmore Ave., and then veer right on Hwy. 99. Near the coast, keep right on the Leong Hwy. (Haleiwa by-pass) which merges with Hwy. 83, the Kamehameha Hwy. Follow Hwy. 83 north, past the traffic light in Pupukea. *For Sunset Beach*, continue for 2 mi., passing Paumalu Pl., and park on the right in a large lot. *For Sunset Point Beach Park*, continue a short distance past Sunset Beach, turn makai on Kahauola, and park at a right-of-way at the end of this street. *For Kaunala Beach*, continue .25-mi. past Sunset Beach and, just north of the low wall for wannabe Sunset Colony development, turn makai on a paved beach access road. If the road is still gated, walk down from the highway. If coming from the north (Turtle Bay) on Hwy. 83, Sunset is south of mm10.

HIKE: Sunset Beach to Sunset Point (1.25 mi.); Kaunala Beach to Sunset Point (1 mi.)

Talk Story: The broad sands and huge combers of **Sunset Beach** open to the highway, an easy place to pull off and discharge busloads of tourists eager snap images of Hawaiian surfers. The name derives from the imagination of 1920s developers, and became famous among surfers in the 1950s when featured in L.A. Beach Boy-era flicks on the mainland. *Note:* If crowds are an issue, for a quieter first impression, use the Sunset Point Beach Park, noted above. *Be Aware:* Stay well back from the surf line on beach hikes. Rogue waves commonly snatch beachcombers. Rip current, heading to the left from Sunset, is notorious.

To walk to **Sunset Point**, take off to the right as you face the water. In less than .25-mile you'll stride by the Sunset Point beach access, where a run of mostly tasteful beach homes are set back from the sand. You'll see the sandy ironwood copse of Sunset point not far ahead. Just before reaching it you'll pass another beach right-of-way that is accessible from the highway by turning on O'opuola. Around the point is the south end of Kaunala Beach. You can keep hiking around the point and along the beach, or double back and move the car to the parking for **Kaunala Beach**, which is described above. From that beach parking, you walk down the access road (assuming it's gated) and take a trail through the grass on the left before reaching the parking lot. A nice grove of beach trees gives way to the sand. Go left, walking in front of a seawall and continue to Sunset Point, which is visible. If tide and surf narrow the beach, use the inland strip of the now-defunct Sunset Colony. *More: Stuff:* Nobody's going to prevent you from going south from Sunset toward the Banzai Pipeline, which is about a mile away. A bike path and paved lane run parallel to the highway, providing the opportunity for a beach-neighborhood loop hike.

SNORKEL: Most of the time in the winter, even getting close to the water is foolhardy on the Sunset coast. During calmer periods, **Sunset Point Beach Park** is a choice place to log beach time. You'll find shade trees and a narrow channel between the shore and the near-shore reef. At **Kaunala Bay**, head for a rocky section to the left of the bulkhead toward the left or south side of the beach. *Be Aware:* Stay out of the water during even moderate surf, and stay clear of the channel in the middle of the bay.

Toward Banzai Pipeline from Ehukai Beach Park

SURF: Sunset Beach has its star on the North Shore's walk of fame. The thick outside break often reaches 20 feet or higher, a foaming avalanche that draws surfers from around the world to competitions. In the 1940s, Waikiki beach boys began riding these monsters, and since the early 1980s Sunset has been one venue for the Triple Crown of Surfing. The inside break at Sunset, called **Val's Reef**, is more of a tube. The next break south—ride the rip current or use an access across from the market—is **Kammieland**, a left-right bone-crusher. Just north, shortboarders like the reef break in front of Sunset Point Beach Park called **Backyards**. Sailboarders also ride the wind offshore.

Kaunala Bay has several popular breaks, not for amateurs but less harrowing than some at Sunset. The main break is known as **Velzyland**, homage to L.A. producer, Dale Velzy, who shot a movie here just a few years after the opening of Disneyland. Just north and farther out is a huge winter break surfed less often called **Phantoms**. Not many tourists gawk at Kaunala, though seawall is ready made for spectators, and the surf scene is international.

40. PIPELINE HIKE, SURF

WHAT'S BEST: Many great surfers ride famous waves all over the world, but there is only one Banzai Pipeline it's on the North Shore of Oahu. Come out standing from this tube and you are daddy.

PARKING: From Waikiki, follow H-1 West. Take Exit 8A-H-2 to North Shore. From H-2, take Exit 8, Wahiawa, Hwy 80. Follow Hwy. 80 through town, past Whitmore Ave., and then veer right on Hwy. 99. Near the coast, keep right on the Leong Hwy. (Haleiwa by-pass) which merges with Hwy. 83, the Kamehameha Hwy. Follow Hwy. 83 north past Waimea, to the traffic light in Pupukea. Directions continue below.

HIKE: Pipeline stroll (up to 2.25 mi.)

Talk Story: So *this* it? That may be the query if you catch the Banzai Pipeline on a flat day, since there are no neon signs or hip people carousing chic shopping centers and foodie eateries—at least not yet. To understand Pipe you need to come when the surf is up—10, 18, 25 feet and up—and preferably when a competition is taking place. Then settle in to witness one of the world's great sporting events. Traffic can be a mess on those days, but it can be avoided if you play it right.

Pipeline (or Banzai Pipeline or just plain Pipe) is the name of the mammoth tubular reef break that is accessible via a right-of-way, just south of Ehukai Beach Park, which is about a mile north of the supermarket in Pupukea. The Banzai part came from post-WWII soldiers applying the enemies' eternal battle cry to these dangerous, incessant waves; the Pipeline part was added by filmmaker Bruce Brown in the early 1960s, when a pipeline was being put in the highway opposite these tubular breaks. There are a few ways to do the **Banzai stroll.** As you go north on two-lane Highway 83, both a bike path and paved lane road run between the beach and the highway. This is public property that was once part of the railway easement. Along the paved lane are numerous right-of-ways to the beach. So, you can walk the bike lane from Pupukea, drive by the whole scene and ditch the wheels anywhere and start walking,

Banzai Pipeline

or, perhaps the most fun, rent a beach bike. Across from the supermarket is Country Cycles, where you can snag a beach cruiser for about 10 bucks a day. *Be Aware:* Stay well above the surf line when walking the beach. Unsuspecting visitors are knocked down daily. Rip current is fierce.

Heading north from Pupukea, stay on the first frontage lane, Ke Iki Road, which then gives way to a second, Ke Waena. The first beach access is on the left, after only .1-mile, and leads to the sharp lava reef that is Kalalua Point. The 8-foot-high lava plugs sticking up like a row of molars are called Pele's Followers, frozen in place by the volcano goddess to guard the beach. North from here is 2 miles of sloping sand, all the way to Sunset Point. Banzai Beach (not Pipeline) is the name given to the first .25-mile. The paved lane becomes Ke Nui Road, and you'll see four or five more access points between beach cottages before reaching Ehukai Beach Park, which is across the highway from Sunset Beach Elementary School. Ke Nui and the bike lane continue for another .5-mile, again with a handful of access points, before popping out to the highway just south of Sunset Beach Park. The bike lane continues north.

The Banzai Pipeline is the first right-of-way south of Ehukai Beach Park, at address 59-359 Ke Nui Road. A short sand path leads between cottages to concrete stairs. Sloping sands of the beach create a perfect stadium, complete with shade trees, to view the rolling wall that is Pipe, breaking at a reef only a couple hundred feet offshore. During competitions a PA announcer calls the wave-by-wave from the judges booth and gives color commentary as heats of surfers rise from their nests of friends, don jerseys, and head out to face the wave. Another booth, featuring surf wear and power drink logos, is normally set up at Ehukai Beach Park. Today's surfing legends—like Kauai's Andy Irons, Florida's Kelly Slater, and many others—face the challenge of Pipe, including during World Pro Tour events. Aussies, Japanese, Mainlanders, Brazilians, and French join Hawaii's favorite sons. In 2005, the first-ever women's competition took place, T&C Surf Women's Pipeline Championship.

Photographers are almost as big a part of surfing as boards, and many of the top guys rely on their shutterbug friends to capture the magazine shots that bring endorsements. Many

Banzai Pipeline

long lenses are set up along the beach. In the water, photographe[r]
and wetsuits are free falling below the board riders. It's not eas[y]
man and lover of the sea, Haleiwa's John Mozo, lost his life in puɪ[s.]
perfect pic. His photos live on in a gallery in Mililani. For surfers and photog[.]
the max moment at Pipe is when a rider, having been lost inside the curling tube, ɪ[s]
spit out into the open again and slices triumphantly toward shore. The bummer, and
more frequent moment, is when a surfer slides down the steep face and is hammered
into the reef by a thundering turbulence of white water. This wave is job security for
surfboard makers.

SURF: Does Rome have churches? Over the .75-mile from Pupukea to the southern
end of Sunset are 12 individual breaks. Starting from the south is **Pele's Followers**,
which actually right-breaks off Kulima Pont toward Pupukea. Just south of Pipeline is
a fast right called **Log Cabins**, and farther out is a big, tow-surfing wave called **Outer
Log Cabins**. **Off the Wall** is a reef break just south of Pipeline. The rolling tube of
Banzai Pipeline is normally a left (north) break, but occasionally they catch a shorter
right break off Pipe, called **Backdoor**. Going north from Ehukai (with right-of-ways
to reach them) is the sandy-bottom **Ehukai**, then **Pupukea**, **Gas Chambers**, and
Turkey Bay. **Rocky Point**, opposite the Chevron station, separates Ehukai from
Sunset, and serves up a shallow break for shortboarders and bodyboarders. **Arma
Hurt** is the name given to an inside left break at Rocky Point.

41. PUPUKEA   HIKE, SNORKEL

WHAT'S BEST: Snorkeling is king in Pupukea. Get wet, and then head mauka for the
North Shore's best forested hike and a visit to Oahu's largest heiau, set on a cliff with a
view of Waimea Bay.

PARKING: From Waikiki, take H-1 West. Take Exit 8A-H-2 to North Shore. From H-
2, take Exit 8, Wahiawa, Hwy 80. Follow Hwy. 80 through town, and then veer right on
Hwy. 99. Near the coast, keep right on the Leong Hwy. (Haleiwa by-pass) which merges
with Hwy. 83, the Kamehameha Hwy. Follow Hwy. 83 north past Waimea, to the traffic
light in Pupukea. *For snorkeling,* see descriptions below. *For Pu'u O Mahuka Heiau and
Kaunala Trail,* turn right at the traffic light on Pupukea Ave. *For the heiau,* continue uphill
fɪ[or] 5 mi., turn right at signs, and drive in on a one-lane road for .75-mi. *For the Kaunala
Trail,* continue up on Pupukea Ave. fɪ[or] .75 mi, and park outside the entrance to the Boy
Scout Camp Pupukea.

HIKE: Pu'u O Mahuka Heiau State Monument (.25-mi.), or to Danny Camplin
(Waimea Bay) Overlook (up to .75-mi., 100 ft.); Kaunala Trail (5.25 mi., 650 ft.)

Covering nearly two acres, the **Pu'u O Mahuka Heiau** is the largest on Oahu, although
you'll have to use your imagination to see the structures that once stood within the
remaining low walls—a 20-foot tower, ki'i (war god) statues, a lele platform, and

several pole-frame, thatched buildings. Original rocks were laid in the early 1600s, though, as was often the case, the heiau was modified over the years and used for different purposes. In early times, signal fires were used to communicate with a heiau at Wailua on Kauai. In 1793, three British seamen, crewmembers of Captain George Vancouver's expedition, were sacrificed after being captured in a skirmish. This was the first landing by Europeans since the first-ever one had taken place 14 years earlier, when Captains Cook's crew stopped by for water after the battle at the Big Island's Kealakekua Bay that ended in Cook's slaying.

There are blue-water views from the rise above the walls, but for the eagle's nest, head for **Danny Camplin (Waimea Bay) Overlook**. Start down the dirt road, to the right as you face the heiau from the parking area. Keep right after a short distance down the rutted red-dirt track. The short trail gets steep and hands will help on the last bit down to a rocky perch. Below is a panorama of Waimea Bay. On the way down is a marker commemorating Camplin, a local surfer claimed by the waves in 1994. The overlook sits a few hundred feet above the highway.

Much of the mauka access on the North Shore has been closed, making the forested **Kaunala Trail loop** that much more of a find. Begin along a treed corridor, passing a Na Ala Hele trailhead sign. After about .5-mile, you'll reach a clearing amid stately paperpark trees, where on the left is the signed beginning of the Kaunala Trail. The road continues to the right, which will be the return leg of the loop hike.

The Kaunala Trail follows the contours of four dry (by Hawaii standards) gulches, at times well within a canopy of kukui, guava, koa and other trees, and at other times breaking out to ferny banks with sea views. Botanists will even spot a few sandalwoods that escaped the sawyers in the early 1800s. After 2.5 undulating miles and a switchback, you come to a road, where you go right (to the left is a Girl Scout camp). The route then ascends through native ohia trees, and reaches a flat that yields a view of the Waianae Mountains. You then drop down, pass a gate, and hit the road in a stand of Norfolk pine that is the return route; go right. *More Stuff:* The road continues up to the left, toward the Pupukea summit on the southerly portion of the Ko'olau Range—almost 2 miles distant, with several hundred feet of elevation.

SNORKEL: During the winter months, snorkeling is iffy at best, but during calm periods and the summer months, Pupukea is right up there among Oahu's best snorkeling sites. The most popular is **Shark's Cove**—relax, it's only a name derived from the shape of the reef as seen from above. Pass the traffic light and fire station, and turn left into the Pupukea Beach Park. The Shark's Cove tidal pool lies below the rest rooms, on the other side of a low wall. The pool can be a sheltered wade-snorkel area when the cove is too rough. The most common entry to Shark's Cove is via a path that leads to a sandy beach that is to the right of the tidal pool; enter on the end of the sand closest to the beach park. Waters are 4- to 6-feet deep near shore, dropping to 20-plus feet in the middle of the cove. Green sea turtles may join you in

the swim. The cooler-water areas result from freshwater entering the cove at underground springs. *Be Aware:* Surf even as low as 2 feet can bring current to Shark's Cove, so use caution.

The second-fiddle, yet still a major player, is **Three Tables**. Parking is at a 20-car turnout just south of the traffic light in Pupukea, across from Kapuhi Place. If this is full, park at the lot across from Foodland supermarket (to the left of the fire station) and walk a path back. From Three Tables parking, head down a short path and get in on the left side of the beach. The three tables are flat rocks, often wave-washed, that sit not far offshore. Depths are

Waimea Bay, Three Tables

about 10 feet within the cove formed by these tables, and most snorkelers will want to stay within them. Swim to the right toward the fire station. During flat-calm periods, count yourself lucky and swim out past the tables to the vast flat reef that lies beyond, in depths of 15 to 25 feet. *Be Aware:* This area is Marine Life Conservation District—feeding fish is not lawful.

WHAT'S BEST: You won't find a better valley-beach, one-two punch in all of Hawaii. The Waimea Valley shows off a waterfall with swim pool and a river valley resplendent with tropical gardens and cultural sites. Waimea Bay invites the international surfing set to gigantic waves, but also presents snorkelers with enticing possibilities.

PARKING: From Waikiki, take H-1 West. Take Exit 8A-H-2 to North Shore. From H-2, take Exit 8, Wahiawa, Hwy 80. Follow Hwy. 80 through town, and then veer right on Hwy. 99. Near the coast, keep right on the Leong Hwy. (Haleiwa by-pass) which merges with Hwy. 83, the Kamehameha Hwy. Follow Hwy. 83 north about 3 mi. and pass Iliohu Pl. on an uphill grade. The highway curves right and into the valley. *For Waimea Bay Beach Park*, turn left at the bottom of the grade. *Note:* If the lot is full, not to worry. Continue around the bay and up the grade. At the top, pull right into the lot for St. Peter and Paul Catholic Church, the blocky white tower of which is a landmark. A path across the highway leads along the guardrail and then down to Waimea Bay. *For Waimea Valley*, pass the beach park and turn right after the bridge. Drive in .25-mi. to the center's large lot. *Note:* Admission is about $10, less for kids and seniors. Hours are 9:30 to 5.

HIKE: Waimea Valley (up to 2.5 mi., 150 ft.); Waimea Bay stroll (up to 1.25 mi.)

Talk Story: Give yourself half a day to wander in **Waimea Valley**, which is operated by the state's Office of Hawaiian Affairs. A main path curves for .75-mile along Kamananui Stream, passing through 1,900 luscious acres—300 of which are planted with 35 individual gardens—and ending at a natural swimming oval beneath Waihi Falls (a.k.a. Wahihe'e or Waimea Falls). Only 100 acres have been surveyed by anthropologists, but efforts so far have yielded some 70 cultural sites, sketching a history that goes back to the 11th century. It was then that the kahuna (high priest) Pa'ao built the island's first temples and agricultural terraces, and set up a priesthood system that would last 800 years.

Begin your visit at the Hale O Lono Heiau, which is outside the center off the parking lot. Lono is the Hawaiian god of fertility, apropos Waimea Valley, which was the breadbasket for the region. The site was not discovered until 1974, and some historians believe it dates from 1100 AD. Once inside the park, you'll be greeted by affable Hawaiian Moorhens, billed birds who hang around at the lily pond, apparently oblivious of being endangered. One strategy for visiting Waimea Valley is to stay on the main path to the waterfall, which crosses several bridges along he way, and then take side jaunts to various gardens on the return. *Be Aware:* A lifeguard is on duty, and swimming is available at the falls. Conditions aren't always right.

The ginger-and-heliconia garden is one not to miss. It's to the left on your return from the falls at the upper end of the valley. After that, cross a major bridge and go right to see the duck pond, which lies below the confluence of Kaiwikoele and Kamananui streams. Farther along is a side trail through a streamside tropical rain forest—but

Waimea Valley

you'll miss the sublime gardens at a huge banyan tree if you don't backtrack a little after taking this trail. Also make sure to step up from the main path to see Kauhale, the ancient Hawaiian living site. Burial caves have been discovered in the valley's rock walls, making Waimea Valley a primary sacred spot. Ti and other Polynesian plants grow amid stone-and-thatched structures. After a day absorbed in Waimea Valley, expect a mild case of culture shock when re-emerging to the world outside. *Be Aware:*

No hiking trails lead out of the park areas. About 5 percent of the 6,000 different plant species is endangered. Many insects, birds, and fish in the streams are native only to Hawaii.

The beach at **Waimea Bay** is as good as any for chilling out, but it also begs for a stroll. A huge deposit of sloping sand curves from Jump Rock, at the left side of the shore, around to Waimea Point, a scramble over rock that is at the north mouth of the bay. In between is Kamananui Stream, the surface waters of which are commonly blocked by a sand dam. The slack water ponds lie inland for more than .25-mile, a placid home to bird life. You can use a pedestrian bridge over calm waters near the highway to explore this section of Waimea Valley, outside the entrance to the gardens. You'll see hibiscus gardens as well as numbers of loulu palms, the only palms native to Hawaii. *Be Aware:* Lifeguards cordon the shore during epic surf, but you always need to keep an eye peeled for rogue waves when walking the shoreline.

SNORKEL: Though **Waimea Bay** is primarily a surfing beach, you'll find days all year-round when waters are safe for swimming. Don't be shy about asking the lifeguards. One reasonably calm spot is to the right of the bay, opposite the sand dam that normally blocks the stream (bracing freshwater dips are also an option at Waimea). A rocky shoreline along the north side of the bay to **Waimea Point** is healthy habitat for marine life. The south coastline of the bay, starting at the left side of **Jump Rock**, is even rockier, and requires paying attention to wave swell as

Waimea Bay

you swim your way out along the submerged reef. This end of Waimea gets the nod, if you only try one spot. *Be Aware:* Make sure your insurance is paid up before attempting to climb and leap from Jump Rock. It's not a gimme.

More experienced snorkelers can try the tiny **Wananapaoa Islands**, big rocks really, that lie off the south mouth of Waimea Bay. It's a long swim out, or you can use a different access. Drive south from the beach park. As you make the left at the top of the hill, turning away from the bay, make a right on Iliohu Place. At the end of the place (not Iliohu Way) look for a right-of-way. Entry is over rocks and not easy—this spot is for only the calmest of conditions. All of Waimea Bay is in the Pupukea Marine Life Conservation District.

Not as easy to find, but worth the effort is **Alligator Rock**. Go south on Highway 83, about .5-mile beyond Iliohu Place and just north of little Ikuwai Way, which is mauka the highway. You'll see a 12-car turnout by concrete barriers on the makai side. Make your way to the right, where a small sand beach lies at the base of Alligator Rock, a short-snouted peninsula that provides protection from the swells. Water is clear, with depths 10 to 25 feet along a rocky shore extending to the point. *Be Aware:* Surfers are around for possible help, but you are mostly on your own when it comes to water safety. Wave action will bring rip current.

If you're interested in face time with turtles, take the Kamehameha Highway about 1.75 miles south of Waimea to **Laniakea Beach**, a.k.a. **Turtle Beach**. Look for a large dirt turnout mauka the highway, about .25-mile south of Ashley Road, where the south end of Pohakuloa Way pokes out on the makai side of the highway. It's just north of address 61-647. Tour buses and surfers park here and create a bit of a scene. High surf can bring current, so be careful. Turtles can often be seen from the shore. Seems the word is out that this is a good place to spot humans.

SURF: **Waimea Bay**, which attracts big-wave riders from around the globe, was the home surf for Eddie Aikau, who is on the short list of Hawaiian surfing legends. Eddie had made countless rescues here, and elsewhere on Oahu, and had already attained heroic status at by age 32 when, in 1978, he was selected to be an original crewmember of the *Hokulea*. This replica of an ancient Polynesian sailing outrigger has since duplicated the trans-Pacific voyages of the ancients, but on her maiden voyage the ship encountered a severe storm its first night out. The *Hokulea* was capsized and helplessly taking a beating off Lanai. Knowing currents were taking them into open seas, Eddie mounted a surfboard in the dark of night and paddled toward shore. The *Hokulea* was rescued, but Eddie was never seen again. Now "Eddie Would Go" is a battle cry that extends beyond surfers into folklore, and beyond that to bumper stickers, and beyond that to become a registered slogan of Quiksilver, the surf wear people. The Quiksilver in Memory of Eddie Aikau Big Wave Invitational is one of surfing's most prestigious events. Wave faces must be at least 20 to 40 feet

Waimea Bay

during a winter period for the event to take place which has only happened once every three or four years. Previous winners have been Florida's wunderkind Kelly Slater and Eddie's brother Clyde Aikau. In 2005, after three years of no competition, Kauai's Bruce Irons (brother of three-time world champ Andy Irons) rode 50-foot monsters to victory.

Pinballs is the name given for the smaller break inside of Waimea Bay, and the shore break also flings bodyboarders about. The reefy, intricate two-mile coastline south of Waimea Bay creates many surfing spots, noted by surfmobiles parked willy-nilly along the highway. **Uppers**, **Marijuanas**, **Alligator Rock**, **Leftovers**, and **Baby Sunset** are all within the first mile south. For Leftovers, use a makai-side turnout just north of little Iku Wai Place. **Chun's Reef**, which is just south of Kawailoa Beach and across from Ashley Road, is maybe the most popular. **Jocko's** and **Pidley's** are two of the breaks on either side of Chun's. Just south of Chun's, on the south end of Pohakuloa Way, is **Laniakea Beach**, offering a board-busting break along with a fierce rip current.

43. HALEIWA   **HIKE, SNORKEL, SURF**

WHAT'S BEST: The Surfing Capital of the World is also Oahu's best walk-around beach town. The surfing quality rivals Haleiwa's more glamorous cousins to the north, and a varied coastline presents a host of beach walks and snorkeling coves.

PARKING: From Waikiki, follow H-1 West. Take Exit 8A-H-2 to North Shore. From H-2, take Exit 8, Wahiawa, Hwy 80. Follow Hwy. 80 through town, and then veer right on Hwy. 99. Near the coast, pass the Leong Hwy. and then go left toward Historic Haleiwa. In the roundabout (Weed Junction) keep right on Hwy. 83, Kamehameha Hwy. *Note:* Directions continue in the activity descriptions.

HIKE: Haleiwa Town stroll (up to 1.5-mi.); Haleiwa Beach Park to Police Beach (2.25 mi.); Papailoa Beach (1.25 mi.); Haleiwa Aliʻi Beach Park to Kaiaka Beach Park (2 mi.)

Talk Story: Haleiwa Town is an assemblage of wood-frame buildings, some quaint and some unremarkable, strung out along about a mile of Highway 83. You have to pick a few stopping points and do some poking around to find the eccentricities of the surfing culture that give the town its undeniable allure. Haleiwa began as a small missionary settlement on Anahulu Stream in 1832, but its real growth came with the

Steven Gould at the Surf Museum, Haleiwa Beach Park, Rainbow Bridge

pineapple and sugar industries that brought the railroad later in that century. And with the rail came weekenders from Honolulu who sought a getaway at the Hale Iwa Hotel, built by Benjamin J. Dillingham. Agriculture receded, but an infinite supply of waves remained, which became the town's new economic product. The beach business was given a boost by the surfer-Joe movies of the 1950s and 60s. Although developers faithfully hatch schemes of greed and grandeur, the North Shore has so far resisted and retained its rural vibe of benign neglect.

Your first stop, not far after the turn, should be Deep Ecology, a family-run dive shop offering unique tours at a storefront that doubles as a community center and art house, with a photo gallery in the back. Across the highway is Celestial Natural Foods, where you can make the smart choice for today's goodies and also pick up something at the Paradise Café in the back, if it happens to be open.

Haleiwa

Haleiwa's main walk-around attractions are in the North Shore Marketplace, a quarter-mile down the road. First impression is a humdrum strip mall—shops built around a parking lot—but this impression will be upgraded as you nose around. Snag a cup and check the scene at the Coffee Gallery—or a cup of something else at Cholos Restaurant next door. Then wander over to the North Shore Surf & Cultural Museum, a big name for an laid-back place that is filled with an evolving collection of flotsam and surfing folklore—vintage boards, aloha shirts, photos of Eddie and Duke, sunrise shells, a necklace of lost car keys, a surf-video room, and anything else that strikes the fancy of hey-dude curator Steven Gould. Next door is Patagonia, a mountain shop you say, but step inside for surf wear and to see photos and memorabilia of women's longboard surfing dynamo Rell Sunn, who helped set up the shop in 1994—before breast cancer took her way too early. Around the corner, appropriately on the fringe of the marketplace (look for a land-locked lifeguard station) are the broken-surfboard art and classic cars at Crossroads and the Travis Talamoo galleries. Keep surfing the pavement and you'll find lots more at the marketplace—jewelry, chic surf apparel, boutiques, bona fide surf sport outfitters, and one-of-a-kind gift stores, like Twelve Tribes International Imports.

Continuing down the highway, you'll find some more prosaic shopping opportunities and good-deal eateries (try Waialua Bakery next to Malama Market) before coming upon several historic buildings. *Cool tip:* People line up on hot afternoons for the shave ice at Matsumoto's, which has received some good press, but the cones offered at Aoki's and H. Miuras on either side are every bit as good. The old buildings that house these stores date from sugar cane days. Iwa Art galley is next to Aoki's and across the street is Liliuokalani Church, worth a look just to see the clock bearing the great queen's name that tells not only time but also phases of the moon. Haleiwa's number one browser shop sits at the far end of town, the Surf-N-Sea, the one with an army of surfboards at attention outside an amped-up shop crammed with beach garb. This is the place to set up your first surfing experience. Walking distance to the north of the shop are the arches of narrow Rainbow Bridge, the town's signature structure that spans the slack water of the Anahulu Stream. Local canoe clubs paddle by, a traditional subculture of Haleiwa that goes unnoticed amid all the surfing stuff.

In and around Haleiwa are several beach walks that blend people-watching with wild seascapes. For the **Haleiwa Beach Park to Police Beach walk**, continue through Haleiwa on Highway 83 and cross Rainbow Bridge. Then turn left into the park, noted by a 40-foot obelisk, a memorial to Vietnam Vets. A fringe of coco palms rim inner Waialua Bay. Head to the right along the 13-acre, developed portion of the park and you soon come to a grove of ironwoods and palms that mark a second, more appealing beach, which is also accessed by driving in on Kahalewai Place—a makai turn from the highway just past the beach park. You leave people behind as you continue to Puanea Point, a westerly prominence with a look toward Kaena Point. Around the point is reefy Police Beach, leased for recreation by the boys in blue since 1975. The relatively wild coast extends north to Papailoa.

Off the main drag, pretty **Papailoa Beach** is a run of reef-protected white sand that fronts the gardenscapes of one of the North Shore's earliest and nicest beach-cottage communities. You'll find quietude even on busy weekends. To get there, take Highway 83 north from Haleiwa, past where it merges with the Laana Highway bypass. Less than a mile later, make a left on Papailoa Road and continue almost .5-mile to its end, where you'll see right-of-way parking. A short, shaded path pops out at the beach. Snatch your honey's hand, if available, and take off barefoot. Massive offshore surf provides counterpoint to the mellow beachscape as you walk north (to the right), peeking into the gardens of expensive homes that are modest by today's jumbo standards. You can walk this beach all the way to Turtle Beach-Laniakea, but the highway comes in to interrupt the faraway feel.

Big **Haleiwa Aliʻi Beach Park** is the locus for all the water-born sports that keep Haleiwa hopping—a boat harbor for fishing, sailing, and outrigger canoeing; and endless waves for bodyboarding and surfing that ranges from keiki rollers right up to the giant offshore break that rivals any on the North Shore. To get to the beach park, take Highway 83 though town and hang a sharp left on Haleiwa Road just before the arched Rainbow Bridge. On your right will be the Haleiwa Boat Harbor, which has a breakwater to walk. Across the channel is Haleiwa Aliʻi Beach Park. A sprawling lawn is scattered with palms and beach trees that border a deep-sand beach. The two-story, Dutch-gabled building to the left is the John K. Kalili Surf Center, named for Haleiwa's famed waterman and community leader from the 1940s. Location shots for the *Baywatch Hawaii* were filmed here.

Haleiwa Alii Beach Park

The coast to the south (left) can be accessed via Haleiwa Road, but the walk to **Kaiaka Beach Park** will feel like you've been someplace. At the far end of the beach from Aliʻi is little Haleiwa Army Beach, noted for the best rest room on the North Shore. From there the coast is backed by homes and gets rockier as you approach Kaiaka Point. The 50-plus green acres of the beach park offer a scenic campground in ironwoods and palms, as well as enormous spreading mangos and leafy beach trees. You might spot a few car-sleepers, but this is mainly a serene spot to kick back for awhile. On the south side of the park, on the mauka shore of silty Kaiaka Bay, is Pohaku Lanai, a 12-foot-high, oval rock, now partially overgrown, that was used as a fish observation platform in ancient times. *Note:* Drive directly here by taking Haleiwa Road for .5-mile and turning makai on Fresh Air Camp Road, at a sign for Kaiaka Beach Park.

More Stuff: If staying in Haleiwa, you'll want to know about Aweoweo Beach Park and Pu'uiki Beach. Continue south on Haleiwa Road as it veers mauka, and then turn right on Wailua Beach Road. This road rejoins the shore in a condo-rich zone. Turn makai on Apuhihi, which ends at Au Street. You can use one of several right-of-ways along Au or drive to the end for the beach park itself. To get to pleasant and forbidden Pu'uiki Beach, go right, or north for a short distance. Although the beach is public, the inshore park is only for Dole employees and retirees.

SNORKEL: The cove on the north side of **Haleiwa Beach Park** is hard to beat, with interesting and usually safe snorkeling and a scenic beach scene. Either walk over from the park or use the parking just north via Kahalewai Place. Enter in the middle

Haleiwa

of the cove, where waters are about 5 feet deep, and swim inside of the rocks that are near the shore. In calmer weather, you can flipper seaward toward Puaena Point, but keep an eye out for boaters.

Haleiwa Ali'i Beach Park isn't quite a tropical paradise but the snorkeling will not disappoint. As you face the water, walk to the left past the surf center building to where the grassy shore curves inland and a rock formation provides a sheltered nook. Get in to the left of the rocks. A reef runs for several hundred feet close to the shore, and you may see a turtle among smaller reef fish. In calmer weather, swim seaward across the reef and you'll reach the deep blue water of the Haleiwa Trench, a wide channel 75- to 100-feet deep. A second reef lies in deeper water across the trench, but this one is best left for scuba divers. **Pu'uiki Beach** (see *More Stuff* above) has a reef fronting the park and is an underrated snorkeling spot due to its obscure access. Local spear fishermen know about it. Watch out for rip current during high surf, but otherwise this place may be your weekday paradise.

SURF: Offshore the north end of Papailoa Beach is a mountainous break given the moniker **Himalayas** in the 1950s. Farther south, near the beach right-of-way is a tamer, sandbar break called **The Point**. From Haleiwa Beach Park, the best surfers ride a hard-right break off **Puaena Point**, which is also a good place to be a spectator. The inside break is called **Puaena**, and, outside of Waikiki, it's probably the best beginners spot on Oahu, where surf instructors take newbies.

When the big ones roll in, the big boys head for **Haleiwa**, offshore Haleiwa Aliʻi Beach Park. Surf competitions take place in the winter, and the breakwater on the harbor side of the park is a front-row seat. Surf can be 30 feet, and wave heights in the teens are common. **Avalanche** is a foamy break to the left at the park. Farther down by the condos, accessed usually from Kaiaka Beach Park, is **Walls**, a.k.a, **Fresh Airs**. Off Puʻuiki Beach is a tubular reef break known as **Hammerheads**, not for an injury that may occur, but because these sharks really do breed there.

44. MOKULEIA COAST   HIKE, SNORKEL, SURF

WHAT'S BEST: The wall of the Waianae Range rises above miles of beaches on a wild coast, inviting hikes and high-flying adventure sports. Is this Oahu? Where is everybody?

PARKING: *From Waikiki*, take H-1 West. Take Exit 8A-H-2 to North Shore. From H-2, take Exit 8, Wahiawa, Hwy 80. Follow Hwy. 80 through town, and then veer right on Hwy. 99. Near the coast, pass the Leong Hwy. and then go left toward Historic Haleiwa. In the roundabout (Weed Junction) take Hwy. 830, Kaukonahua Rd. toward Mokuleia-Waialua. Continue a short distance and go right on Hwy. 930, the Farrington Hwy. Continue about 2.5 mi. to Mahinaʻai Rd. Directions continue below in hiking descriptions. *From Haleiwa*, take Haleiwa Rd. south from the Haleiwa Aliʻi Beach Park and turn right on Waialua Beach Rd. From there, you can take a left on Goodale out to the Farrington Hwy. or stay on the Waialua Beach Rd. all the way to Mahinaʻai Rd., where you turn left to join the highway.

HIKE: Mokuleia Access Road to: Peacock Flat (7 mi., 1,450 ft.), or Pahole Natural Area Reserve (9.25 mi., 2,100 ft.); 'Lost' Beach to Devil's Rock (1.5 mi.); Mokuleia Beach to Camp Erdman Beach (up to 4.5 mi.); Kealia Trail to: Dillingham Overlook (2 mi., 900 ft.), or Makua Valley Overlook (7.25 mi., 2,100 ft.); Mokuleia to Kaena Point (5.25 mi., 200 ft.)

Talk Story: Extending eight miles due west from Haleiwa, the Mokuleia Coast is the island's most pristine, especially since roadside trash and illegal camping have been all but eliminated in recent years. Farrington Highway passes numerous beaches that grow increasingly more wild and reefy, culminating at windswept Kaena Point, Oahu's most westerly land that is reachable only by a for-real four-wheel drive tract. Meanwhile, on the mauka side of the road, the Waianae Range declines from Oahu's high point of 4,020 feet at Mt. Ka'ala to sea level at Kaena Point, coming closer to the highway in the process and presenting hikers with some opportunities. Dillingham Airfield, no longer a military base, is now a site for sky diving, hang gliding, and gliders, adding flair to the air, while along the coastline kiteboarders and surfers shred the waves.

Kealia Trail, Dillingham Airfield

Kealia Trail

The wide, paved **Mokuleia Access Road** is just the ticket for exercise walkers to step on the gas and reach the Waianae ridges in 60 to 90 minutes, less than half the time it would take on a typical mauka trail. Park at a gated, signed trailhead that is mauka the highway .25-mi. past Mahinaʻai Road, at the border of a vast grove of coco palms. *Be Aware:* The route is sunny and exposed, so avoid mid-afternoons going up and bring plenty of water. When entering the natural area reserve, stay on the trail.

For both hikes, begin on the string-straight road for .5-mile as it passes the Dillingham estate's coco palm grove, the largest in Hawaii. The road then begins its upward curves. Things get hotter as the road gets steeper, pointing toward Norfolk pines on the ridge. Just before the 3-mile mark, you pass a block building on an outside turn and begin the final push. At last you reach the oasis at **Peacock Flat**, where a dozen campsites with shelters are spaced nicely about a sloping glade that is amply forested with eucalyptus, Norfolks, sugi pine, and other non-native trees. To reach the **Pahole Natural Area Reserve**, hang a left on the Mokuleia Trail at the gate, and continue up through the campground and beyond. The road transitions to a trail as you near the 658-acre reserve, beginning less than a mile from Peacock Flat. Pick your own turnaround spot. You'll make good time down the access road, enjoying an airborne coastal view without thinking of foot placement. *More Stuff:* Going to the right on the road at Peacock Flat connects with the Kaena Point Tracking Station, accessed from the Waianae side.

For the highly scenic beach jaunt from **'Lost' Beach to Devil's Rock**, look for a right-of-way just west of the Mokuleia Access Road. It's where a wood-rail fence ends, near address 68-434. Horses may noticed as you walk .25-mile along a pasture to undeveloped Makaleha Beach Park. The Hawaiian translation is "to look around in awe," and you are free to do so. Scenes from the TV program *Lost* are filmed on these sloping sands, backed by ironwoods and palms. You may see the cables and stuff used by the film crew, unless the whole deal has gone south by the time you get there, ala

North Shore. (To the right on the beach is Kaiahulu, the private enclave for employees of Castle and Cook, one of Hawaii's large land corporations.) Devil's Rock is to the left at the beach, around the first dip in the sandy shore and offshore rounded Kolea Point that protrudes from the green expanse of Mokuleia Polo Field. The wave-washed rock is a few hundred feet offshore, the coast's only island, albeit tiny.

A signed, paved road marks the entrance to **Mokuleia Beach Park**, just past private Camp Mokuleia and the entry to the drop zone for sky divers. (For an entertaining point-blank look at the freefall, pull in to Pacific Skydiving Center and Sky Dive Hawaii, which are side by side.) From the open parking area at the beach, make your way through the low-lying vegetation and walk to your left. **Camp Erdman**, a YMCA youth center, is about 2.25 miles away, and Mokuleia Army Beach is midway. About .5-mile along the narrow strip of sand from the beach park is a rounded point, called Kealia Beach, which yields views up a foaming coast toward Kaena Point. *Be Aware:* On weekends, ATVs will be seen and heard on the coast west of Kealia Beach. Also, beginning at Army Beach, the coast is accessible from the highway, so this beach walk works better as a car-shuttle than as an up-and-back.

The **Kealia Trail** is one of Oahu's best, switchbacking up the pali above the ocean, transecting the forested valleys of the Waianaes, and ending with a bird's-eye view of the West Side's Makua Valley. To get to the trailhead, pass Mokuleia Beach Park and turn left past the glider area, just before the fence at Dillingham Airfield ends. Follow the road as it loops around to the left, and park in the lot for the squat control-tower building. The trailhead is a five-minute walk away, on a road that passes upright pipes and continues to the left past a concrete structure used by the nearby quarry. On the way, look mauka to see the steep canyon that is the trail's route; the incoming road points at it before turning left to the parking lot. *Be Aware:* As signs note, rockfall is a hazard on this trail.

The trail begins in tree cover, but opens up after the first few switchbacks. You need to take giant steps in rocky areas, including a crumbling overhang where you may want to quicken the pace. After about a half-hour of ascent, the trail reaches a grassy open area with a panoramic view, the **Dillingham Overlook**. If the day is fair, you'll be able to hear the whoosh of gliders as they pass not that far overhead. From there the trail climbs for less than .25-mile and reaches a view flat amid ironwoods and near a picnic shelter, there could be of Boy Scout Troop 167. From the shelter, you've done more than half the climb, but only one-third the distance to the **Makua Overlook**. Head up the road, which is fairly steep, to a T-junction where you go right. Soon the route flattens to reveal looks across the interior to the Waianae crest. The trail undulates and, after a decrepit water tank, enters the Kauokala Hunting Area. You'll reach a junction where you stay left. After another climb you reach another junction, where you go left again toward Makua Valley (this is the Kuaokala Access Road, which to the right goes to the Kaena Satellite Tracking Station). Not far ahead you

Mokuleia Beach Park

reach a four-way junction. Jog to the right, on the Kuaokala Trail, and you'll get to the summit for a look down the green bowl of Makua Valley.

Where the Farrington Highway ends is the beginning of a four-wheel drive track, cobbled with rocks and dipping into lakelet-sized puddles on a 2.5-mile journey to **Kaena Point**. The route was part of Dillingham's Oahu Railroad, as the utility poles and track fragments suggest. The rutted trailhead is also an excellent park 'n' stare, particularly during whale migrations and winter surf. At the beginning you can walk a long, flat shelf below the trail, checking out tide pools. The lower route is also nonmotorized, a particular benefit on weekends. About halfway to the point, look for an unsigned trail to a nice sandy beach that is pocketed into the rocks—a choice for shorter hikes. The wall of the Waianaes hovers mauka, but tapers to sea level a distance before the point, creating a flat toe of land within the park that is Kaena Point Natural Area Reserve. *Be Aware:* Stay well back of wet areas on the reef, which indicate where the waves are breaking at the moment—and keep an eye peeled for the occasional rogue (larger) wave. Wind can be brisk on this walk, and sun exposure can be extreme.

More Stuff: One of the north shore's better known trails, the Dupont Trail to Oahu's highest peak, Mt. Ka'ala, requires special permission. See *Resource Links*. The trail covers more than 11 miles, with a biscuit over 4,000 feet of climb. The trailhead is in Waialua off the Farrington Highway. Turn mauka on a plantation road that is just past the school, but don't get excited since you reach the Kamananui Ranch gate after only a mile.

SNORKEL: A reef runs near shore at **Mokuleia Beach Park**. Walk through the dune path in the center of the parking area and enter via the sloping sands. You should be able to see channels in the coral. The best and safest snorkeling is close to shore. Mokuleia is quietly one of the better snorkeling venues on the island. A little father up the road, **Mokuleia Army Beach** can also be good for snorkeling and swimming, but usually only during the summer months. The sandy shore elbows to create a protected spot that is a family favorite. The beach is near the highway, just after the entry to the Kealia Trailhead. *Be Aware:* At both of these beaches, wave action, particularly in winter, brings a swift rip current that runs parallel to the shore. Stay out during high surf, and pay attention to which way you may be drifting. Although not known for snorkeling, **Makaleha Beach Park**, a.k.a. Lost Beach, is just the ticket for a day at the beach spent dipping, lazing about, and beachcombing. High winter surf pops that bubble, however, and you need to be aware of current.

SURF: Walk to the right at Makaleha Beach Park, toward Kaiahulu, and you'll come upon **Silva Channel**, not one of the more reliable breaks. (Silva can also be accessed off Crozier Drive; backtrack on the highway and go makai on Mahina'ai.)

At **Mokuleia Beach Park**, kiteboarding is often king as intrepid board riders harness themselves to sails and go winging away.

Mokuleia Beach

Give them plenty of room when watching this colorful spectacle, since take-off time is on the edge of out-of-control. Mokuleia also draws surfers. **Park Rights** is a longer paddle straight out from the park. **Day Star** is farther left, or west, coming off another reef break. The ride can get wild, as the uniformity of the surf dissipates the closer you get to Kaena Point. **Army Beach** has a fast left break, and also one a little farther west called **Crushers**, named for the quarry that is across the highway.

West Side

Pokai Beach Park

Wanting for water and scorched by the sun, the remote leeward coast of Oahu historically has been land of the dispossessed. In the 1700s, the Waianae Coast is where Oahu's chiefs made a futile last stand against Chief Kahekili and the invading forces from Maui. When Kaheliki later died, warriors of Waianae sided with his son, Kaeo, and were again on the losing side. The other son, Kalanikupele, became chief. In 1795, when Kamehameha the Great and his forces from the Big Island rousted Kalanikupule, the vanquished warriors once again gathered on the West Side.

In the early 1800s, when the sandalwood trade flourished under Kamehameha, the conscripted workers of Waianae secretly yanked saplings in the forest, ruining the crop and forcing Kamehameha to leave them in peace. Cattle and sugar cane, industries that went wild in Hawaii beginning in the mid-1880s, survived around Waianae, but never really flourished. And same goes for post-war tourism. In 2005, when illegal campers were rousted from Ewa, and in 2008, when a poor economy struck the working class first, where were many to go but Waianae?

Of course, that's the appeal of the West Side. It may not be little-grass-shack Old Hawaii, but it is Real Hawaii, real-to-the-bone. Waianae's hard-edged reputation is earned, but, as is the case with many tough guys, a big heart resides within. With the exception of Ni'ihau, a greater percentage of Native Hawaiians live here than anywhere else in Hawaii. Yes, the West Side is beholden to the laws of the state, but the real order is kept more by the old way, by the rule of aunties and uncles, rather than cops and lawyers. Visitors, even Hawaii veterans, may feel the culture shock of a haole. Many will turn those gleaming Hertzmobiles around and hightail it back to Waikiki. Others who settle in will come to like the West Side most of all.

In not-so-recent history, the leeward coast was not the land of the vanquished, but the center of things. Maui, the demigod so prominent in Hawaiian mythology, was a real man who lived in Nanakuli. Pokai, a navigator and farmer who helped Tahitians gain a foothold in their new world, lived in Waianae. In geophysical terms, the West Side is also central. The Waianae Range is but a remnant of what probably was Hawaii's oldest and largest volcano, and Mt. Ka'ala remains Oahu's tallest, even though it's had a few million years longer to erode than the neighboring volcano of Ko'olau.

On the east side of the Waianaes is the Wahiawa Plateau, known mainly as a scenic viewshed that extends across to the Ko'olau Range, covered in recent history by pineapple fields. Most people stop, if at all, to grab a pineapple cone or whatever at touristy Dole Plantation and keep on truckin' to the North Shore. Those people miss the Kukailoko Birthstones State Monument, a reminder that the Wahiawa Plateau was a central gathering place among ancient royalty. They also miss Wahiawa Botanical Garden, a quick floral escape set along a ravine on the east side of the town.

Waianae Range from the West Side

To the west on the plateau is Kolekole Pass, infamous as a reputed route for Japanese warplanes during the attack on Pearl Harbor. The pass, once a major route for the ancients from the leeward coast to central Oahu, is gated now, part of Schofield Barracks. But hikers can take the short walk to the pass after visiting Tropic Lightning Museum. Schofield Barracks was the setting for the novel and Oscar-winning movie, *From Here to Eternity*, and today its spacious grounds and historic buildings evoke a 1950s quietude.

Dropping toward Pearl Harbor from the Wahiawa Plateau, amid the freeways and suburban malls, is the unlikely site of Hawaii's Plantation Village, part of Waipahu Cultural Garden. This is Hawaii's best museum on the sugar cane industry. A re-created block of preserved cottages depicts life among the half-dozen different cultures that came across the seas to labor in the fields. For a century the dominant economic force in the islands, sugar cane operations have dwindled to only one on Maui, since Kauai's last mill closed in 2009.

Technically, Ewa is not considered West Side, although traditionally 'Ewa' is interchangeable with 'west' when giving directions on Oahu. A large military base was mothballed in recent years, opening Ewa beaches to the public. Nimitz and White Plains beach parks will be a find for visiting surfers, swimmers, and strollers, and most tourists don't find their way here. Inshore at Ewa is the Hawaiian Railway Society, a chance for visitors to take an open-air ride on vintage cars along the coast to Kahe Point.

Across Barbers Point to the west of Ewa is Ko Olina Resort, a series of four man-made lagoons and resorts. Safe, sunny swimming is a big draw for tourists. Developers are warming up the bulldozers to add more towers, designer shopping, and an enormous aquarium with an artificial swimming reef. A grittier recreational opportunity awaits inland from Ko Olina, at the southern tip of the Waianaes. Trails at Camp Timberline, a nonprofit school camp, present hikers with the easiest access to this end of the mountains, to an overlook of the Nanakuli Valley.

The true West Side begins west of Ko Olina at Kahe Point and extends through Nanakuli, Maili, Waianae, and Makaha to the western tip of the island at Kaena Point State Park. Developers still have plans to

Barber's Point Lighthouse, Ko Olina

spritz up the West Side, but for now the busy Farrington Highway runs along weatherworn communities, a highway with few left-turn lanes or bus turnouts that keeps drivers on their toes when not bogged down in traffic. Guys ride on couches in the back of pickup trucks, motor scooters whiz the shoulder against traffic, and flip-flopping jaywalkers dart at dusk unexpectedly across four lanes. Yeah baby, this is Waianae.

Kahe Point Beach Park, along with nearby Electric and Tracks beaches, are very good snorkeling and surfing venues, easily reached. Beaches at Nanakuli and Maili see weekend parties of huge extended families, a Hawaiian tradition, as well as a constant supply of surfing waves. Pokai Beach Park in Waianae, one of the most scenic in all of Hawaii, is the best bet for a safe swim at any time of the year. Makaha Beach, next up the coast, rivals any in Hawaii among surfers who know what they're talking about. Makaha is the home foam for a band of local-boy legends, including patriarch Buffalo Keaulana and his sons, Rusty and Brian, as well as goddess of the longboard, the late Rell Sunn. Tourists will feel snug at nearby Papaoneone Beach, a hidden treasure behind the Hawaiian Princess, the coast's only high-rise.

Hawaii's Plantation Village, Makaha Beach

Beyond Makaha, development ends, although homesteading campers find places to squirrel away. Much of this coast is part of the Kaena Point State Park, including beautiful beaches at Makua and Yokohama bays. A trail and the end for the highway leads to the wave-battered rocks and dunes that form Oahu's most westerly point.

As pretty as they are, West Side's beaches play a scenic second-fiddle to the mauka views, where spur ridges from the Waianae Range dive toward the shore and end at a series of heads, between which are majestic valleys. The military grabbed much of the land after Pearl Harbor, and much of the upper regions remain off-limits to mere citizens. But that doesn't mean you can't look. Basked by a long western exposure, clouds often hang above these sweeping uplands that are burnt-blond during the summer and ripened to spring-green by winter rains. Rural roads take independent visitors in for a view. In Makaha Valley is Kaneaki Heiau, a centuries-old homage to Lono, the god of peace and fertility that was converted to a war temple in the late 1700s, when Kamehameha and his men sojourned there prior to launching an unsuccessful invasion of Kauai.

Kaneaki Heiau, Hawaiian Railway Society

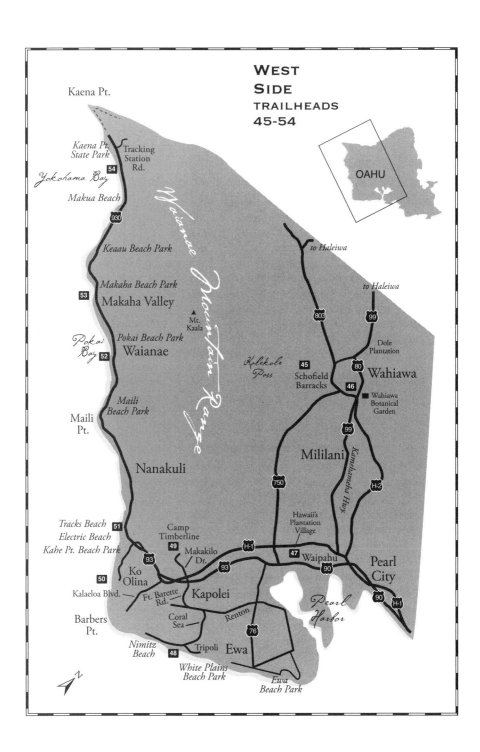

WEST
SIDE
TRAILHEADS
45-54

OAHU

Kaena Pt.

Kaena Pt.
State Park
54
Yokohama Bay
Makua Beach

Tracking
Station
Rd.

930

Keaau Beach Park

Makaha Beach Park
53
Makaha Valley

Waianae Mountain Range

Mt.
Kaala

to Haleiwa

to Haleiwa

803

99

Dole
Plantation

Kolekole
Pass

45
Schofield
Barracks

80
46

Wahiawa

Wahiawa
Botanical
Garden

Pokai
Bay
52
Waianae

Pokai Beach Park

Maili
Beach Park

Maili
Pt.

Nanakuli

99

Mililani

Kamehameha Hwy.

750

H-2

Tracks Beach
Electric Beach
Kahe Pt. Beach Park

51

Camp
Timberline
49
Makakilo
Dr.

Hawaii's
Plantation
Village

H-1

47
Waipahu

Pearl
City

50

93

Ko
Olina

93

90

90

H-1

Kalaeloa Blvd.
Ft. Barette
Rd.

Kapolei

Pearl
Harbor

Barbers
Pt.

Coral
Sea

Renton

76

Nimitz
Beach
48
Tripoli

Ewa

White Plains
Beach Park

Ewa
Beach Park

TH:	TRAILHEAD
HIKE:	ALL WALKING, FROM SHORT STROLLS TO FULL-FLEDGED DAY HIKES
SNORKEL:	BOTH FISH-VIEWING WITH MASK AND FINS, AND PLACES TO SWIM
SURF:	BOARD, BODYSURF, BODYBOARD, WINDSURFING, KITEBOARDING
MAKAI:	TOWARD THE OCEAN
MAUKA:	INLAND, TOWARD THE MOUNTAINS
MM:	MILE MARKER, CORRESPONDS TO HIGHWAY SIGNS

PLEASE NOTE:
All hiking distances in parentheses are ROUND TRIP. Elevation gains of 100 feet or more are noted.
See *Resource Links* page 232 for telephone numbers for all attractions and public agencies.
Admission prices listed are for full-price adults. Leave your car free of valuables at EVERY parking spot.

45. KOLEKOLE PASS   HIKE

WHAT'S BEST: A short walk leads to a gap in the Waianae Range that legend says Japanese planes flew as part of the bombing of Pearl Harbor. Get there by touring historic Schofield Barracks, home base for the novel-movie, *From Here to Eternity*.

PARKING: *From Waikiki*, take H-1 West (which merges with H-78 West) and continue to Exit 8A-H-2 to North Shore. Stay on H-2 until it ends and becomes Hwy. 99, North-Schofield Barracks. Then veer left on Hwy. 750, Kunia Rd.-Schofield. Now on Kunia Rd., pass Foote Gate and turn right into Lyman Rd. *Note:* You reach a guard station. Tell the man you want to visit the Tropic Lightning Museum. A security and ID check will be performed. Afterwards, if you are not locked up, make the second right, on Flagler Rd., and follow until it ends at Waianae Rd. Turn left and then left again into the museum parking lot. Further directions to Kolekole Pass follow below.

HIKE: Tropic Lightning Museum (up to .25-mi.); Kolekole Pass (.5-mi., 150 ft.)

A pass to enter **Schofield Barracks** is a ticket to a kinder, gentler Hawaii, traffic-free, with sprinklers misting the expansive lawns and gardens of buildings that date from the early 1900s and the art deco period of 1930s. The barracks is named for General John M. Schofield, who in 1872 fancied a plan to build a harbor at the mouth of the Pearl River and put a military base inland. The plan had to wait until the U.S. annexed Hawaii in 1898, after which a military camp was set up and, in 1909, named for the general. The **Tropic Lightning Museum**, in the barrack's only lava-rock structure, memorializes the actions of the Army's 25th Infantry Division. *Note:* Hours are 10 to 4, closed Mondays. Admission is free.

The museum is surprisingly atmospheric, blending touch-screen tech with plenty of historic and modern warfare paraphernalia. Photos show that Schofield Barracks was heavily bombed on December 7, 1941. At the time, eyewitnesses reported Japanese planes used nearby Kolekole Pass as a stealthy entry for the attack. But a subsequent review of the Japanese battle plan belies those reports, and historians now believe the planes may have been skimming along the Waianae Range, only appearing to come through the pass. Schofield's fighting forces were nicknamed 'Tropic Lightning' after storming Luzon in the Philippines in 1945. James Jones' 1951 novel, *From Here to Eternity*, is set here, and many of the scenes from the Oscar-winning movie were shot in and around the barracks. A Viet Cong tunnel recreation will give the sweats to vets of that war, and more recent displays on Bosnia, Afghanistan, and Iraq remind visitors that war is not history.

Schofield Barracks, Shirley Temple in Hawaii

A historic guide is available at the museum, which will be helpful for touring Schofield. To reach **Kolekole Pass**, go back on Flagler and then turn right on Kolekole Avenue. You'll pass a golf course and a neighborhood that makes Army life appealing. Then, at a stop sign, go right on Lyman Road. Lyman curves and climbs, becoming more rural and approaching the Waianae Range. At about 4.75 miles from the museum, the road is gated. Park on the left at a sign for Kolekole Pass Rock. Under the branches of ironwoods and native koa trees, a trail leads steeply up, slick in places and improved by steps in others. At the top is a view to the leeward coast and the pointed, smaller peak that sits due west in the notch of the pass. Pohaku Hupeloa, a dimpled rock the size of an eight-foot coconut, rests near the top of the trail. Accounts vary, but the lore on this big stone involves beheadings, and you can see a nice smooth indent, perfect for resting a neck.

More Stuff: Other trails lead north and south into the Waianaes from Kolekole Pass, but permission to access is required; see *Resource Links*. North of the pass a dirt road curves up and joins the Kalena Ridge Trail—a rugged and narrow ascent of 2,200 feet over 2.75 miles to the summit of Puʻu Kalena, Oahu's second highest ground at 3,504 feet. Permission is needed from Schofield Barracks. Going south from Kolekole Pass, the Hapapa Trail is a little easier, but still no cakewalk. It goes 3-plus miles and climbs 1,650 feet to the summit of Puʻu Kanehoa, which stands at 2,728 feet. The route begins past the Pohaku Hupeloa; go down steps and take a left on a dirt road. Permission from both The Nature Conservancy and Schofield Barracks is required to hike this trail.

46. WAHIAWA PLATEAU   HIKE

WHAT'S BEST: The pineapple-growing uplands between the Koʻolau and Waianae mountains are known mostly for the open scenery on the way to the North Shore, but several spots along the way are worthy of the brake pedal.

PARKING: From Waikiki, take H-1 West, which merges with H-78 West. Continue and take Exit 8A, H-2 to the North Shore. From H-2, take Exit 8-to Hwy. 80, Wahiawa. Directions continue below.

HIKE: Wahiawa Botanical Garden (up to .75-mi., 125 ft.); Kukaniloko Birthstones State Monument (.25-mi.); Dole Plantation (up to .5-mi.)

Wahiawa Botanical Garden added a new visitors center in 2005, the entranceway to 27 acres of mature trees and flowering plants that are terraced over a deep ravine. To get there, turn right on California Avenue, a few blocks after entering Wahiawa on Highway 80. You'll see the entrance on your left, about .75-mile up the avenue. Wahiawa is in the top tier among the five city-run Honolulu Botanical Gardens, with railed pathways connected by staircases and footbridges, and a number of benches to bird watch under huge autograph trees and other spreading broadleafs. Don't miss the footbridge that is downstream, or behind you as enter the garden. The mature trees and vintage lampposts speak of the garden's 1920s origins, when the ravine was an experimental arboretum for sugar growers. Wahiawa is an excellent family R&R stop. *Note:* Hours are 9 to 4. Admission is free.

More Stuff: The Schofield-Waikane Trail makes a steady-but-sane ascent of 1,350 feet over 7 miles of wild forest land, reaching the Koʻolau summit. Among backcountry , it is a favorite—but you need to get permission from Schofield Barracks to access the public lands. To scout the trailhead, head up California for about a mile past the gardens. After the avenue makes a 90-degree right turn, followed by a left, look on the right for an opening in a chain-link fence. Enter, turn left, and continue for about .25-mile to an office for the 25th Infantry Division. The trail, beginning as a road, is straight ahead.

To get to the five-acre **Kukaniloko Birthstones State Monument**, pass through Wahiawa on Highway 80 and turn left at the traffic signal on Whitmore Avenue.

Halemano Plantation, Kukaniloko Birthstones

A dirt track leads to the rather forlorn monument in the middle of fields long since devoid of heaius, seeming more like an afterthought than a centerpiece. Still, the short walk out to the stones that rest in an eucalyptus grove will capture a moment for the respectful visitor. *Talk Story:* The smooth rocks were for 700 years, until 1800, the centerpiece at the crossroads of civilization on Oahu. When a chiefess gave birth to a royal infant, the moment was witnessed by 36 ali'i (chiefs) from throughout Oahu and other islands who gathered on the Wahiawa Plateau. Several heiaus were constructed in the surrounding gulches of the Waianaes. To the west is the crest of the Waianae Range, the peaks of which were used to note the passing of the seasons in the fertile plateau. In 1925, this monument became Hawaii's first officially recognized historic site.

You can't avoid the **Dole Plantation**, set on Highway 99 on the way to the North Shore, about 3 miles from Wahiawa. It's parklike grounds, familiar logo, and prime location draw busloads of visitors, about a million per year, seeking all things pineapple. Don't expect free juice or displays depicting history or production methods. The gift shop hums with commerce. Outside are the 'World's Largest Maze,' a hedge that families can attempt to navigate; a small garden to stroll; and the Pineapple Express, an open-car, 20-minute ride around an orchard—all with admissions of five to ten bucks. Children may be enthralled, and if you've ever had a hankerin' for a pineapple butterhorn, this is the place. Before you buy souvenirs, check out the **Halemano Plantation** next door. The nonprofit school offers job opportunities for retarded young people and opportunities for tourists to buy quality T-shirts at 3 for $10, along with inexpensive Hawaiian giftware.

More Stuff: One of the state's Na Ala Hele hiking system's best offerings is the Poamoho Ridge Trail, a 7-mile round-trip jaunt that begins east of the Dole Plantation and climbs about 800 feet to the Koʻolau Ridge. It is accessed by a 5-mile-long drive on a plantation road, beginning near a bus stop—the first right after passing the visitors center and Halemano. Sadly, Dole has closed the road to the public. See *Resource Links*, and call the DLNR for current access status.

47. HAWAII'S PLANTATION VILLAGE   HIKE

WHAT'S BEST: A 'main street' from the sugar plantation days of the early 1900s is Hawaii's best window to a time when sugar was king.

PARKING: From Waikiki, take H-1 West, which merges with H-78 West. Pass the H-2 turnoff and take Exit 7, Waikele-Waipahu. Turn left (makai) on Paiwa St., continue for several blocks, and turn right on Waipahu. Pass the older section of town, with sugar refinery chimney, and turn left at signs for Waipahu Cultural Park and Plantation Village.

HIKE: Hawaii's Plantation Village (up to .25-mi.)

Bordered by busy highways and set within a Waipahu Cultural Garden Park that needs some growing, **Hawaii's Plantation Village** doesn't cast the best first impression. But that impression will be dispelled upon entering the authentic museum and gift shop, and then vanquished altogether when you walk through the nearby 'time tunnel' and enter the tree-lined row of plantation cottages. Of varying design, the cottages are furnished as though workers walked away yesterday. *Notes:* Hours are Monday through Friday, 9 to 3, opening an hour later on Saturdays. Tours begin on the hour; admission about $13, less for kids and seniors. The village is nonprofit.

Talk Story: From the late 1800s and well into the 1900s, Hawaii's sugar cane industry grew along with America's sweet tooth, but at the same time Native

Hawaii's Plantation Village

Hawaiian workforce declined by 80 to 90 percent due to the ravages of Western diseases. As a result, workers came from around the globe—Japan, Okinawa, Korea, the Philippines, Puerto Rico, China, Portugal—and each population brought a way of life that was melded with others by the rigors of the sugar plantation to form the 'calabash' of cultures that still describes modern life in Hawaii. A docent leads the way (you can get a personalized tour when the buses are not around) from cottage to cottage, as well as to the infirmary, bathhouse, field office, and general store. Each cottage is another layer of time, reflecting both the spiritual beliefs as well as the day-to-day lives of the workers. This is the kind of place that teaches effortlessly by osmosis. By the end you can almost hear the fieldworkers singing the holehole bushi, Japanese spiritual songs that are reminiscent of cotton-field workers of early America.

48. EWA BEACHES   HIKE, SNORKEL, SURF

WHAT'S BEST: Two miles of undeveloped coast invite beachcombers, surfers, and snorkelers. Check the weekend scene or have it to yourself on weekdays. On Sundays, enjoy one of Oahu's best deals, a coastal ride on the Hawaiian Railway.

PARKING: From Waikiki, take H-1 West, which merges with H-78 West. Pass the H-2 turnoff and take Exit 2, Kapolei-Makakilo. From the off ramp, turn left (makai) on Ft. Barrette Rd. (to the right it's called Makakilo Dr.). Continue for 1.5 mi. and turn left on Roosevelt Ave., which is just past Renton. *For Ewa Beaches*, continue less than .75-mi. on Roosevelt and turn right on Coral Sea Rd. Continue 1.75 mi. on Coral Sea to a stop sign at Tripoli. *For Nimitz Beach Park*, continue straight on Coral Sea as it curves along the coast. The beach park is another 1.5 mi., just past the air station. *For White Plains Beach*, turn left on Tripoli, go .5-mi., and turn right on White Plains Circle. *For the Hawaii Railway Society*, continue past Coral Sea Rd, for a little over a mile on Roosevelt, turn left on Philippine Sea, and go one block. *Be Aware:* My god, during late afternoon commute times, the drive from the freeway onto Ft. Barrette Rd. can be a parking lot.

HIKE: Nimitz Beach to White Plains Beach (up to 3.5 mi.); Hawaiian Railway Society (.25-mi.)

Talk Story: The zone from **Nimitz Beach to White Plains Beach**, part of the Barbers Point Naval Air Station, is a wild space of kiawe trees and scrub, with open beaches, buffered inland by the instant-suburbia of Kapolei—a serious contender for Oahu's most underrated coastline. Many visitors are students, military personnel, and the occasional tourist gather at two beaches. You may wind up stopping here and there to explore rather than making this an up-and-back beach walk.

From Nimitz Beach Park, walk the lawn beside the picnic pavilions to the earthen breakwater on the right, which forms the west end of the beach. You'll see an ample strip of sand running the nearly 2 miles to White Plains Beach, along a shore buffered by ironwoods and grassy dunes—and giving way to a long view of Diamond Head. Begin the walk by passing the flat-topped vacation cottages of the Coast Guard, and .5-mile later reach the large ironwood forest of rough-hewn Eisenhower campground. (The campground, one of the best coastal camping spots in Hawaii, is a left turn off Coral Sea Road, after passing Tripoli Road.) Continuing on the beach, palms mingle with heliotropes as you approach the pleasant picnic grounds of White Plains Beach. You can mingle at a beachside restaurant that serves up local-style plates.

The **Hawaiian Railway Society** operates a vintage, open-car train ride (13 miles round-trip) on a section on tracks that used to continue around Kaena Point to connect Honolulu with the agriculture of the North Shore. Don't expect a lot of pizzazz at the all-volunteer, nonprofit society museum, which is inside a Quonset hut. But do expect a fun time and a great value. The yard has a shaded picnic area that boasts some restored beauties. Railroad buffs and photographers will enjoy walking the huge boneyard out back, their open-air museum, where decrepit survivors of the Oahu Railway await sprucing up. The four-car train, with the uniformed crew providing narration, goes through a treed

Nimitz Beach, White Plains Beach, Hawaiian Railway Society

portion of Barber's Point, past swanky Ko Olina resort, and reaches the coast at Kahe Point. *Notes:* Public rides are Sundays at 1 and 3. Cost is $10, $7 for kids. Food and beverages *are* allowed.

More Stuff: Thorough adventure travelers may by tempted to check out Ewa and Onelua beach parks, but most will agree that these locals' beaches have less to offer visitors. If you insist, take Renton Road east to Fort Weaver Road-Highway 76 and turn makai. Ewa is at the end of Ft. Weaver; Onelua is to the right on Papipi Road.

SNORKEL: Current can be an issue during periods of high surf, but normally **Nimitz Beach Park** is a better-than-decent spot to flipper around. Water clarity is good, and coral and sea life are ample. One of the safer spots is inside the earthen breakwater at the beach park. Better coral, however, lies to the west side of the breakwater—which you can also access past the beach park, before the road ends. You'll find both reefy snorkeling and a nice **Nimitz Keiki Pond**. This shore is also well-known haunt for shell collectors.

It may seem silly to come all the way to the islands to visit a water park, but **Hawaiian Waters Adventure Park** is 25 acres of slides 'n' spills that may be of interest to families. From H-1 Westbound, take Exit 1, Campbell. Curve around to the right and drive a short distance on the Farrington Highway.

SURF: The Ewa coastline is definitely on the map for surfers. The long lefts at **Barbers Point Beach Park** don't require an expert on most days. To get there, from Nimitz, backtrack to Renton, turn left, and then turn right on Ft. Barrette. Then make a left on Kapolei Parkway and follow it to Kalaeloa Blvd., where you go left. (Kalaeloa is also reachable via Exit 1, Campbell from H-1 West.) Follow Kalaeloa all the way to Olai and turn right. With a lighthouse and straggly palm next to Germain's Luau, Barbers Point looks like a place Gilligan may have gone to retire, after the divorce and the drinking problem, but the site is really where salty-dog Captain Henry Barber shipwrecked in 1796.

The breakwater at Nimitz Beach Park creates a nice grandstand to watch the waves known as **Swabbieland**. A break farther down the beach, accessed via roadside parking, is known as **Officers**. **White Plains Beach Park** has a multi-tiered easy break that draws beginning surfers, particularly wahines it seems, from all over Oahu. The snack restaurant and inviting picnic areas add to a mellow hook-up or chill-out beach scene. Farther east on the coast, off 30-acre Onelua Beach Park (see *More Stuff* above) are a few spots known mainly to locals. **John's**, **Sand Tracks**, and **Chicken Creek** are off the front of the fishermen's reef. On the west end of the park, toward White Plains, are **Hau Bush** and **Shark Country**, always an inviting moniker.

WHAT'S BEST: Oahu hiking veterans appreciate this chance to get high in the Waianaes. A trail climbs an arid ridgeline and serves up a West Side panorama.

PARKING: From Waikiki, take H-1 West, which merges with H-78 West. Pass the H-2 turnoff and take Exit 2-Kapolei, Makakilo. Turn right and follow Makakilo Dr. 2.4 mi. to the top. Turn left on Kikaha, continue to its end at a stop sign, and turn left on Umena. *Note:* You reach a gate to Palehua Rd. that is fastened by a combination lock. Call Camp Timberline at 808-672-5441 to get the combination. They welcome visitors. A nominal fee may be charged to hike. After the gate, continue 1.6 mi. and veer left at a junction. Continue for another mile, keep right between the walls, and then go left on a dirt road to Camp Timberline; the right fork continues to Palehua Solar Observation. Check in at the office.

HIKE: Camp Timberline to: Palehua Lookout (2.25 mi., 450 ft.), or Mauna Kapu (3.25 mi., 1,450 ft.)

Camp Timberline is operated by Kama'aina Kids, a nonprofit that provides outdoor learning for children. Perched at nearly 2,000 feet on 150-forested acres, the camp also offers rustic lodging and camping. They'll give you a map and directions. **For both hikes**, head mauka through the cabins, veer left beside the fire pit, and you'll come out on the road that ends at the Palehua Solar Observatory (one of only six in the world). The trailhead is before the observatory gate—across a little footbridge on the right if you were driving up the road.

The Waianaes

Interpretive signs and blue markers punctuate the trail as it ascends through eucalyptus and paperbark trees that hold together the eroding, red-dirt slopes. Past the sandalwood sign, you'll veer left at a gully recovering from a forest fire, and come upon cables that lie on the ground and extend up the ridgeline. **For the Palehua Lookout**, cross over the cables and follow the trail as it curves right and descends. The terminus is an overlook of the green bowl of the Nanakuli Valley. To reach **Mauna Kapu**—a 2,776-foot bump on the southern end of the Waianae Range—go to the right when you reach the cables. This route is steep, much less traveled, although the country is open and traversable by mere mortals. Another road leads mauka to military communications sites on this ridge, so don't expect wilderness. After Mauna Kapu, the ridge rollercoasters up to 3,098-foot Palikea before falling 1,000 feet to Pohakea Pass. Routes continue northward to Kolekole Pass. The blue-water views coming down Mauna Kapu take in all of eastern Oahu.

50. KO OLINA LAGOONS   HIKE, SNORKEL

WHAT'S BEST: Throw a zillion dollars and some imagination at a limestone coastline and you get sunny Ko Olina—four man-made lagoons with beaches, the premier JW Marriott Ihilani Resort, and high-end, beach-club condominiums.

PARKING: From Waikiki, take H-1 West, which merges with H-78 West. Pass the H-2 and continue about 9 mi. H-1 ends and becomes Hwy. 93, the Farrington Hwy. After about 1 mi., exit on Ali'inui Dr. to Ko Olina. Stop at a security station to gain admission. *For Lanikuhonua Cultural Park beach*, turn right after Paradise Cove into a parking lot and then turn right into Shoreline Access parking. (A second security guard may greet you.) *For Lagoon 1*, turn right at either Olani or Kamoana, which are within .5-mi. of the guard station. *For Lagoon 2*, turn at the next right, on Waiali'i. *For Lagoon 3*, turn right on the following road, Mauloa. *For Lagoon 4*, veer right before the marina of Waipahe. *Notes:* All of the lagoons have separate parking, with attendants. Arrive early on (busy) weekends. The cultural park and the marina are your best bets at busy times.

HIKE: Lanikuhonua to Ko Olina Lagoons (up to 3.25 mi.)

The **Lanikuhonua Hawaiian Cultural Park**, where community groups and private parties gather, was staked out in 1939 by Alice Kamokila Campbell, daughter of super-rich James Campbell, who practically owned the air on this side of the island. Before then, the beachside oasis had been a retreat for Hawaiian royalty. The wave-battered limestone reef to the east was blasted into lagoons by developer Herbert Horita in the mid-1980s and the JW Ihilani (now a Marriott) Resort came to be in 1993. Plans are in the works to pump a billion dollars more into Ko Olina, adding a four-tower Grand Ko Olina Resort, an aquarium, and an artificial snorkeling reef, plus the obligatory commercial village. The **Ko Olina Lagoons** walk begins at the far west end of the shoreline; you can shorten the hike by beginning at Lagoon 1.

From the Lanikuhonua parking, a short path leads to a cove that lives up to its Hawaiian translation, "Where Heaven Meets the Earth." To the right at the shore is a gardenscape and the chapels of Paradise Cove, a wedding mill for Japanese couples. For the lagoons, go to the left, and you'll pass a smaller sand beach with a keiki pool that borders the lovely grounds. You'll have to rock-hop a bit before reaching the lawns of the resort. Take a detour to check out the grand ocean-view terraces.

Lanikuhonua Cove

Lagoon 1, a.k.a. Kohala or "Whale," lies in front of the resort. You can trod the imported sand or a paved path, called the Sea Walk, which skirts all four lagoons. Palms and other plantings boder this sunny excercise jaunt. The Grand Ko Olina and aquarium are slated for the ground mauka the next section, where a 10-story beach club looms over the shore at the second lagoon, named Honu (Turtle). The next lagoons are Naia (Dolphin), and Ulua (Fish). The path ends at a marina and the point for Barbers Point Harbor.

SNORKEL: Sweet **Lanikuhonua Cove** is protected and boasts scenery worthy of whiling away a day. The natural cove is smaller than the Ko Olina Lagoons and can be too shallow at low tide, but even so it is probably the top choice at Ko Olina. An even smaller **keiki pool** lies to the left along the shore. In calm sea conditions the rocks and reef outside the protected area are good for snorkeling, but be wary of wave action and current.

All four **Ko Olina Lagoons** are a sure thing for snorkelers looking for a safe and easy place to test warm Hawaiian waters and sunshine. Water clarity, although good, is not the best, due to silting, and you won't see a lot of marine life inside the reef. All three lagoons are similar, ovals several hundred feet across with openings to the sea that are sheltered by breakwater islets. Lagoon 1 gets the most action, since it is closest to the resort and is accessed by two parking lots. Lagoon 2 has about a dozen small shade cabanas. The gardens and palmy backshore of Lagoon 3 may make it the pick of the bunch, although the new high-rise, time-share resort adds more flesh to the sand. The most recently constructed, Lagoon 4 has the most room to roam, and the waters outside the lagoon draw shore scuba divers and snorkelers, under calm conditions. Enter to the right of the lagoon and swim outside the rock barrier and reef, where waters are 10- to 15-feet deep.

51. KAHE POINT   SNORKEL, SURF

WHAT'S BEST: Tour boats cruise to these snorkeling reefs, but all you have to do is drive up and park it. Mid-level surfers make tracks to a reliable offshore break.

PARKING: From Waikiki, take H-1 West, which merges with H-78 West. Pass the H-2 and continue about 9 mi. H-1 ends and becomes Hwy. 93, the Farrington Hwy. Pass the turnoff for Ko Olina. Directions continue below.

SNORKEL: Boatloads of tourists cruise the Oahu coastline and anchor a couple hundred feet off **Kahe Point Beach Park.** To drive there, take the left-hand turn lane as Highway 93 curves to the right and joins the coast, about .5-mile past the Ko Olina turnoff. You'll see the park's covered pavilion that is across the street from the Hawaiian Electric Company. Walk through the covered area past the rest rooms and enter via the tiny cove that has the power plant's large concrete holding tank as one border. Swim out and explore the reef and lava rocks to the left, along the cliffs of the beach park. Marine life is drawn to the warmed water that surfaces about 200 yards offshore from the plant's large cooling conduits. *Be Aware:* Wave action can create current at Kahe Point. More scuba divers than snorkelers use the point.

Nearby **Electric Beach** is a better choice for snorkelers—even easier entry, a nice run of sand, and a less-obvious location that screens out most tourists. To get there, pass Kahe Point Beach Park. Just past the power plant, take a left-turn lane, which is the entry to Tracks Beach. Hang a U-turn at Tracks, backtrack about .25-mile, and then turn right into an opening that will take you across the old railroad tracks to a parking area next to a low rock wall. Head down the long slope of sand. Beach trees to the right provide adequate nesting spots away from highway noise. You'll want to swim to the right, away from the power plant, where a reef runs parallel to shore in depths of 10 to 12 feet. You may see spinner dolphin and turtles at Electric Beach. Local spear fishermen may be on hand to offer advice.

SURF: On most days you'll see hopeful surfers riding the swell at **Tracks Beach**— use the left-turn lane after Kahe Point Beach Park, and just past the power plant. Tracks is easily reached from central Oahu and the break is reliable without being too hairy. There's room for lots of surfmobiles in the undeveloped parking lot. Local surfers and bodysurfers also gather at sandy **Nanakuli Beach Park** and at long, reefy **Ulehawa Beach Park**, which is the next beach to the north. Concrete walls extend seaward at Ulehawa Stream, on the northern end of the park, at a surf site called **Channels**. Hard times have brought increased beach campers to Nanakuli.

52. WAIANAE
HIKE, SNORKEL, SURF

WHAT'S BEST: First-timers might feel culture shock before getting a feel for Waianae, the reigning capital the West Side. Pokai Beach Park offers a inspiring beach walk and this coast's best snorkeling and swimming. Inland, above Waianae Valley, is a walk on the wild side to Mt. Ka'ala, the lush bog that rests atop the highest peak on Oahu.

PARKING: From Waikiki, take H-1 West, which merges with H-78 West. Pass the H-2 and continue about 9 mi. H-1 ends and becomes Hwy. 93, the Farrington Hwy. Continue for 6 mi., passing through Nanakuli and rounding Maili Point. Directions continue in the activity descriptions below.

Nanakuli Beach Park

HIKE: Waianae Kai Trail to: Kamaileunu Ridge (5.25 mi., 2,200 ft.), or Mt. Ka'ala (8.5 mi., 3,650 ft.); Pokai Bay to Kuilioloa Heiau (1.5 mi.)

Be Aware: Think of the Waianae Kai Trail as more of a journey than a destination, since reaching the top at Mt. Ka'ala—a misty bog inside the extinct crater—will be a challenge to even seasoned hikers who are traveling without local guides. It's doable and well worth the effort, but double the stats when figuring the toll it will exact physically. You'll also want to know that a private road also reaches the top to service a FAA and Air Force installation. Even so, this trail gets high marks for gung-ho hikers, and accommodates everyone else who wants to climb into native forests rich with bird life. This is the only trail to the 1,100-acre Mt. Ka'ala Natural Reserve —one of three natural areas on Oahu—that does not require special permits.

To reach the **Waianae Kai Trail**, drive through Maili on the Farrington Highway and pass the Waianae Mall. Then, about 3 miles after having rounded Maili Point, turn mauka on Waianae Valley Road. Continue for about 2.25 miles and veer left as Haleahi Road goes right. Continue on the now one-lane road for .75-mile and park at a dirt turnout on the left, at the locked gate for the Waianae Kai Public Hunting Area. **For both hikes**, start up the concrete ramp at the trailhead and get used to going up. Koa trees fringe the road, as it rises several hundred feet over the first 1.5

miles, while passing two water pumping buildings. The road ends at a picnic shelter and the real trail begins. With roots and rocks underfoot, you'll be enveloped by ti and guava in your face, and kukui, koa, and other trees overhead. After the ridge narrows, the trail passes a utility pole and drops left into a gully and through a relatively flat zone. You then ascend fairly steeply for the last 850 feet and top out at **Kamaileunu Ridge**, which separates the Waianae and Makaha valleys. To the right on the ridge is an overlook of Waianae Valley, in a clearing made for utility poles.

Take a read on the weather and decide whether to go for **Mt. Kaʻala**, another steep 1,300 feet up. Bear in mind that the Kaʻala Trail has one section over rocks that requires handholds and use of a rope cable. If you should lose the trail in overgrown sections, return to your last known point. Okay, time to take off. Pink plastic ribbon will mark the sketchy trail in places. You'll ascend through low-lying flora and ohia trees. The notorious trail section lies ahead, where boulders and ropes provide a challenge. Be sure to test these ropes before trusting them. After this most difficult stretch you still have some muddy ascent before reaching the boundary of the Mt. Kaʻala Natural Area Reserve. Finally the trail levels as you approach the lip of the plateau, and the best part of the hike begins—the .75-mile boardwalk across the otherworldly mists of the Kaʻala Bog. Delicate awaʻawapuhi flowers, hapuʻu tree ferns, and red bottlebrush ohia provide a home for several native birds. On the far side of the bog is the paved Mt. Kaʻala Road. If the clouds cooperate, you can steal a view from an overlook. Go right on the road and keep left where a gate blocks entry into the facility.

The walk along **Pokai Bay to Kuilioloa Heiau** takes in a big slice of life on the West Side—especially on sunny weekends when the place is popping—and ends with one of the most sublime seaside spots in all of Hawaii. To begin the hike, pass Waianae Valley Road and less than .25-mile later turn left on Army Road, which is just after Guard Road and before the 7-11 store. Go to the end and park outside a guard station of an R&R camp for the military. An Army recreation center and beach cabins lie left and right at the beach, which is fronted by a sandy pathway and a pleasant array of beach trees. Go left on the path or drop to the sand—you'll soon pass the middle section of Pokai Bay, which is bordered by a breakwater. You then come upon the grassy fields of Pokai Beach Park. Weekends bring a flood of locals, with lots of huli huli chicken on the grill. In the late afternoons on weekdays, the bay is the training ground for outrigger canoe teams.

Continue around the sand and out to the treed peninsula that ends at Kaneilio Point—the site of Kuilioloa Heiau. Grass terraces supported by low walls are all that remain of what for centuries was the heiau devoted to the teaching of fishing. The coastal views from the heiau are great, but the big look is mauka across a breakwater and bay at the yawning Waianae Valley surrounded by the ramparts of a nuanced ridgeline. *Talk Story:* This park is named for Pokai, a navigator among the first Tahitian voyagers, who arrived as early as 200 AD. For several centuries, these open-canoe mariners made round-trips of more than 5,000 miles, sailing back with the plants and animals vital to survival. *Be*

After canoe practice, Pokai Beach Park

Aware: Locals consider this heiau is a sacred spot, so you don't want to picnic or play Frisbee. Treat it like a church.

SNORKEL: Pokai Beach Park has the safest swimming on the leeward coast. Get there directly by turning makai on Lualualei Homestead Road, which is just past the venerable Tamura Market. To the left side of the bay is a long riprap breakwater, which provides shelter for both fish and people even during high surf. Get in near the base of the breakwater and swim towards its tip. A mostly sandy bottom means visibility will not be optimum during higher surf. During calm conditions, you can flipper to the seaward side of the breakwater and along the rocky Kaneilio Point. For a swimming spot to call your own, head to the middle of Pokai Bay, between the beach park and the Army's beach. *More Stuff:* Legendary slack-key singer, the late Israel Kamakiwiwoole (better known as Iz) chose Waianae as his home. A memorial statue is at the Neighborhood Commuity Center near 85-670 Farrington Highway.

Maili Beach Park birthday party, Israel (Iz) Kamakawiwoole

SURF: Running for nearly .5-mile on the north side of Maili Point, between Nanakuli and Waianae, is **Maili Beach Park**, site for West Side surfing competitions and normally a weekend venue for local-style parties. First-year birthday parties are a big deal, where extended families gather in droves with aluminum baking dishes the size of birdbaths. **Maili Point** serves up a long left for long- and -shortboard surfers. **Green Lanterns** is at the south end of the park, near Maili Stream. **Tumbleland**, mostly for bodysurfing and bodyboarding, is in the middle of the beach. North of Maili, along Lualualei Beach Park, is **Sewers**, since the treatment plant is across the highway (surfers don't do euphemisms). Pokai Bay is not a surfing haven, but beginners and bodysurfers head to the easy rollers offshore **Army Beach**.

53. MAKAHA   HIKE, SNORKEL, SURF

WHAT'S BEST: In Makaha Valley is the island's most dramatic heiau, and on the coast is a short and exciting adventure hike to Lahilahi Point. But the real deal is Makaha Beach, the right-of-passage for Oahu wave riders, even considering the glamorous offerings at Waikiki and the North Shore.

PARKING: From Waikiki, take H-1 West, which merges with H-78 West. Pass the H-2 and continue about 9 mi. H-1 ends and becomes Hwy. 93, the Farrington Hwy. Continue on the busy, 4-lane highway for about 12 mi. passing Waianae High School on the left. Directions continue below in the activity descriptions.

HIKE: Kaneaki Heiau (.25-mi.); Papaoneone Beach to Mauna Lahilahi (1.25 mi., 250 ft.)

Couched in a tangle of ti plants and tropical greenery below the high ridges of Makaha Valley, **Kaneaki Heiau** is Oahu's most realistic, adorned with re-created thatched structures and pole platforms. To get to the heiau, turn mauka from the right-turn-only lane to Makaha Valley Road at a 7-11 store. Continue (the road changes names twice on curves) for more than a mile, pass the right turn for Makaha Valley Country Club, and take the next right on Maunaolu Street. *Notes:* After .25-mile you'll reach a security station, where you'll be asked for identification and be given list of rules and regs. Hours for the heiau are Tuesday through Sunday, 10 to 2. The heiau is about .75-mile from the station; following signs, continue up Maunaolu, go left and park.

The Kaneaki Heiau is a two-minute walk. Its six-foot-thick, low-walled terraces sit above Makaha Stream and under a canopy of native trees that filter sunlight to banana, ti plants, and other Polynesian imports. Some five periods of construction—now enclosing about 15,000 square feet—have been identified at the site, beginning in the 1300s when the agricultural terraces were dedicated to Lono, the god of peace and fertility. The place did the big flip in the late 1700s, when Kaneaki became a war temple, dedicated to the god Ku. Kamehameha the Great and his legions encamped here waiting to invade Kauai and unite the islands—an invasion that failed twice, once because of high seas and once due to disease among the warriors.

Papaoneone Beach to Mauna Lahilahi is a small hike with a big payoff. To begin, pass Makaha Valley Road and Orange Street, and park at the dirt turnout on your left opposite Jade Street—and just past the high-rising Hawaiian Princess and dreary apartments. (There's also a right-of-way off Lahilahi Street.) Walk the wide sandy pathway to Papaoneone Beach, which caters mainly to the guests at the Princess. These sands are also known as Turtle Beach, since the lovable reptiles munch the seaweed on the reef offshore. At the far end of the beach, hop up to a rock ledge that once supported the old Waterhouse Estate. To scale the 250-foot summit, backtrack on a trail inland, to your left from the beach through brush and kiawes. You'll come around to the base of the point, where an unsigned trail goes right up the shoulder of the pu'u. Hands are required in a couple places. You get a winning mid-distance view of the coast as well a wide-angle toward the inviting recess of Makaha Valley.

SNORKEL: Wave action normally rules out swimming in Makaha, especially during the winter months. During flat surf, **Papaoneone Beach** (Turtle Beach) will

Makaha Valley

do just fine for snorkelers, although this is mainly a scuba diver's haunt—Turtle Reef and Ulua Cave are offshore. At all times, Papaoneone is a very scenic beach, the most comfortable West Side beach for tourists to hang around. Makaha Beach Park is also more of a surfing beach that doubles as a scuba beach when surf is lower. The **Makaha Cavern** lies to the right of the wide sandy channel in the middle of the bay, which during even moderate surf is a one-way ticket on rip tide to the deep blue sea. For some dry-land tide-pool action, and a short walk to wave-bashed **Kepuhi Point**, drive about .25-mile past the beach park and the Makaha Shores condos, and turn left on Makau Street. You'll see a right-of-way on the left between homes that leads to a sandy swath fronted by the north reef. You need to rock hop a bit to Kepuhi Point, which is the north boundary of the beach.

The best bet for snorkelers, yet still far from ideal, is rough-hewn **Kea'au Beach Park**, which .5-mile north of Makaha. A rocky shore, blue-tarp campers, and prevailing current normally dissuade swimmers. But experienced snorkelers, under calmer conditions, can join the occasional scuba diver and enter at a marginal beach that is at the far-north end of the open, grassy park. A flat reef is near shore, in depths beginning at 10 to 15 feet. Take a path that diagonals right through trees at the far end of the parking lot.

SURF: Massive waves, 25 feet and up in the winter, break off Kepuhi Point and roll in tiers toward **Makaha Beach Park**, creating a venue for world-class contests. The Makaha International Surfing Championships began in 1952. In January, Makaha is the site for the Quiksilver Makahiki surfing competition. But the main event, normally taking place on the last two weekends in March (after the NFL Pro Bowl), is the Buffalo's Big Board Surfing Classic, presided over since 1976 by West Side patriarch, Richard Buffalo Keaulana and his family—along with the aunties and uncles of Makaha's extended family. Take a seat in the sand and you'll never forget it, for the Buffalo's Big Board Classic is a moveable feast. Buffalo is a legendary surfer and original crewmember of the Polynesian sailing voyager, the *Hokulea*. He is gradually

Makaha Beach Park

PICTURE LIFT SHEET

-1 Cradle
-2 Shoulder sit
-2 Swan
-3 Knee Stand
-3 Reverse Knee Stand
-4 Hand Knee Stand
-4 1-Leg Knee Stand
-5 Fake Arm-to-Arm
-6 Fake High Stag
-6 Elbow Aerobesque
-7 One-arm Back
-7 Camel
-8 Shoulder Stand
-8 High Swan
-9 High Stag
-9 Grass Shack
)-10 Kennedy
)-10 Side Bird
)-11 Aerobesque
)-11 Reverse One-Arm Back
)-11 Falcon
)-12 High Reverse Stag
)-13 1-Leg Shoulder Stand
)-14 Buddha or Chair
)-14 Front Angel
)-14 Helicopter (backspin)
)-15 Attitude
)-16 Statue
)-16 1-Arm Kennedy
)-17 Back Angel
)-17 Straddle-L
0-17 Arrow
0-18 Americano
0-18 Pyramid
0-19 Arm-to-Arm
0-19 Foot-to-hand
0-19 Star

*Tandem surfing, canoe surfing,
Picture Lift Sheet, Brian Keaulana,
new* Hokulea *crew member with original
crew Richard Buffalo Keaulana at
Buffalo's Big Board Surfing Classic.*

handing the baton to sons Rusty and Brian—the latter destined to surpass his father's fame, thanks to innovative, heroic efforts on jet skis as a life-saving waterman and a hot career as a Hollywood stunt coordinator and director. The Buffalo's Classic is a potpourri of events that include six-man outrigger canoe surfing, beach boy (standing up with a paddle) surfing, a 250-pounds-and-up division, team bodysurfing, and the amazing tandem surfing, where a man rides the big foam ashore with his petite female partner posed overhead on his outstretched arms. Rain or shine, the PA announcer prattles on with slack key in the background and plate lunches off the grill.

If the Keaulanas and other families are today's ali'i, then the Queen of Makaha is Rell Sunn. Beginning in the early 1970s, she helped pioneer women's professional surfing. A photo of lithe Rell hanging ten toes off a two-ton longboard combines power and grace in a way that has become an icon for the sport. An exotic mix of Hawaiian and Chinese ancestry, Rell was a 200-watt bulb in a 60-watt world. In 1998, at age 48, Rell Sunn lost a long battle with breast cancer. Her legacy lives on, both in a big-sister-type program in which older women befriend younger girls in the community, and a play, *The Queen of Makaha*.

You may miss an official competition, but local boys gather at the Makaha Beach Park every evening. Visiting surfers are well advised to get friendly before paddling out, since violations of etiquette are not taken lightly. But the tough-guy reputation masks the heart of Makaha, where a dime's worth of politeness and respect gets you about a buck-fifty in return. Bodysurfing is also popular at Makaha, where shore break combines with outgoing surf to create a unique backsplash ride taken, oh, ten-million times by locals. It's dangerous for beginners. On occasion, you'll see board surfers riding the backsplash wave *away* from shore. To get a different and closer perspective on the Makaha surfers, try the right-of-way access to Kepuhi Point, described in the snorkeling section above. With cliffs rising inland and waves rushing by the reef, this is one of those sublime spots.

Bodyboarders and bodysurfers also like the left-break off Lahilahi Point, coming into **Papaoneone Beach**. Beginners can give it a try on lower-surf days. The shelf at the end of the beach, site of the old Waterhouse Estate, is one of the better places to watch. On the other side of Lahilahi Point, at roadside at Mauna Lahilahi Beach Park, is a break called **Shark Island**, peeling off an offshore reef.

54. KAENA POINT STATE PARK   HIKE, SNORKEL, SURF

WHAT'S BEST: The end of the road is the beginning of a wild coastal trail to the windswept natural area that is Oahu's most westerly point. Take a hike, and then kick back at Makua and Yokohama, both beautiful beaches au naturel.

PARKING: From Waikiki, take H-1 West, which merges with H-78 West. Pass the H-2 and continue about 9 mi. H-1 ends and becomes Hwy. 93, the Farrington Hwy. Continue

Kuailai marker at Makua Beach

on the busy, 4-lane highway for about15 mi. passing Waianae and leaving development behind (but picking up homeless camps) after Makaha. Directions continue below.

HIKE: Makua Beach loop (up to 1.75 mi.); Yokohama Bay to Kaena Point (4.5 mi.)

Beginning after mm17 north of Makaha, **Kaena Point State Park** includes about 850 undeveloped, coastline acres, bordered inland by sweeping valleys and the Waianae Mountains, which dive into the sea at the point. At land's end is one of Hawaii's last sand dune ecosystems—one of only three Natural Area Preserves on Oahu.

Many tourists stop at beleaguered Kaneana Cave after mm17 and breeze right on by **Makua Beach**, since a guardrail borders the highway on the makai side and mauka are U.S. Military fences and an observation tower. Inland is a panorama of Makua Valley, a green triangle that slopes steeply to the high ridges of the Waianae Mountains. So, slow down. Just before the guardrail begins and mm18, take a bumpy turnout to the left that leads to a rocky shelf that is the south point of a long sweep of sand. Running parallel between the highway and the beach is a paved lane, closed to cars on weekdays, which pops out again to the highway after .75-mile. You can make a nice beach-and-backshore loop, weaving in and out of an interesting shoreline.

At the south end of Makua Beach, off the point, is Pohaku Kulailai, a coral outcrop named by the ancients for a female demigod, and said to symbolize the sacred unity of the land and the sea. In 1962, some nimrod spray-painted "Pray for Sex" at the base of the rock, and the name, of course, caught on as a nickname. Along the paved lane are several stream spillways, a historic cemetery, remains of a fishing shrine, and Gail's Garden, where Gail, her son, and others have restored vegetation to the valley

Yokohama Beach

that had been used as a bombing range by the military. Beginning in 2001, locals have been able to gain limited access to archeological sites in the upper valley. Idyllic settings under mature trees along the beach were shown in the 1966 movie *Hawaii*, adapted from James Michener's novel.

A little more than a mile from Makua Bay, the highway rounds Pukano Point and reveals the inviting sands of Keawaula Bay Beach, more commonly known as Yokohama Bay and Beach. The name derives from a Japanese fisherman who operated a store in the early 1900s; he and his compatriots hailed from that port city across the Pacific. For the awesome hike from **Yokohama Bay to Kaena Point**, you can drive to trailhead parking that is about .5-mile from the beach parking lot. But more secure parking will be in the first parking lot or along the roadside before the spillway at the lifeguard station. *Be Aware:* Bring plenty of water and adequate sun protection.

The trail, now a puddle-pocked track, follows the abandoned bed of the Oahu Railway, which linked agricultural Haleiwa the seaport at Honolulu. The trail continues around the point, making a 150-degree bend that bottlenecked trains in the old days, while passengers kept a wary eye on rogue waves that would splash the tracks. In 1946, a tsunami on the Mokuleia Coast finished the railway for good.

The Mokuleia end of this trail is described on page 180. Those giant techno golf balls on the ridge are part of the military's tracking station. About .5-mile into the walk you'll probably hear the exhale of a blowhole, sounding like a whale, and not long after that is a small sea arch. You'll see decrepit sections of the railway, now claimed by tidal erosion and landslides. At one point a mile into the walk, the sea has blasted the trail down to a hands-on footpath, closing the route to even die-hard Jeepsters.

With the low Kaena Point clearly in view, you pass the toe on the falling ridgeline where prevailing winds normally add a new element to the hike. The trail skirts the dunes of the natural area. Broad-winged Laysan albatrosses, looking like enormous gulls, nest amid the orange blossoms of ilima papa, leafy naupaka kahakai, and other low-lying flora. At the point, a 30-foot steel-tower lighthouse braves the wind, next to a toppled concrete tower. During the winter and early spring, keep an eye out for breaching whales. Off Kaena Point is a turbulent current that gives way to the Kauai Channel, the deepest water along the 1,600-mile Hawaiian Archipelago. Among Hawaiians, the point is known as 'leiana a kauhane,' or 'leaping of the souls,' the place where the spirits of the recently deceased left the earth to be with their ancestors.

Waianae Range ends at Kaena Point Natural Reserve

More Stuff: The Kaena Tracking Station Road heads up the mountain to the right as you reach Yokohama Bay, leading to trails that are part of the state's Na Ala Hele hiking system. Although readily reached via two trailheads on the Mokuleia Coast (see page 178-79), the military treats this side like the Berlin Wall in the '50s. Hiking permits are available through the state's website (see *Resource Links*). The advantage to this access is driving up about 2.5 miles and 1,200 feet to the parking lot. From there is forested loop hike of about 7 miles and 1,100 feet that combines the Kuaokala Trail with the Kuaokala Access Road. The loop connects at the far end with the Kealia Trail. The road continues for several twisting miles beyond the end of the loop to Peacock Flat, the terminus of the Mokuleia Access Road.

SNORKEL: With no protective reef, the waters offshore Kaena Point State Park are most often subject to wave action and rip current, neither being a friend to snorkelers. But that's not always the case. At **Pray for Sex Beach**, the eastern end of Makua Beach, is a swimming area and jumping rock used by local youths. On the calmest of days, snorkeling tour boats stop in at Makua Bay, but it's not a common sight. Entry is difficult over sharp rock. Visibility is excellent, with depths ranging from 15 to 25 feet. The real treat here, one of Oahu's secret goodies, are the spinner dolphins cruising Makua Bay. Often you'll see them from shore, and they are not averse to saying howdy to swimmers.

Snorkeling is not unheard of at **Yokohama Beach**, but shore break is usually a deterrent. An entry point for divers is to the left, across from the military road just

Kaena Keiki Pond

as you reach the bay. Enter at generous sand patches between large rocks, and swim along the margins of Pukano Point. The best chance for getting safely in the ocean during the winter is the **Kaena Keiki Pond**. Drive past the first parking lot and the lifeguard tower, and park along the road, near the spillway—about .25-mile before the end of the road. A reefy section opens to a few pools, bathtub-sized and larger, that look better when you get down there than they do from the road. Throw in a great view down the beach toward the Waianae escarpments and you've got yourself a nice spot to enjoy life in Hawaii.

SURF: Wave riders, clever guys, have dubbed the left-break off Pohaku Kulailai at Makua Bay, **Pray for Surf**. More popular is the bodyboarding shore break at **Yokohama Bay**, to the left just as you get there. A curving slope of sand makes for a grandstand to watch these guys get pounded. (Sand that uplifts at the base of the waves is an indication of a shallow landing.)

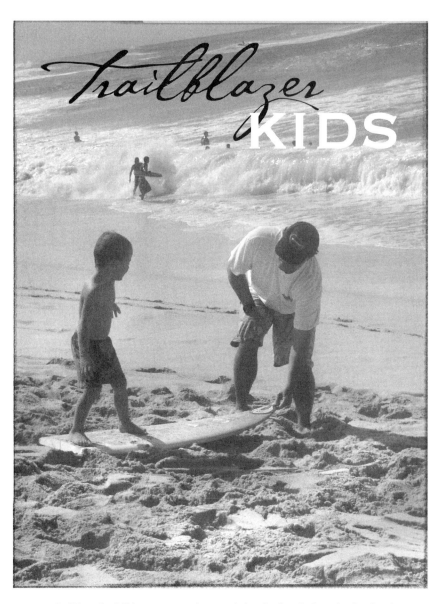

Trailblazer KIDS

In Hawaii, children are reared not only by the family, but also by the ohana—the extended family of 'aunties' and 'uncles' that make up the community. First-year birthday parties are large celebrations, usually taking place at beach parks. The Hawaiian word keiki (KAY-key) means both 'child' and also the green shoot of a new banana plant. Bananas are plants, not trees, and each year a new generation must be nurtured to maturity, just like children.

TH = TRAILHEAD. SEE RESOURCE LINKS FOR PHONE NUMBERS NOT LISTED BELOW. THE ACTIVITIES ARE LISTED IN ORDER OF TRAILHEAD NUMBER.

KEIKI POOLS
YEAR ROUND SAFE PLACES
TO SWIM AND SNORKEL

MAGIC ISLAND TH3, page 42
*Ala Moana's man-made lagoon is
hopping on weekends*
KAHANAMOKU BEACH TH4, page 48
*A shady park backs this beach next
to the Hilton on Waikiki*
KUHIO BEACH PARK TH4, page 44
*Huge concrete pools make for gentle
(sometimes crowded) ocean dipping*
MOTHERS BEACH TH7, page 58
*Plenty of quiet places to spend the
day at long Kahana Beach*
HANAUMA BAY TH20, page 89
*Like taking the kids to a Hollywood
summer blockbuster*
MAKAPU'U KEIKI PONDS TH23,
page 105 *A splash-around pool in the reef*
PAHONU POND TH24, page 109
*Ancient fishpond at Kaiona Beach Park
has a view of Rabbit Island*
KAILUA BEACH PARK TH25, page 110
Perfect for a Windward Coast day at the beach
SECRET ISLAND TH33, page 130
*Tour companies take guests to this quiet
spot at Kualoa Regional Park*
**KULIMA COVE, KAIHALULU
KEIKI POOL** TH38, page 156
*Fill the family album with fantasy
shots; a small sandy pool in the reef*
NIMITZ KEIKI POND TH48, page 196
Quiet tide pool is off the tourist radar
KO OLINA LAGOONS TH50, page 199
*Four man-made and one natural
lagoon are well suited for tourists*
POKAI BEACH PARK TH52, page 203
*The kids may meet some Hawaiian
keikis at the West Side's safest swim spot*
KAENA KEIKI POND TH54, page 213
*Scenic and secluded; not easy to spot
from the car*

NATURE WALKS

KEAIWA HEIAU TH10, page 64
MOANALUA VALLEY TH11, page 65
The seven bridges spell fun
**KANEALOLE TRAIL-HAWAII NATURE
CENTER** TH14, page 75
LYON ARBORETUM-MANOA FALLS
TH15, page 78
Tropical fairyland with a choice of easy hikes
KOKO CRATER BOTANICAL GARDENS
TH21, page 92
*Cacti look like they were invented by
animators*
LIKEKE WATERFALL TH29, page 119
A quick adventure at the base of the pali
HO'OMALUHIA BOTANICAL GARDENS
TH30, page 120
KAWELA BAY TH38, page 155
*Take little tropical walks while
enjoying a day at the beach*
'LOST' BEACH TH44, page 178
*Scenes from the TV program are
filmed around this beach.*
WAHIAWA BOTANICAL GARDEN
TH46, page 191
*Footbridges, vintage lamp posts and wandering
walkways make this freebie the best picnic stop
on the way to the North Shore.*

KIDS VIEW HIKES

DIAMOND HEAD TH6, page 54
*No one in the family will forget this
hike to a Honolulu panorama*
**TANTALUS-PU'U UALAKA'A STATE
LOOKOUT** TH14, page 76
*Tantalus is an easy achievement;
the lookout is a gimme from the car*
MAKAPU'U LIGHTHOUSE ROAD TH22,
page 101
The road is easy for beginners
KAWAI RIDGE TH25, page 109
A doable challenge for the little ones
OLD PALI HIGHWAY TH28, page 116
*A quick getaway on an old road being
swallowed by the jungle*
KEANIANI LOOKOUT TH34, page 132
An ancient fisherman's bay view

BEST BEACH PICNIC PARKS

ALA MOANA BEACH PARK TH3, page 40
*Safe swimming, spacious grounds, and close to
fancy shopping. Jumpin' on weekends.*
DUKE KAHANAMOKU BEACH PARK
TH4, page 45
Tucked into Waikiki

KAPIOLANI BEACH PARK TH5, page 50
*The zoo and aquarium, plus outdoor events,
liven things up. Walk from Waikiki*
WAIALAE BEACH PARK TH7, page 57
*Good swimming with shaded arbor; close to
dolphins*
KAWAIKUI BEACH PARK TH18, page 85
*The best stop going to or coming
from Hanauma Bay*
KAILUA BEACH PARK TH25, page 110
Kayak and swim. Big spreading lawn and trees
KOKOLOLIO BEACH PARK TH36,
page 148
*What a beauty: rolling parklands and a
crescent of sand*
HALEIWA ALI'I BEACH PARK TH43,
page 174
All kine water sports in Haleiwa
WHITE PLAINS BEACH PARK
TH48, page 194
*Easy-going surf scene, nice park,
and a snack bar*

FORESTED PICNIC SPOTS

WA'AHILA RIDGE RECREATION AREA
TH16, page 81
A forest with a view close to Waikiki
**WAIMANALO STATE RECREATION
AREA** TH24, page 107
HO'OMALUHIA BOTANICAL GARDENS
TH30, page 120
*A flowered arboretum with the Ko'olau Pali in
your face*
MALAEKAHANA RECREATION AREA
TH37, page 152
Goat Island floats offshore
KAIAKA BEACH PARK TH43, page 174
Spacious lawn and trees, near Haleiwa

FAMILY ATTRACTIONS

HAWAII MARITIME CENTER TH1,
page 32
HONOLULU ACADEMY OF THE ARTS
TH1, page 39
*Each child gets to hunt for 'heroes and heroines'
and other art treasures.*

FREE FAMILY ATTRACTIONS

Dolphin Quest at Kahala Mandarin

RESORTS WITH KEIKI PROGRAMS
Most of the activities are for kids aged 5 to 12.

ASTON HOTELS & RESORTS 800-655-6055—*Kids stay and eat for free when Mom & Dad rent a 1 bedroom suite, and they also get an ID card that's good for free admissions.*

STARWOOD HOTELS 931-8232—*The Keiki Aloha program means 'good-bye' for the day as children go off on excursions to Waikiki Aquarium, Diamond Head, and many other indoor and outdoor fun places. Parents may wish to tag along. Several resorts participate, including the Royal Hawaiian and Moana Surfrider, Waikiki's vintage beauties.*

HYATT REGENCY 800-233-1234—*An on-site Camp Hyatt has Hawaiian games and crafts and a classics library, plus the stuff kids really want to do: watch Disney DVDs and play Nintendo.*

JW IHILANI(MARIOTT) RESORT 800-679-0079—*The younger ones will be ready for beddy after a day in the Keiki Beachcomber Club, spent on treasure hunts, doing hula, and crafting.*

KAHALA MANDARIN ORIENTAL 738-8911—*Hawaiian crafts and traditional games give the Keiki Club high marks for spreading aloha. Dolphins in the resort's lagoon are a big thrill.*

OUTRIGGER RESORTS 923-0711—*Cowabunga Kids Club likes to teach beginning water sports, like bodyboarding and fishing, but lei making and other crafts are in the mix. Mom & Dad can take part in some of the fun.*

WAIKIKI BEACH RESORT 922-6611—*Who wants to make a model of an erupting volcano, dance the hula, and paint on Hawaiian tapa club? The Keiki Klub kids, that's who.*

free advice & opinion

DISCLAIMER

Think of this book as you would any other piece of outdoor gear: It will help you do what you want to do, but it depends solely upon you to supply responsible judgment and common sense. Weather and new rules may alter the condition of trails and beach access. The publisher and authors are not responsible for injury, damage, or legal violations that may occur when someone is using this guidebook. Please contact public agencies to familiarize yourself with the most current rules and regulations. Posted signs and changes in trail status determined by public agencies supersede any recommendations in this book. Okay, now be careful and go out there and have fun.

HIKING

Always stay on the trail ... Walking off-trail in Hawaii leads to getting lost or injured ... If you lose the trail, go back to a known spot ... Look back as you hike to memorize your return route ... Leave a marker as you pass confusing junctions ... Then remove the marker on your return ... Never take a guess to make a loop trail ... Note your departure time and know how many hours of daylight you have to hike ... Turn around before half the hours are used up ... Always carry an equipped day pack, see *Packlist* below ... Cell phone coverage is good on Oahu: 911 ... Know what trail you are on ... Carry at least two liters of water per person ... And drink it ... Never drink untreated stream water ... Stay calm if you get lost ... Food, rest, and water will lead to clear thought ... You won't freeze on Oahu ... Stay put if darkness settles in and you are without a flashlight ...

Never walk downhill with your hands in your pockets ... Accidents are more likely coming back from a peak hike ... Your legs are tired and your eyes are farther away from the ground going downhill ... And you're thinking about a beer or ice cream rather than concentrating on the climb ... Wear mud-colored dark shorts ... A retractable hiking pole is a helping hand on Hawaiian trails ... Roots, rocks, and slick surfaces are tough on footing ... Look where you step ... Always stay back from drop-offs ... Greenery disguises cliff edges ... Old lava tubes are also booby traps under greenery ... Dirt and rocks are unstable ... Never trust an embedded rock ... Watch the keikis at all times ... Flash floods occur in valleys and gulches ... Don't hike gullies in the rain ... You will hear a flash flood coming ... Get to high ground ... Never cross a high stream ... If caught on the wrong side, wait until the flow subsides ... Don't linger under cliff faces or waterfalls: landslides and falling rocks ...

Hike with a buddy or two ... And stay together on the trail ... Let someone know about your hiking plans ... Check the weather report ... Keep an eye on the sky... Rain makes trails very slick, and visibility becomes zero ... Wear white or bright colors ... You'll be easy to spot if lost ... And hunters are out in forest reserves on weekends and holidays ... Always yield the trail to an enraged wild pig ... Use boot brushes located at many trailheads to keep weed seeds out of native forests and natural areas ... Don't take risks if your gut says no ... Know your capabilities ... Eat before you're hungry, drink before thirsty ...

When beach hiking, always keep an eye on the waves ... Stay well back of the surf line, especially on sloping sand ... Rogue waves—freak waves that are larger than others—arrive without warning and snatch beachcombers ... Don't forget sun protections ... Wind will disguise the heat: keep drinking fluids ... Barefoot beach walking is the ultimate foot massage and treatment ... If caught on hot sand with bare feet, dig down a few inches to where the sand is cool; then continue and repeat as necessary ... Beaches are public property ... Unless the military says keep out ... Now drink some more water.

SNORKELING

Waves bring rip current ... All that water coming in has to go back out: Look for blue channels through the reef, and foamy areas where the wave pattern is broken down ... Float and look at the bottom to see if you're being carried away ... Also note a fixed point on the shore ... Throw a stick in before you jump in, to see if it floats away ... Higher surf means stronger current ... Don't try to swim against a rip current ... It will release you not far offshore ... To escape a rip current, swim perpendicular to the current (usually you swim almost parallel to the shore) ... Don't panic or tire yourself out; saltwater is easy to float on ... Always swim with fins ... Swim with a buddy ... Or have a swimming partner stay on shore to watch you—and your stuff ... Don't be shy about asking lifeguards about safe places to swim ... Just because you see other people in the water doesn't mean it's safe ... Every beach is both safe and dangerous, depending on the day ...

Don't' take your eyes off the kids ... Sloping sand means deeper water at the shore, and the likelihood of an undertow ... Dry your beach towel by pining it in the rolled-up car window ... You can buy inexpensive swimsuits and snorkeling equipment in Hawaii ... Longs Drugs is a good place ... Use a liquid defogger to keep your mask from clouding up ... Or spit in it ... Snorkeling is usually best at high tide ... Don't step on coral: It's alive and you will kill it ... Monk seals are the only mammals allowed to be naked on Hawaiian beaches ... It is both impolite and illegal to approach a beached monk seal ... Wet suit booties (or surf shoes that fit inside the flippers) help with rocky entries ... Only professional clowns can walk forward with fins on ... Try entering the water with your mask on and putting on the flippers when bobbing in waist deep water ... Don't feed the fish; you disturb the ecological balance of the reef ...

Watch for boat traffic ... Touching a finger to the top of your head is the diver's sign to say you're okay ... When snorkeling offshore, have a buoy with a diver's flag ... Don't touch sea turtles ... Sticking your hand in a hole in the reef is also a bad idea ... At out-of-the way, rocky places, watch the surf for at least five minutes before going in ... If in doubt, don't go out ... Good judgment beats the most dangerous conditions.

SURFING

Get friendly with local guys before getting out there ... Especially on the West Side ... Beginners should always hire an instructor ... Longboard surfing will be easiest for beginners ... on small waves ... Bodysurfing attracts beginners, and also has the most neck and head injuries ... Sand being drawn up the face of a wave is an indication of a shallow break ... Eddie would go ... See *Best Of* section for surfing spots ... The big waves hit the North Shore in the winter... High surf rolls in without storms or wind ... Surfing is life.

DRIVING AROUND

More than a million people live on Oahu, well over ten times the population of Kauai, which is of similar size. Drivers on Oahu are less cutthroat than those in the typical metropolitan area on the mainland, but road rage is not unheard of and gridlock is commonplace in certain areas at certain times. Given the oddball topography of Oahu—two mountain ranges, steep ravines, coastal marshlands—visitors at times will marvel at the achievement of the road system, particularly the H-3 freeway, a Disney ride that penetrates the windward pali with no exits for a dozen miles. At other times, drivers will recoil in horror at a Byzantine nightmare, where freeway exits have no corresponding on-ramps, roads intertwine like spaghetti, street names change indiscriminately, and signage is inscrutable.

To Drive or Not to Drive? For independent adventure travelers, a rental car is nearly essential. But on Oahu, many attractions are within walking distance of Waikiki, and major attractions like the USS Arizona Memorial at Pearl Harbor and Polynesian Cultural Center are serviced by shuttle buses and tour companies. Oahu also has a very good system of public bus transportation servicing the entire island (see *Transportation* in *Resource Links*). So, visitors here for a short time could opt out of a car.

Car Break-ins: Among all the states, Hawaii ranks at or near the top when it comes to property crime, mainly due to car break-ins and thefts on Oahu. (Relax; Hawaii ranks at or near the bottom when it comes to robbery, assault, and other crimes against people.) Ask your car rental company about their policy concerning break-ins. Call your insurance company before leaving to make sure you are covered. Also, many credit card companies offer supplemental insurance, but to collect  from them is like squeezing blood from a turnip. American Express has customer-friendly policies. If you have coverage, be sure to decline the car rental company's insurance when you pick up your car.

Avoiding Car Break-ins: Thieves on the neighbor islands know to just rip off tourist cars, but Oahu is an equal-opportunity island. Locals get hit along with tourists, even the cars of professional surfers. Statistically speaking, you are not likely to be a victim, but you might as well take precautions: *Always leave your car free of valuables.* Have your stuff in a knapsack that comes out of the car when you do. Don't think the trunk is safe, and certainly avoid putting items in there at a parking space. Look around when you park. These days, thieves commonly are a guy and girl working together. Also, a guy parked with his hood up may be scoping cars to break in. It's best not to leave a cooler or anything that might contain a valuable that's visible in the car; even though you may not lose anything, filing an insurance claim and picking up a fresh car is a hassle. Red cars and convertibles are more likely to get broken into. Avoid parking in an area that has broken glass on the ground, the telltale sign of previous break-ins. You can "localize" your car by hanging beads or a lei from the rearview mirror and adding a bumper sticker to the back window—and by not leaving maps spread out—but these techniques are less effective on Oahu. Some people leave their car unlocked. Also, it won't hurt to leave a note: "This car is free of valuables."

Road rules: Remember that for many Hawaiian drivers, red stop lights are just a suggestion, so look both ways before proceeding on a green. Drive aloha: allow lane changes and merges. The late-evening and pre-dawn hours see more than the average numbers of driving whackos, so be extra careful.

Maps: The directions and maps in Oahu Trailblazer are good enough. But should you miss a turn, you can easily become lost. Street names are unpronounceable to newcomers and roads connect illogically. Independent travelers will want to buy a roadmap or map book, preferably the Hawaii TMK's Oahu Mapbook, XXL edition. See *Supplemental Maps* in *Resource Links*. Outside the metro Oahu area, maps are not as important. In all areas, drivers will benefit from having a map-savvy co-pilot.

Directions: Old-timers still say 'Ewa' to mean 'West' and 'Diamond Head' for 'East,' regardless of whether you happen to be east or west of these places. On all the islands, left and right are avoided in directions. People instead say 'mauka,' meaning turn inland or toward the mountains; and 'makai,' to turn toward the coast. Nowadays, 'McDonalds' is used frequently, as in, "take Vineyard Avenue to the left, Honolulu turn right, go two McDonalds, and make a left." If all the McDonalds on Oahu were on the coast (thankfully they are not) you could grab a Big Mac every two miles.

Touring Time: In many vacation spots, sightseers wishing to avoid crowds can head out at dawn. On Oahu, that strategy will put you in commute traffic. If you leave earlier than the commuters, you will get places too early, since the island is not that large. A departure at 8:30 seems to work well—after commute and before shopping and most tourist traffic.

Driving the Freeways and Highways: Hawaii has four freeways, affectionately known as H-1, H-78, H-2, and H-3. H-1, the longest, runs east-west, from near Hawaii Kai to Kapolei. H-78 is a short, east-west segment that runs mauka H-1, by-passing the airport; it veers away from H-1 and then rejoins it. When coming to and from Honolulu on H-1, the H-78 signs can be confusing as all get out—but no sweat. Unless you are going to the airport or Pearl Harbor, it doesn't matter which road you take. H-1 generally has less traffic, however. During morning commute hours and from late afternoon until dinnertime, both H-1 and H-78 are jammed, commonly in both directions from Hawaii Kai to west of the airport—where H-3, H-78, and H-1 merge hellishly. Outside of this freeway corridor the commute traffic is straightforward: toward Honolulu in the morning, away in the evening. This pattern works well for tourists, who are generally leaving Honolulu in the mornings and coming back in the evenings.

H-3, accessible from both H-1 and H-78 west of Honolulu, essentially connects Pearl Harbor with Kaneohe Marine Corps base on the Windward Coast. H-3 is the fastest way over the Ko'olau Mountains—and also an astounding engineering achievement. During your stay, make sure to take H-3 from the Windward Coast to Honolulu. You'll speed airborne toward a head-on collision at the vertical mountains before entering a long tunnel. Highway 61 (the Pali Highway) and Highway 63 (the Likelike Highway) are roads with cross traffic that go through tunnels in the Ko'olaus, also reaching the Windward Coast; these highways run parallel, fairly close together from Honolulu. H-2, west of Pearl Harbor, is the fast track to the North Shore, as long as you're not trying it during evening commute time.

Highway 72 begins where H-1 ends, going east from Honolulu. A two-lane scenic road, Highway 72 loops around Koko Head to Waimanalo. Sightseers often take Highway 72 east, and then return to Waikiki via H-3, Highway 61, or Highway 63.

Kamehameha Highway: Let's start simply by saying the Kamehameha Highway is Highway 83, a scenic two-lane blacktop that goes around the North Shore from Kaneohe to Haleiwa. Sightseers commonly take H-2 to Wahiawa, drive the Kamehameha Highway around the North Shore, and return to Honolulu s via H-3. Now let's complicate matters by saying that the route of Kamehameha Highway is also chopped to smithereens by newer roads on Oahu, and, depending where you are, is also shown as Highway 830, 99, or 80.

Farrington Highway: This four-lane road with plenty of cross-traffic that runs from the west end of H-1 in Kapolei, through Waianae, and around Kaena Point to Haleiwa— except for a five-mile section around the point that is closed to passenger vehicles and used by hikers. On the north side, the Mokuleia Coast, it's Highway 930, a very scenic, undeveloped two-lane road. On the West Side (where the Farrington starts out as four-lane Highway 93 and becomes two-lane 930 north of Makaha) the route is also scenic, although often congested in the evenings coming into Waianae. But this is one traffic jam you might want to get in, kind of like cruising the main drag, *Waianae Graffiti*, if you will. Sunsets are beautiful, as are the valley views toward the Waianae Range. You're crawling along, able to take in the scenery as well as the unique sights of the West Side—a world unto itself. Traffic ends at Makaha, and you can continue to the wild beaches at Kaena Point State Park. Returning to Honolulu is a breeze on a traffic-free freeway.

The H-1

STRATEGIES FOR VISITING OAHU

More than any other Hawaiian island, Oahu can yield a vastly different vacation experience, depending on where you choose to stay.

Waikiki Monk Seal: Most visitors to Oahu jet into Honolulu and stay amid the high-rises of Waikiki, which is a fantastic place. This can be the least-expensive way to visit Hawaii: Shuttles and buses are available from the airport, and visitors can find plenty to do within the Waikiki area, using the downtown trolley system and buses to visit nearby attractions, such as the USS Arizona Memorial, Hanauma Bay for snorkeling, Ala Moana, Bishop museum, historic Honolulu, and so forth. Room packages are available. And you don't have the expense of a rental car or an inter-island flight. Hawaii first-timers, especially those staying for a week or less, may like this option. People who want to stay put and relax, interrupted only to do glamour shopping and enjoy dinner and nightlife, may also prefer the life of a Waikiki Monk Seal. You'll find plenty of safe swimming beaches year-round. If you have a car, you'll have ready access to the metro-mauka trail system—many of the best trails on Oahu lie in the mountains above Honolulu. And you can always jet around the island for the day—via rental car, private tour, or public bus. *Downside*: Most hiking trailheads are not readily accessible via public transportation. A much different, rural Oahu and more remote beach parks await outside of greater Waikiki, and independent travelers need wheels to get out there and see it. And, if that's your preference, driving back to Waikiki every night doesn't make sense.

North Shore Surfer Dude: The North Shore is opposite Waikiki more than just geographically. Restaurants are few, nightlife is minimal, and dressing up means adding flip-flops and a T-shirt to the bathing suit. Kamehameha Highway is a two-lane country blacktop. Beach cottages are strung along a rural landscape and a shoreline that is almost a continuous run of beaches. During the winter months, you'll be in the thick of monstrous waves that attract professional surfers. From the North Shore, you can readily access the Windward Coast, and the Mokuleia coastline—both offering good surf 'n' trail recreational opportunities. You can also make day trips into Waikiki and Honolulu to see those sights. Turtle Bay Resort is one of Oahu's best, and features hiking trails and remote beachscapes. Otherwise, you'll need to stay in a B&B, cottage, or one of the rustic lodging places, like Camp Erdman or Malaekahana. *Downside:* If nightlife is your thing, the North Shore will be lacking. You will also miss easy access to Honolulu's museums and attractions. There are some excellent hikes in nearby Molukeia and Kahana, but you will not be close to many of the tropical valleys and waterfall hikes. In the winter, ocean conditions are not the best for swimming, although Turtle Bay has year-around possibilities. There are few resorts or condos to provide a compromise destination—between big-time Turtle Bay and small-time B&Bs.

Other-Shore Surfer Dude: The Windward Coast and the West Side are two other options to staying in Waikiki—and these are vastly different from each other. On the Windward Coast are excellent beaches at Makapu'u, Waimanalo, Lanikai, and Kailua. Kualoa Park, Kahana, and Malaekahana are not far up the coast. Honolulu-Waikiki is not far away, via either Highway 72 around Koko Head, or Highways 61 or 63 through the pali. Close by are tropical hikes beneath the pali, and into some of the valleys. Lodging will be mainly in B&Bs or cottages. *Windward Downside:* Sunset comes early and rains gather against the pali. Kailua-Kaneohe, though not Honolulu, is fairly densely populated. Nightlife is scarce (though there are a number of good bars and restauanats), but then Honolulu is a reasonable drive away.

On the West Side, you will find far fewer tourists, but among them are people who would stay nowhere else. Traffic can be a hassle, but if you time it right, Honolulu with its attractions and trails is less than an hour's drive. The West Side gets beautiful sunsets, and the Waianae valleys are underrated scenically. Cheap restaurants abound, but there's little touristy nightlife. The Hawaiian Princess is right on a nice beach, and the Makaha Valley Towers (six high-rise buildings) stand alone in an otherwise undeveloped valley—one on Oahu's most dramatic places to stay. Pokai Beach Park and nearby Ko Olina Resort have good swimming all year. Kaena Point State Park is a wild, undeveloped seascape. *West Side Downside:* The ambiance, to use a non-West Side word, will be far too gritty for many visitors. For short vacations, the driving may be cumbersome, although Ko Olina Resort is a nice (pricey) alternative it's located at the end of the H-1 freeway with easy access to Honolulu and the North Shore, and the tourist atmosphere will suit visitors.

Bi-Coastal: If the above options create a dilemma, the obvious solution is to do a stint in Waikiki, followed by a stay on the North Shore, Windward Coast, or the West Side. You can catch the city sights, and perhaps avoid renting a car until it's time to move. *Downside:* The Bi-Coastal option works best for vacations longer than a week.

PACKLIST
For one- to two-week visit.

Slippers
    (a.k.a flip-flops, go-aheads, zories)
Airport & dress-up shoes
    (clean athletic shoes, sandals)
Hiking shoes (cross-trainers, lightweight
    hikers; to get muddy)
Surf shoes (bootie style or Teva; optional)
Khaki pants plus aloha shirt or polo shirt
    (men, for airport and dress-up)
One piece dress or Dri-fit pants and jacket
    (women; for airport and dress-up)
Swimming suit
Sarong to wrap around waist
    (women, optional beach wear)
Shorts (two pair)
Short sleeve tops
    (3 or 4, quick-dry synthetic)
Long sleeve tops
    (1 or 2, quick dry synthetic)
Windbreaker (Gore-Tex or equivalent)
Sun hat
Sunglasses
Hiking pole (retractable; optional but useful)
Snorkeling gear (mask, snorkel, fins, mask
    defogger; fins with heel straps and
    booties are good for rocky entries and
    the snorkel-hikes to offshore islands.
    Gear can be purchased cheaply in
    Hawaii.)
Rash guard (Lycra top for surfing and
    snorkeling)
Umbrella (for shade and rain optional)
Daypack
    Antibiotic ointment
    Band Aids
    Camera
    Cell phone
    Flashlight or headlamp
    Food (energy bar for emergency)
    Handkerchief/bandana
    Mosquito repellant
    Sunscreen/lip balm
    Swiss Army knife
    Water (at least two liters per day)
    Water pump or water treatment tablets

GETTING TO KNOW OAHU AFTER THREE DATES

All of the Hawaiian islands tell of being the world's most-isolated landmass, 2,500 miles of open sea in all directions, islands that are actually the tips of the world's tallest mountain range, born of molten lava spewing to this day from the an underwater crack in the earth's crust. All of these islands tell the story of physical transformation by incessant waves, torrential downpour, and winds, along with a consistent barrage of nature's epic events, like tsunamis, volcanic eruptions, earthquakes, landslides, and hurricanes.

All of Hawaii tells of being the last place on earth to be discovered by man, by the seagoing Polynesians, around 200 AD. Finding a land devoid of metals or even clay suitable for pottery, the Polynesians voyaged back and forth across the South Pacific, bringing back with them the plants and animals to make these turbulent lands a perpetual garden. Then the South Pacific migrations ceased, and the Polynesians became the Hawaiians, furthering the bounty of nature, learning the myriad physical details of their new home, and living in comfortable isolation in the middle of the Pacific for some 500 years.

All of Hawaii tells the above story. But only Oahu tells clearly the modern history of Hawaii that is hinged around three years: 1795, 1893, and 1941.

In 1795, after nearly a century of inter-island warfare, Kamehameha's forces came ashore at Waikiki Beach and drove a coalition of Oahu defenders into the mountains, hundreds of them clubbed to a freefall over the Nu'uanu Pali. Although more than a decade would pass before chiefs on Kaua'i capitulated without warfare, the Oahu invasion effectively made Kamehameha the first Hawaiian monarch. Kamehameha succeeded, in part, because a little more than a decade earlier, Western Civilization in the form of British Captain James Cook finally found Hawaii, and Kamehameha was quick to use their weaponry to ensure his victory. Absent the appearance of the Western World, the alternate-universe fate of the Hawaiian Kingdom is open to speculation. Would these people, numbering a half-million or more, have been able to maintain their prosperity without resource depletion and overpopulation, as happened on other island nations? At any rate, the Western World arrived and The Great One died in 1819. The next few years saw the coming of missionaries from the eastern United States, as well as hundreds of whaling ships. Under the successive reign of three of Kamehameha's sons—and aided greatly by the influence of two queens who had been wives of Kamehameha—the Kingdom of Hawaii prospered. Old ways, including the oppressive kapu system of laws, were discarded, and the education and the written language fostered by the missionaries were embraced. In the mid-to-late 1800s, wealthy folks in the American West sent children to Hawaii for an education, which had a higher English literacy rate, even though the Hawaiians had no written language at all prior to the missionaries' arrival.

In 1893, a group of politicians—led by Sanford Dole and others, many of whom were landowners who were the offspring of missionaries—staged a revolt and, with the aid of U.S. Marines, overthrew the monarchy and established a provisional government. During the previous decades, sugar cane had become king in Hawaii, and the monarchs had partnered with Americans rather than the British, French, and Russians, who had other designs on the islands. Hawaiian royalty had traveled the world, and King David Kalakaua, an enlightened Renaissance man who also had a fondness for the finer things, presided over a nation that had modern conveniences in the Iolani Palace before they were installed in the White House. Kalakaua died in San Francisco and his sister, Queen Liliuokalani, became Hawaii's first and only woman monarch. When she tried to alter the kingdom's constitution on behalf of native Hawaiians, the overthrow took place. The Hawaiian army at the time may well have won the battle, but Liliuokalani chose to avoid bloodshed and appeal to the rule of law. Indeed, President Grover Cleveland, after a lengthy inquiry, sided with the Hawaiians and ruled that the monarchy be restored. But Cleveland's ruling was rebuffed. Queen Liliuokalani was imprisoned in Iolani Palace for eight months. The provisional government waited for Republican William McKinley's election in 1898, at which time Hawaii was annexed as a Territory of the United States.

In 1941, on December 7 of course, Japanese warplanes swarmed Oahu and in two hours crippled almost all the Pacific forces of the United States. In the decades leading up to Pearl Harbor, the United States had protested Japan's expansion into Pacific island territories, and the Japanese sneak attack was to delay any interference with Japan's plans. At this point, 90 percent of the native Hawaiians had died due to cholera and other western diseases, and the Hawaiian population was comprised of a 'calabash' of ethnicities who immigrated to work in the cane fields—Chinese, Korean, Filipino, Portuguese, but mainly Japanese, who comprised more than 40 percent. The U.S. had ceased Japanese immigration in the decade prior to Pearl Harbor attack. World War II cemented Oahu as the most strategic piece of ground on earth and military bases and airfields and defense systems popped up everywhere. The G.I.s fell in love with Hawaii, creating a post-war tourist boom that eventually led to statehood in 1959. Ironically, a contingent of Hawaiian-Japanese servicemen who had distinguished themselves in Europe became central in post-war politics that saw the end of the Republican stronghold and the beginning of a Democratic-voting state.

Most visitors don't realize that the issue of Hawaiian sovereignty is still an open legal question. A resolution of the sovereignty issue will add a fourth year of significance to the above three in the history of the Kingdom of Hawaii. Queen Liliuokalani wisely chose the rule of law. Had she chosen war, Hawaii would have been a defeated nation, with greatly diminished legal status in the world court. The metaphorical candle of the monarchy, therefore, has never gone out and that flicker can be seen, among all the islands, most vividly on Oahu.

Resource links

RESOURCE LINKS
All area codes are 808, unless otherwise noted

MUSEUMS & HISTORIC BUILDINGS
Ali'iolani Hale (Judiciary Center) 539-4999
Army Museum, Ft. DeRussy 438-2821, 438-2822
Hawaii Army Museum Society 955-9552
Bishop Museum 847-3511
Membership and contributions 848-4187
Hilton Kalia Tower annex 947-2458, 947-4321
Bowfin Submarine Museum & Park 423-1342, 423-1341
Byodo-In Temple 239-9844, 239-4724
Contemporary Museum, The 526-0232
Hawaii Chinese Museum 595-3358
Hawaii Maritime Center 521-2829
Falls of Clyde 523-6151
Hawaii State Art Museum 586-0900
Hawaii State Capitol 586-0178, 586-0146
Hawaiian Chinese Museum 595-3358
Hawaiian Railway Society 681-5461
Hawaii's Plantation Village 677-0110
Honolulu Academy of Arts 532-8700
  Academy Shop 532-8703
Doris Duke at the Academy (theater) 532-8768
Iolani Palace 522-0832
Friends of Iolani Palace 522-0821
Kawaiahao Church 522-1333
Mission Houses Museum 531-0481
Mormon Temple Visitors Center 293-9297
North Shore Surf & Cultural Museum 637-8888
Queen Emma Summer Palace 595-3167
Royal Mausoleum 536-7602, 587-2590
Tropic Lightning Museum 655-0438

ATTRACTIONS
Aloha Stadium Swap Meet 486-6704
Aloha Tower Marketplace 566-2337
Buffalo's Big Board Surfing Classic 668-9712
Dole Plantation 621-8408
Dolphin Quest 739-8918
Duke's Canoe Club 922-2268
Halemanu Plantation 622-3929
Hawaii Children's Discovery Center 524-5437

ATTRACTIONS CONT'D—

Hawaiian Waters 674-9283
Honolulu Zoo 971-7174, 971-7171
HURL (Hawaii Undersea Research Laboratory) 956-9772
Makai Pier 259-9646
Kualoa Ranch 237-7321
Maunakea Marketplace 5243409
National Memorial Cemetery of the Pacific
Punchbowl 532-3720
Oahu Market 841-6924
Oceanarium 922-1233
Oceanic Institute 259-7951, tours 259-3146
Polynesian Cultural Center 800-367-7060, 233-3333, 293-3305
Sea Life Park 259-7933
Shangri La (Doris Duke's) 866-385-3849, 532-3853
Sunset on the Beach (movies) 923-1094
Top of Waikiki 923-3877
Tropical Farms 877-505-6887
USS Arizona Memorial National Park 422-0561,
Pearl Harbor Memorial Fund 866-332-1941
USS Missouri 973-2494, 423-2263
Waikiki Aquarium 923-9741
Special programs 440-9007
Wee Play & Learn, Hawaii Kai, 396-2100
Windward Open Market (Heʻeia) 948-1111

GARDENS
Aliʻi Tour (Kualoa) 237-8508, 781-2474
Hawaii Nature Center 955-0100
Honolulu Botanical Gardens 522-7060, 522-7064
Foster Botanical Garden 522-7066, 522-7065
Foster Garden Gallery & Bookstore 533-6335
Friends of Honolulu Gardens 537-1708
Hoʻomaluhia Botanical Garden 233-7323
Koko Crater Botanical Garden 522-7060
Liliʻuokalani Botanical Garden 522-7060
Wahiawa Botanical Garden 621-7321
Lyon Arboretum 988-0456
Lyon Arboretum Association 988-0464
Moanalua Gardens Foundation 839-5334
Senator Fong's Plantation Gardens 239-6775
Waimea Valley 638-7766
Waipahu Cultural Garden 677-0110

HAWAII VISITORS BUREAU MARKER

ULUPO HEIAU

HAWAIIANA SHOPS AND GALLERIES

HONOLULU

Ala Moana Shopping Center 955-9517
Aloha Tower Marketplace 566-2337
Bestsellers 528-2378
Bethel Street Gallery 524-3522
Got Art? 521-1097
Hawaiian Quilt Collection 800-367-9987
Hawaiian Ukulele Company 536-3228
Pacific Traditions Gallery 531-5122
Sharky's Tattoo 585-0076

WINDWARD

Rightstar (Byodo-In) 239-9844
Tropical Farms 877-505-6887, 237-1960

NORTH SHORE

H. Miura Store 637-4845
Ron Artis Collection 637-1211
The Only Show in Town 293-1295

ALOHA STADIUM SWAP MEET

On Saturdays, Sundays, and Wednesdays the parking lot around Aloha Stadium comes alive with hundreds of outdoor vending booths catering to souvenir-hungry tourists, as well as locals looking for a good deal. Even moving at a brisk walk, you'll need a couple hours to scan the dizzying array of T-shirts priced at 10 for 20 bucks, koa porpoises, aloha toe rings, Suzy Wong dresses, bobble-head hula dolls, a forest of Hawaiian fabric rolls, vintage ukuleles, and dozens of objets d'art that say "Mahalo for removing your shoes." The scene becomes a blur. Lose your wits and you can become a novelty item back home, attired and accessorized in aloha from head to toe. Food stands are few, although you will find exotic Japanese snacking treats, jars of litchi-mint jam, and dried mangos. On the north end of the stadium are a few lunch wagons serving local-style plates.

The rest room is inside the stadium on the north side at gate six— a chance to peek into the arena that hosts the NFL's Pro Bowl, as well as the home games for the University of Hawaii Rainbow Warriors (whose logo is represented by swap meet vendors). *Tips for visiting:* The Aloha Stadium Swap Meet is a great rainy day event, if you have an umbrella, since the booths are covered. In fact, an umbrella comes in handy on sunny days, when the asphalt bakes and shade is scarce. Buses service Aloha Stadium from Waikiki: routes #20 and #42. To drive, take either H-78 or H-1 west from Honolulu; and watch from stadium exits. Things get started around 6 a.m., but there's no need to be an early bird since goods are abundant and there are no fresh fruits and veggies that get snapped up.

Another tip: For island-fresh produce, head the *Kamehameha Swap Meet*, held on weekends not far away. You'll find fewer tourists at this affair. It's located on the Highway 99 (the Kamehameha Highway) going west from Aloha Stadium. From H-1, take Exit 13A-Aiea and 78 West. (Or take H-78 west; this freeway ends and becomes the Kamehameha Highway.) A mile west of the stadium, turn right (mauka) on Kaonohi. Go up the hill and—across from Macys and before you reach Monanlua Road—turn left into the Kamehameha Swap Meet. The fruit-and-veggie vendors occupy the grounds of an old drive-in movie.

All area codes are 808

HIKING & CAMPING PERMITS, CLUBS
STATE
Department of Land & Natural Resources
   Camping permits 587-0300
Forestry and Wildlife (maps, hike permits) 587-0166
Conservation hotline 587-0077
Makiki visitors center 973-9778
Na Ala Hele trails (hikes permits) 973-9782, www.hawaiitrails.org
Ahupua'a O Kahana State Park 237-7766
Friends of He'eia State Park 247-3156
Division of State Parks and Recreation (permits) 768-3440
COUNTY
City & County of Honolulu 523-4523
Hanauma Bay information 396-4229
White Plains 684-5133
Stairway to Heaven-Haiku Stairs 233-7303, 527-6637
PRIVATE
Camp Timberline 672-5441, 877-672-4386
Dole Company 621-3204
Hawaii Nature Center 955-0100
Hawaii Reserves, Inc. (BYU-Laie) 293-9201
Hawaiian Trail & Mountain Club 674-1459, 377-5442
James Campbell National Wildlife Refuge 637-6330
Moanalua Valley 839-5334
The Nature Conservancy,
   537-4508
Sierra Club 538-6616
Waialua Sugar Co. 637-3521
MILITARY
Poamoho Ridge 656-1028
Schofield-Waikane 656-1027,
   ext. 113, fax 656-8200

CAMPING AND RUSTIC ACCOMMODATIONS

Call for rates and availability. City & County of Honolulu beach parks 768-3440, www.co.honolulu.hi.us/parks/permits. For state park sites call 587-0300; www. hawaiistateparks.org Many state and county campgrounds normally do not allow camping on Wednesday and Thursday nights.

HONOLULU

Keaiwa Heiau State Recreation Area, Aiea
> *Easy access to central Oahu. Nice campground in gardenlike setting on 400 acres.*

Sand Island State Recreation Area
> *Open campground with a great view across the water at downtown Honolulu. Nice beach sunsets. Only open Friday, Saturday, and Sunday, and can be crowded.*

WINDWARD

Camp Kokokahi, Kaneohe 247-2124
> *A 10-acre conference center on Kaneohe Bay. Tent sites and lodge that accommodates groups.*

Ahupuaʻa O Kahana State Park
> *Beautiful tropical setting, but it does get rain and the facilities are not well maintained.*

Bellows Field Beach Park, Waimanalo
> *Campground with 50 sites in scenic forest with a great beach. Only open on three weekend nights and it gets heavy use.*

Hauʻula Beach Park, Hauʻula
> *Close to highway in town, but not bad.*

Hoʻomaluhia Botanical Garden (county), Kaneohe
> *Magnificent setting below the pali on wide-open grassy camp area with a cooking pavilion. Only open three weekend nights.*

Kokololio Beach Park, Laie
> *One of the prettiest beach parks in Hawaii. Just south of town, with 5 campsites. Nice beach with large treed landscaping.*

Kualoa 'B' Regional Park
> *About 30 sites at a nice forest-and-beach country, with scenic mauka views. Historic park with Chinaman's Hat island offshore. Good access to the North Shore, and not far south to Kailua.*

Swanzy Beach Park, Kaʻaʻawa
> *Located in quiet commercial area just south of Ahupuaʻa O Kahana State Park. A 5-acre lawn with trees fronts a seawall, and has 9 campsites. Only open on the three weekend days.*

Waimanalo Beach Park
> *More than 20 sites on 40 beachfront acres. Scenic place, just out of town, with good swimming. Popular among locals. (May be closeed.)*

Waimanalo Recreation Area (county)
> *Huge ironwood forest and long, scenic swimming beach make for good camping. Park has night security. (May be closed.)*

NORTH SHORE

Camp Erdman, Mokuleia, 637-4615
> *A YMCA camp with clean cabins and tent sites set on the beach, a few miles west of Haleiwa. Cabins nicely spaced. Among the best beach cabins in Hawaii.*

Hawaii Backpackers, Pupukea, 888-628-8882, 638-7838
> *Located across from Three Tables snorkel site is tropical setting. Close to bus stop and a few minute walk to a supermarket. Accommodations range from $25 hostel rooms to private rooms with kitchen at $125 and up. No camping. Airport pick up.*

Kaiaka Bay Beach Park, Haleiwa
> *Quiet location, just outside of town. Pretty peninsula with ironwoods as huge beach trees. Night security. Better than decent.*

Malaekahana State Recreation Area, Laie
> *Huge forested campground on a beautiful beach. Very scenic spot with nicely kept campground.*

Malaekahana, Friends of Laie, 293-1737
> *Yurts, funky cabins, and tent sites on the beach, right next to the state recreation area. Not exactly aesthetic, but not bad.*

Mokuleia Beach Park, Mokuleia
> *The park's 15 open sites are along the low dune of an undeveloped coast a few miles west of Haleiwa. Good place but may be closed.*

Surfhouse Hawaii, Haleiwa, 637-7146
> *Walking distance from beaches. Tropical setting in town. Tent spaces, shared rooms and cabins, and private cabins with baths. Clean.*

WEST SIDE

Camp Timberline, Kapolei, 672-5441, 877-672-4386
> *Nonprofit school for kids set on 10 acres at 2,000 above Ewa. Several group cabins and a few tents. Safe and hang-loose with central-island location. You'll need a car.*

Camp Waianae, Waianae, 595-7591
> *A Seventh Day Adventist camp in Waianae Valley with a half-dozen cabins and tent spaces. Kitchen and dining hall, along with a swimming pool.*

Eisenhower Beach Park 684-5133
> *Large campground in ironwood forest on the beach in Ewa between Nimitz and White Plains beach parks. No facilities but, some of the best beach camping in Hawaii. Operated jointly by the county and the military.*

Keaʻau Beach Park, Makaha
> *Open bluff out of commercial area has 25 campsites. Will be a bit too 'local' for many visitors.*

Lualualei Beach Park, Waianae
> *The 6 sites are along the highway in a commercial district. Not bad, but it will be too 'local' for most tourists.*

Maili Beach Park, Maili
> *Within a commercial district, but the park has 12 sites on a large open lawn that fronts a pretty sand beach. Surfing competitions take place. Big parties on weekends, the only days camping is available.*

ADVENTURE TOURS, BIKE RENTALS, SPORTS SHOPS
HONOLULU

Aloha Dive, Honolulu 395-5922
Adventures Extreme Hawaii 573-5100
AquaZone, Waikiki 923-3483
Big Kahuna (bike rentals, weekly rates) 924-2736
Boca Hawaii (bike rentals) 591-9839
Coconut Cruisers (bike rentals, good weekly rates) 924-1644
Bike Hawaii, John Alford (also snorkel, hike)
    877-682-7433, 734-4214
Breeze Hawaii Diving Adventures 735-1857
Dino Ching, Waikiki surf instructor 922-2993
Discover Hidden Hawaii Tours 946-4432
Hans Hedemann Surf School 924-7778
Hawaiian Fire Surf School 384-8855
Hawaiian Ocean Promotions, Hawaii Kai 369-9169
> *Shuttle service to Hanauma Bay*

Hawaiian Watersports 255-4352
Hike Oahu 955-4453
Oahu Nature Tours 924-2473
Paradise (bike rentals) 946-7777
Snorkel Bob's 735-7944
Town & Country Surf Shop 483-8383

WINDWARD

Kailua Sailboards & Kayaks 262-2555
Kualoa Ranch 237-8515
Mauka Makai Excursions 593-3525
Two Good Kayaks 262-5656

NORTH SHORE

Country Cycles (bike rentals) Pupukea 638-8866
(inexpensive daily rates and great weekly rates)
Deep Ecology, Haleiwa 800-578-3992, 637-7946
Glider Rides 677-3404
North Shore (Quiksilver) Boardriders Club 637-5026
Patagonia 637-1245
Surf-N-Sea, Haleiwa 800-899-7873, 637-9887
Tropical Rush 687-8886

WEST SIDE

Hale Nalu Surf Company (also bike rentals) 696-5897
Wild Side Specialty Tours (marine) 306-7273

VISITOR INFORMATION & LOCAL CONTACTS

Haleiwa Main Street 637-4558
Oahu Visitors Bureau 877-525-6248
Office of Hawaiian Affairs 594-1888
Surf Reports 596-7873 (SURF)
Weather 973-4380

SUPPLEMENTAL MAPS

The maps and descriptions in *Oahu Trailblazer* are enough to get you by. People staying in Waikiki, or anywhere for that matter, who mainly want to relax and hit a few highlights will do okay with this book and the maps provided for free in various tourist publications. But independent adventure travelers who want to take a good look around will need a road map, preferably a map book. *Recommended:* The TMK Oahu Mapbook and the Map of Oahu by the University of Hawaii Press work well together.

MAP BOOKS

Hawaii TMK's Oahu Mapbook, XXL edition, 533-4601,
www.hawaiitmkmaps.com Large format (8.5 by 11 inches) and clean graphics cover the island in 99 maps. This is the best available and a very useful tool for independent travelers.
The Oahu Mapbook by Phears, 877-828-4852, www.booklines.com
Readily available and popular. Graphics are good. This one uses 164 maps to cover the island, which involves more flipping around.
Rand McNally also publishes a mapbook that is adequate; check on-line.

MAPS

Map of Oahu, The Gathering Place, 956-8255, www.uhpress.hawaii.edu
Indexed place names and trail locations. Will work as a road map in a pinch. The U of H maps are a must for Hawaii visitors.

The Oahu Travel Map by Phears, 877-828-4852, www.booklines.com
A poor man's map book that gives more street detail than any other foldout map. Since much detail is given, the graphics bit crammed.

AAA Honolulu (city series), and Hawaii, 800-736-2886, www.aaa.com
These two maps double up to provide an adequate road map as well as general reference.

USGS Topographic Map of the Island of Oahu, 888-ASK-USGS
A single map (scale 1:62500) gives hikers the big picture on island topography.

The Island of Oahu, Oahu Visitors Bureau, 877-525-OAHU
A comic book version, really, but useful for locating hotels and points of interest. It's free.

Franko's Oahu Surfing Map, www.frankosmaps.com
Surfers and surf fans will like this one. Has island-wide map, plus details for the North Shore and the greater Waikiki coastline.

Franko's Map of Oahu, The Gathering Place, www.frankosmaps.com
Has an excellent Waikiki section and fairly good detail on trail locations. Not a must-have, however.

Oahu Recreation Map, Department of Land & Natural Resources, 587-0300
The state park's map needs updating and difficult to come by. Give them a call to see if a new version is available.

Trail Maps, State Division of Forestry & Wildlife, 587-0166
Trail maps—7.5 series topos printed on letter-sized paper—are available for free, along with summaries of the routes; a handy source for hikers.

TRANSPORTATION

AIRLINES

America West 800-235-9292
American 800-433-7300, 833-7600
Continental 800-523-3273
Delta 800-221-1212
Hawaiian Airlines 800-367-5320, 838-1555
United 800-864-8331

THEBUS (route information, fares) 848-5555
Public bus service to all of Oahu; fare is $2 per adult; no change. Excellent maps and printed schedules available. www.thebus.org
Bus passes 848-4444, customer service 848-4500
24-hour recorded information 296-1818

Popular routes from Kuhio at Waikiki to:
>Airport #19, #20
>Ala Moana Center #8, #19, #20, #42, #58
>Aloha Stadium #20, #42
>Diamond Head #22, #58
>Chinatown, Downtown #2, #13, #19, #20, #42
>Hanauma Bay #22
>Pearl Harbor-USS Arizona Memorial #20, #42
>Wahiawa-Circle Isle #52 (go to Ala Moana, get transfer)

WAIKIKI TROLLEY 593-2822

Four different lines (pink, yellow, red, and blue) with open-air cars service greater Honolulu from Waikiki. Buy one-day pass from their website and get a second pass at half-off; buy a multi-day (four-day) pass from the website and receive a second pass free:
www.waikikitrolley.com

>PINK LINE-ALA MOANA SHOPPING SHUTTLE—*Loops around Waikiki with pickups every 10 minutes. Goes west to Ala Moana. Fare is $2 each ride.*
>YELLOW LINE-SHOPPING AND DINING—*Take Pink Line to Ala Moana; free transfer to Yellow Line—Service to Aloha Tower and shopping centers. $2 each ride.*
>RED LINE-HONOLULU CITY LINE—*From Ala Moana Center, through downtown and Chinatown and as far west as Bishop Museum. One-day fare, $25; includes unlimited boarding of all lines. Multi-day (four days) is $45, and includes all lines for consecutive days.*
>BLUE LINE-OCEAN COAST LINE—*From Waikiki to Diamond Head, Hanauma Bay, and Makapu'u. Fares are the same as the Red Line.*

CAR RENTALS

All major companies plus a few others, serve Oahu, most of which have offices at the airport as well as at Waikiki—giving you flexibility when planning your trip. Shop around. See *Driving Around* on page 222 for tips on renting a car.
Make sure your hotel has parking.

Alamo 800-327-9633; airport, 833-4585; Renaissance Ilikai Hotel 947-6112
Avis 800-321-3712; airport, 834-5536; Outrigger East Hotel, 971-3700
Budget 800-527-0700; airport, Outrigger Reef, Hyatt, 836-1700
Dollar 800-800-4000; airport 831-2331; Waikiki. 952-4264
Enterprise 800-325-8007; airport, 836-2213; Waikiki, 922-0090
Hertz 800-654-3011; airport, 831-3500; Hyatt, 971-3535; Hilton, 973-3637
National 800-227-7368; airport, 831-3800; Kahala Mandarin, 733-8888
Paradise, Waikiki, 946-7777;,923-8000
Thrifty 800-367-2277; airport, 831-2277; Waikiki, 971-2660
V.I.P., airport 488-6167; Waikiki, 924-6500, 922-4605

TAXIS
Aloha State Cabs (wheelchairs) 847-3566   Pacific Taxi & Limousine 922-4545
Charley's Taxi & Tours 531-1313   Tradewinds Taxi & Tours 841-5555
Handi-Cabs of the Pacific (wheelchairs) 524-3866

SHUTTLE BUSES
*Several companies offer economical service between Waikiki and the airport, as well
as from Waikiki to the USS Arizona Memorial at Pearl Harbor and the open-air
market at Aloha Stadium.*
H&M, Co. 853-2338   Oahu Airport Shuttle 834-8844
Hawaii Super Transit 841-2928   Reliable Shuttle and Tours 924-9292
Island Express Transport 944-1879

Aloha Stadium Swap Meet

Call to ask about the number of rooms and floors, views, distance from beach, and amenities, such as kitchenettes and room safes. Be sure to ask about discounts to get the lowest rates available. You will almost always get a better rate than the printed 'rack' rate. Also ask about parking. All listings are recommended; **boldfaced** items are preferred lodging. For cabins, see Camping & Rustic Accommodations, *page 236.*

(P) = Pricey, $200 and way up
(M) = Moderate, $100 to $200
(C) = Cheap, under $100

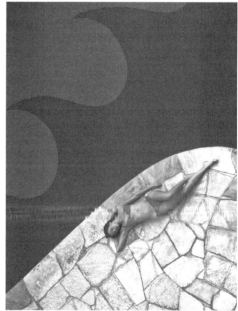

Kahala Mandarin Oriental, Aqua Palms Pool and Spa

Aqua Hotels and Resorts (M-P) 866-406-2782 (reservations)
Hawaii's own Michael Paulin has quietly changed the resort scene over the last decade, with the rennovation of 12 selected properties. You'll have a range of choice, but all will have that "Aqua touch" —first class hospitality and a welcome place to come home to after a day of having fun. Most are around 10 or 15 floors, but a couple rise 40 floors high; the number of rooms ranges from 67 to 740, but most of the resorts have 80 to 200 rooms, small by Waikiki standards. Many rooms and suites have at least partial kithcens. All are within the Waikiki walking circuit, but some are closer to the beach, canal, nightlife, etc. Ask your reservation operator to pick the one that works for you:
Aqua Bamboo & Spa, 922-9473; Aqua Aloha Surf & Spa, 923-0222; Aqua Waikiki Tide, 922-1616; The Equus, 949-0061; Aqua Palms & Spa, 947-7256; Aqua Waikiki Wave, 922-1262; Best Western Coconut Waikiki, 923-8828; Aqua Continental, 922-2232; Aqua Waikiki Marina, 942-7722; Aqua Waikiki Beachside,931-2100; Island Colony, 923-2345; Park Shore Waikiki, 923-0411.

Aloha Punawai (hotel) (C) 866-713-9694, 923-5211
Aston Aloha Surf (hotel) (M) 800-922-7866, 923-0222
Aston Pacific Monarch (hotel) (M) 823-9805
Breakers (hotel) (C-M) 800-426-0494
Halekulani (resort) (P) 800-367-2343, 923-2311
Hawaiian King (hotel) (C-M) 800-545-1948
Hilton Hawaiian Village (resort) (P) 800-221-2424, 949-4321
Holiday Surf (condos) (C-M) 877-923-8488, 923-8488
Hyatt Regency Waikiki (resort) (P) 800-554-9288, 923-1234
Ilima Hotel (M-P) 800-801-9366, 923-1877
Kahala Mandarin Oriental, Kahala, (resort) (P) l 800-367-2525, 739-8888
Kai Aloha Hotel (C-M) 923-6723
Marriott Waikiki Beach (resort) (P) 800-367-5370, 922-6611
Manoa Valley Inn (M) 947-6019
Moana Surfrider, A Westin Resort (P) 888-488-3535, 922-3111
New Otani Kaimana Beach, Kapiolani, (resort) 800-356-8264, 923-1555
Ocean Resort Hotel (hotel) (C-P) 800-367-2317, 922-3861
Ohana Islander Waikiki (hotel) (M) 800-462-6282, 923-7711
Ohana Waikiki Tower (hotel) (M) 800-462-6262, 922-6424
Outrigger Luana Waikiki (condos) (M-P) 800-688-7444, 955-6000
Outrigger Waikiki on the Beach (resort) (P) 800-688-7444-, 923-0711
Pacific Monarch (hotel) (M) 800-922-7866, 923-9805
Queen Kapiolani Hotel (P) 800-367-2317, 923-9805
Renaissance Ilikai Waikiki (resort) (P) 800-245-4524, 949-3811
Royal Grove Hotel (C-M) 923-7691
Royal Hawaiian, Sheraton (resort) (P) 888-488-3535, 923-7311
Sheraton Waikiki (resort) (P) 888-488-3515, 922-4422
W Honolulu Diamond Head, Kapiolani (hotel) (P) 877-946-8357, 922-3734

Waikiki Beach Tower, Aston (resort) (P) 800-922-7866. 926-6400
Waikiki Circle, Aston (hotel) (M) 800-922-7866, 923-1571
Waikiki Grand (hotel) (C-M) 888-336-4368, 923-1814
Waikiki Joy Hotel, Aston (M)800-922-7866, 923-2300
Waikiki Prince Hotel (C) 922-1544
Waikiki Resort Hotel (M-P) 800-367-5116, 922-4911

WINDWARD
Many of the B&Bs have baths, private entrance, kitchenettes.
Affordable Paradise B&B (agent) (C-M) 261-1693
Akamai, Kailua (B&B) (C) 261-2227
Beach Lane, Kailua (B&B) (C-M) 262-8286
Hawaii's Best Bed & Breakfast (agent) (M) 800-262-9912
Hawaii's Hidden Hideaway, Lanikai (B&B) (C-M) 877-443-3299
Laie Inn (motel) (M) 800-526-4562, 293-9282
Papaya Paradise (B&B)(C-M) 261-0316
Manu Mele (B&B) (C) 262-0016
Pat's Kailua Beach Properties (agent) (C-P) 261-1653
Pillows in Paradise, Kailua (B&B) (C-M) B&B 877-657-5745 262-8540

NORTH SHORE
Backpackers, Pupukea (C-M) 638-7838
Ironwoods, Sunset Beach (C) (studio) 293-2554
Keiki Beach Bungalows (C-P) 638-8229
Shark's Cove, Pupukea (B&B) (C) 888-883-0001
Sterman Realty (homes, condos) (C-P) 637-6200
Team Real Estate (C-P) 800-982-8602
Turtle Bay Condos (M) 293-2800
Turtle Bay Resort (P) 866-827-5327

WEST SIDE
Hawaiian Princess, Makaha
 (hotel) (M) 695-5604
JW Ihilani Resort (P)
800 626 4446, 679-0079
Sugar Cane Realty, (M)
 696-5892, 497-3052
Ola Properties, Ko Olina (M) 677-1063

Hilton Hawaiian Village

Where to eat

Both gourmets and chowhounds will find plenty to like on Oahu.
(C) Cheap or takeout (less than $10)
(M) Moderate, family ($10 to $20)
(P) Pricey, special occasion ($20 and up)

WAIKIKI

Ask the bellman, shop workers, guy on the street. The resort grid is packed with eateries of all sorts, many tucked away in hotels and shopping centers that are hard to stumble upon. Each resort will have a signature restaurant.

Banyan Veranda, Moana Surfrider (P) 922-3111
Waikiki's historic beauty; live large at high tea or brunch.
Café Peoni (C-M) 922-2077
Buffet in Miramar Hotel on Kuhio Avenue
Cheesecake Factory (M-P) 924-5001
All tastes met with a 26-page menu. In Royal Hawaiian shopping center.
China Garden Seafood Restaurant (C-M) 923-8383
Diego's Taco Shop (C) 456-7578
Duke's Canoe Club & Barefoot Bar (M) 922-2268
Beachside seats, with a gallery of Duke photos.
Hee Hing Restaurant (C) 735-5544
La Mer (P) 923-2311
In the tropical Halekulani Resort.
Michael's at the Colony Surf (P) 923-6552
French classical cuisine with a sunset view and jazz. Bring the platinum card.
Oceanarium Restaurant (P) 922-1233
While away the evening at a scrumptious buffet in the glow of a gigantic indoor aquarium, Pacific Beach Hotel.
Perry's Smorgy Restaurants (C) 926-0184, 922-8814
Fill the family without emptying the wallet. Open-air décor is better than you'd expect.
Seaside Bar & Grill (C-M) 922-8227
They crank out quality plates. Early bird specials. Voted 'best value in Hawaii.'
Seafood Village (P) 971-1818
In the Hyatt Regency. Past 'best Chinese food' winner.
Top of Waikiki (M-P) 923-3877
Revolving dining room with a view from 18 floors. Sunset dinner specials.
Trattoria Italian Restaurant (M) 923-8415
Early bird specials. Veal dishes and seafood plates.

HONOLULU AND VICINITY
Lots of variety—from culinary pleasures that are worth a flight across the Pacific to plate lunch joints and neighborhood eateries.

Andy's Sandwiches and Smoothies, Manoa (C) 988-2595
A students hangout' near the University of Hawaii.
Angelo Pietro Honolulu (C) 941-0555
Kakaʻako Kitchen (C) 596-7488
Honest local plates and sandwiches; near Ward Center.
La Mariana Restaurant & Bar, Sand Island (C) 848-2800
Working man's district on the harbor near the airport. Fun place.
Pavilion Café, Honolulu Academy of the Arts (C-M) 532-8734
In the courtyard gardens. Critics Choice for lunch.
Restaurant Row (management) 532-4750
In Waterfront Plaza, on Ala Moana Boulevard, a few blocks east from Aloha Tower. A dozen or more restaurants are mixed in with a theater complex and a smattering of gift stores and galleries.
Treetops Restaurant, Manoa Valley (C-M) 988-67838
Asian buffet on the edge of Lyon Arboretum.

WINDWARD
A company town of mostly recent construction, Kailua lacks a great deal of charm, but makes up for it with a range of locally owned places.

Baci Bistro (M) 265-7555
See and be seen; eat and enjoy.
Deb's Ribs & Soul Food (C-M) 275-3993
Mmmm. A good time and good meal.
Down to Earth (C) 262-3838
And good for you. Take a read on community goings on.
Kapapawai Market (C) 262-4359
This gourmet deli in a historic storefront near Kailua Beach Park offers many day's worth of picnic ideas.
Honey's, Koʻolau Golf Club (C-M) 393-1428
View from the terrace of the pali is fantastic, and clubhouse food downstairs is a cut above. Take a hike and work up an appetite.
Kimoz Family Restaurant (C-M) 259-8800
Homemade island-style winners, like kalua pig and lomi salmon. Creative desserts.
Boardrider's Bar & Grill (M-P) 261-4600
Music, nightlife, and drink specials. Don't plan on an early morning.
Pepper's (C-M) 262-3337
See if you can get your face around the cheesesteak.
Pinky's Pupu Bar & Grill (C-M) 254-6255
Bring the group. Everyone's taste buds will be happy.
Teddy's Bigger Burgers (C) 262-0820
Don't worry, be hungry. The special sauce really is.

Banyan Veranda, Moana Surfrider

NORTH SHORE

Peruse an array of places along a two-mile stretch of Kamehameha Highway in Haleiwa. You'll find some chic places, along with a good number of selections that cater to surfers.

Celestial Foods-Café Paradise Found, Haleiwa (C) 637-6729
Select a veggie picnic before exploring the coast.
Cholo's, Haleiwa (C-M) 637-3059
People flock in from the beach cottages and mountain homes for tasty Mexicana.
Coffee Gallery, Haleiwa (C) 637-5571
Cop a caffeine buzz and check out the comings and goings at the North Shore Marketplace.
Grass Skirt Grill, Haleiwa (C-M) 637-4852
Local kine plate and burgers.
Haleiwa Joe's (M-P) 637-8005
Special occasion place with atmosphere and good food, on the water near Rainbow Bridge.
Jameson's by the Sea, Haleiwa, (P) 637-4336
Fine dining with a Hawaiian flair.
Kualoa Ranch (C) 237-8515
Sandwiches and Asian buffet. Lanai with a blue water view makes for a good stopover on the northeast coast.
Punaluu Restaurant (C-M) 237-8474
Stop on the way to the North Shore from the Windward Coast. Satisfying menu and they don't mind serving a beer at lunch.
Shark's Cove Grill, Pupukea (C-M) 638-8300
A great chef concocts gourmet 'fast food,' like pesto shrimp kabobs.
Ted's Bakery, Sunset Beach (C) 638-8207
Fresh sandwiches and baked goods fill the bill any time of the day.
Waialua Bakery (C) 637-9079
Tucked away near Malama Market. Take a whiff and you'll be hooked.

WEST SIDE

Pick up a take-out plate in Waianae and enjoy a sunset dinner at any of many beach parks—priceless. And it will be hard for a couple to spend twenty bucks.

Barbecue Kai, Waianae (C) 696-7122
Germaine's Luau, Barber's Point (P) 949-6626
Old-style Hawaiian entertainment, big appetite plates. Hotel pick-up available. On remote beach in Ewa.
Ho Ho Chinese Cuisine, Kapolei (C) 692-9880
On the way home from Ewa beaches, pull out of the traffic and settle into some potstickers
Kristen's Kitchen, Waianae (C) 678-2579
L&L Drive In, Waianae (C) 696-7989
Makaha Valley Country Club (C) 695-711
Clubhouse faire and a panoramic setting in Makaha Valley
Matsuya's Okazu, Kapolei (C) 676-3757
This is in the instant, fancy suburbia, with other new places nearby
Paradise Cove Luau, Ko Olina, (P) 842-5911
Nice garden setting on the beach, with plenty of hoopla to go with the feast.
Sushi Man, Mililani (C) 625-5775
Take the Kamehameha Highway back from the North Shore.

HAWAIIAN GLOSSARY

The Hawaiian language was first written by missionaries in the 1820s, who transcribed phonetically. One the earliest printing presses can be seen today at Mission Houses Museum in Honolulu. Only 12 letters were used—A, E, I, O, U, plus the consonants H, K, L, M, N, P, and W. Vowels may follow on another, but consonants stand alone. A 'W' is often pronounced as a 'V' when in the middle of a word. The backwards apostrophe (') between some vowels is called an 'okina.' It creates a glottal stop in the word; for instance, in the word 'ahupua'a,' the ending is pronounced 'ah-ah.' Among all words, stress is usually placed on the second-to-last syllable, unless the word has only two syllables, in which case stress the last syllable is stressed.

ahupua'a – a division of land from the mountains to the sea around which a village lived; a watershed
aina – land, country
ala – path, way, or trail
al'i – royalty; blood lineage to the first Polynesian arrivals
aloha – hello or goodbye, welcome or farewell, love and best wishes
aumakua – ancestral spirit, personal or family god
hale – house
hana – work
haole – foreigner, sometimes Caucasian
hau – breeze, dew; type of tree, branches used for poles
heiau – temple, church, worship ground
hono – bay
honu – turtle
hukilau – group net fishing
hula – dance that enacts stories that become myths
huli huli – barbecue
iki – small, little
kahuna – teacher, expert, priest
kai – the sea
kama'aina – native born or longtime resident
kanaka – people
kane – man
kapu – forbidden, no trespassing
kapuna – older, wise person
keiki – child, or young banana plant
ki'i – image, statue
ki'i pohaku – etchings made into rock, petroglyph
kiawe – thorny algarroba tree from South America

koa – largest of the native forest trees
kokua – help
Ku – god of war
kukui – native tree; lamp or torch
lanai – deck, porch, patio
lei – garland of leaves, flowers, or beads worn around the neck
lolo – dumb
lomi lomi – a traditional massage
Lono – god of peace and fertility
luau – feast
mahalo – thank you
makahiki –winter season of peace and fertility; a year's passage
makai – toward the sea
mana – spiritual power in all things
mauka – toward the mountain, inland
mauna – mountain
Mele Kalikimaka – Merry Christmas
menehune – dwarf person; legendary first settlers
moana – ocean
moku – island
Na Ala Hele – 'trails for walking,' state hiking system
nene – Hawaiian goose, state bird
ohana – family
ohia – native tree; lehua blossom bearer
oluolu – please
pali cliff, precipice
Pele – goddess of volcanoes
pohaku – stone
poi – pasty food made from taro
pono – good, blessed; in balance with nature
pu'u – hill or cinder cone
pupu – snack or hors d'oeurves
ohana – extended family, community
tsunami – tidal wave (Japanese)
wahine – woman, girl

surfin' da Web

WEATHER, SURF REPORTS:
Surf Conditions: http://www.surf-oahu.com/
National Weather Service Honolulu: http://www.prh.noaa.gov/hnl/
Climate Charts: http://www.weather.com/weather/wxclimatology/monthly/graph/USHI0026?from=search

COMMUNICATION:
Star Bulletin: http://www.starbulletin.com/
Honolulu Advertiser: http://www.honoluluadvertiser.com
TV: http://en.wikipedia.org/wiki/List_of_television_stations_in_Hawaii
Hana Hou Magazine: http://www.hanahou.com
Honolulu Magazine: http://honolulumagazine.com
Hawaii Public Radio: http://hawaiipublicradio.org

WEBCAMS:
See Hawaii Live: http://www.seehawaiilive.com/sw-cam-sky.cfm
Honolulu: www.co.honolulu.hi.us/cameras/
My Beach Cams: http://www.mybeachcams.com/hawaii/oahu/

EVENTS:
Go Hawaii: http://www.gohawaii.com/oahu/plan/events_on_oahu/
Farmers' Markets: http://hawaii.gov/hdoa/add/farmers-market-in-hawaii
Visit Oahu: http://www.visit-oahu.com/sec/about/festivalscal.aspx

TOURIST BUREAUS:
Hawaii's Official Tourism Site: http://www.gohawaii.com/
Official Oahu Tourism Site: http://visit-oahu.com/

TRAVELERS WITH DISABILITIES:
http://hawaii.gov/health/dcab/docs/TravelOahu.pdf

RESTAURANT GUIDE
http://www.hawaiidiner.com/directory/index.php?island=1

TRANSPORTATION & MAPS:
Bus: www.thebus.org/
Honolulu Airport Delays: http://www.fly.faa.gov/flyfaa/flyfaaindex.jsp?ARPT=HNL&p=1
Oahu Map: http://www.aaccessmaps.com/show/map/oahu
Hawaiian Airlines: www.hawaiianair.com

PLACES TO GO:
Trailblazer Hawaii: www.trailblazerhawaii.com
Gardens: http://www.hawaii.edu/sciref/oahugrdns.html
Go Visit Hawaii: http://www.govisithawaii.com/2007/09/24/10-best-free-activities-and-sites-on-oahu/
Hawaii 's Plantation Village: http://www.hawaiiplantationvillage.org

Go Hawaii, About.com: http://gohawaii.about.com/od/oahuhonolulu/All_About_Honolulu_Oahu_and_Waikiki.htm
Pearl Harbor: http://www.nps.gov/usar/
Bishop Museum: http://www.bishopmuseum.org
Honolulu Zoo: http://www.honoluluzoo.org
Iolani Palace: http://www.iolanipalace.org
Hawaii Museums: http://www.hawaiimuseums.org
Polynesian Cultural Center: http://www.polynesia.com/
Dolphin Swim: http://www.dolphinquest.org/destinations/oahu
Skydiving: http://www.pacific-skydiving.com
Hawaii Maritime Center: http://www.holoholo.org/maritime
Shopping: http://www.alamoana.com/merchcate.htm
Aquarium: http:// www.waquarium.org
Chinatown: http://www.chinatownhi.com/
USS Bowfin Submarine: http://www.bowfin.org/website/index.cfm

HIKING & CAMPING
DLNR: http://www.hawaii.gov/dlnr/dofaw
Trailblazer Travel Books: http://www.trailblazertravelbooks.com
Na Ala Hele Trails: http://www.hawaiitrails.org/island.php?island=Oahu
Sierra Club Hikes: www.hi.sierraclub.org/oahu/oahu-hikes.html
Parks and Recreation Permits: http://www.co.honolulu.hi.us/parks/permits.htm

GOLF:
http://www.808golf.com/oahu/oahu.htm

SAFETY
Guarded Beaches: http://www.aloha.com/~lifeguards/bech_dir.html

ACCOMMODATIONS:
Aqua Resorts: http://www.aquaresorts.com/
Trip Advisor: http://www.tripadvisor.com/AllLocations-g29222-c1-Hotels-Oahu_Hawaii.html
Alternative Hawaii: http://www.alternative-hawaii.com/accom/ocot.htm
About.com: http://www.gohawaii.about.com
Travelzoo: http://www.vacations.travelzoo.com/hawaii-vacations
Vacation Rental By Owner: http://www.vrbo.com

WEDDINGS:
http://www.marriageinhawaii.com
http://www.halekulani.com
http://www.beaumariage.net
http://www.visit-oahu.com/sec/niche/romance/vendors.aspx
http://www.thebigday.com

For publisher-direct savings to individuals and groups, and for book-trade orders, please contact:

DIAMOND VALLEY COMPANY
89 LOWER MANZANITA DRIVE
MARKLEEVILLE, CA 96120
Phone-fax 530-694-2740
www.trailblazertravelbooks.com
www.trailblazerhawaii.com
e-mail: trailblazertravelbooks@gmail.com

All titles are also available through major book distributors, stores, and websites. Please contact the publisher with comments, corrections, and suggestions. We value your readership.

DIAMOND VALLEY COMPANY'S
TRAILBLAZER TRAVEL BOOK SERIES:

ALPINE SIERRA TRAILBLAZER
Where to Hike, Ski, Bike, Fish, Drive
From Tahoe to Yosemite
ISBN10: 0-9670072-6-7
ISBN13: 978-09786371-0-1
"A must-have guide. The best and most attractive guidebook for the Sierra. With you every step of the way."—Tahoe Action

GOLDEN GATE TRAILBLAZER
Where to Hike, Walk, Bike
In San Francisco and Marin
ISBN10: 0-9670072-7-5
ISBN13: 978-0-9670072-7-4
"Makes you want to strap on your boots and go!"—Sunset Magazine

KAUAI TRAILBLAZER
Where to Hike, Snorkel,
Bike, Paddle, Surf
ISBN10: 0-9670072-1-6
ISBN13: 978-0-9670072-1-2
Number one, world-wide among adventure guides.—Barnesandnoble.com

MAUI TRAILBLAZER
Where to Hike, Snorkel,
Paddle, Surf, Drive
ISBN10: 0-9670072-4-0
ISBN13: 978-0-9670072-4-3
"The best of them all."—Maui Weekly

HAWAII THE BIG ISLAND TRAILBLAZER
Where to Hike, Snorkel,
Surf, Bike, Drive
ISBN10: 0-9670072-5-9
ISBN13: 978-0-9670072-5-0
Top three world-wide among adventure guides.—Barnesandnoble.com

OAHU TRAILBLAZER
Where to Hike, Snorkel, Surf
From Honolulu to the North Shore
ISBN10: 0-9786371-2-7
ISBN13: 978-0-9786371-2-5

NO WORRIES HAWAII
A Vacation Planning Guide for
Kauai, Oahu, Maui, the Big Island
ISBN10: 0-9670072-9-1
ISBN13: 978-0-9670072-9-8

"I have tried so hard to do the right thing."—Last words of President Grover Cleveland
After an investigation of the 1893 overthrow of the monarchy, President Cleveland ruled that the rebellion had been unlawful and that the royal Hawaiian government be reinstated. His ruling was ignored. In 1898, after Cleveland left office, Hawaii was annexed as a U.S. Territory.